Criminalization and Prisoners in Japan

Criminalization and Prisoners in Japan

Six Contrary Cohorts

Elmer H. Johnson

Southern Illinois University Press
Carbondale and Edwardsville

Copyright © 1997 by the Board of Trustees,
Southern Illinois University
All rights reserved
Printed in the United States of America
00 99 98 97   4 3 2 1
Photographs courtesy of Corrections Bureau,
Ministry of Justice (Japan)

Library of Congress Cataloging-in-Publication Data

Johnson, Elmer Hubert.
    Criminalization and prisoners in Japan : six contrary cohorts / Elmer H. Johnson.
        p. cm.
    Includes bibliographical references and index.
    1. Corrections—Japan.   2. Prisoners—Japan.
3. Criminals—Japan.
I. Title.
HV9813.J65   1997
365'.952—dc20   96-25707
ISBN 0-8093-2112-2 (cloth : alk. paper)   CIP

The paper used in this publication meets the minimum requirements of American National Standard for Information Sciences—Permanence of Paper for Printed Library Materials, ANSI Z39.48-1984. ∞

To Minoru Shikita
As director general of
the Japanese Correction Bureau in 1985,
he opened the door to this research,
lent active support,
and appreciated its purpose.

Contents

List of Tables   ix

Preface   xiii

1. Introduction: Exceptions to an Exceptional Reluctance to Imprison Offenders   1

2. The Yakuza and Accelerated Criminalization   32

3. Women Drug Offenders and Extended Criminalization   65

4. Traffic Offenders: The Impulse for Penal Innovation   123

5. Juvenile Offenders: Reactions to Drug and Traffic Offenses   157

6. Foreigners in Japanese Prisons: Adaptation and Accommodation   184

7. Elderly Inmates: Demographic Change Creeps into Prisons   217

CONTENTS

8. Deviation from Deviation: A Personal Comment 252

Notes 279

References 287

Index 301

Illustrations following page 148

Tables

1.1	Prisoners Present at Year-End, Japan and U.S., 1926–94	6
1.2	Distribution of Violations of the Antiprostitution Law, 1960–85	30
2.1	Admissions of Male Yakuza to Prison, 1970–94	48
2.2	Representation of Male Yakuza among All Class-B Prisoners at Year-End, 1975–91	50
2.3	Distribution of Offenses for Male Yakuza Admitted to Prison, 1970–94	52
2.4	Ratios of Yakuza to Nonyakuza Male Admissions to Prison, 1970–94	56
2.5	Share of Bosses among Yakuza Admitted to Prison, 1970–94	60
3.1	Average Daily Prison Population of Men and Women, 1926–94	66
3.2	Imprisonment Rate per 100,000 Population, Ages 20 Years and Over, 1945–94	68
3.3	Drug and Nondrug Admissions to Women's Prisons, 1968–94	70
3.4	Distribution of Prison Admissions for Women, With and Without Drug Crimes, 1970–94	80

TABLES

3.5	Female Prison Admissions per 100 Male Admissions, 1970–94	84
3.6	Mean Length of Prison Sentence, 1970–94	88
3.7	Share of First Admissions among Prison Admissions, 1970–94	90
3.8	Mean Number of Exposures to Imprisonment among Prison Admissions, 1970–94	94
3.9	Rule Violations of Inmates Discharged, 1993	102
3.10	Rule Violations by Length of Penal Confinement, 1993	106
3.11	Number of Prison Admissions by Crime, 1993	112
3.12	Rule Violations by Number of Prison Admissions, 1993	114
3.13	Offense Trends of Women Admitted to Probation and Parole, 1993	118
4.1	Sentencing and Imprisonment of Convicted Traffic Offenders, 1979–92	129
4.2	Male Traffic Admissions to Prison for All Traffic Offenses, 1968–94	132
4.3	Male Traffic Admissions to Prison, by Offense, 1968–94	136
4.4	Admissions to Probation of Adult Traffic Offenders, 1968–93	140
5.1	Admissions to Juvenile Training Schools, 1969–94	158
5.2	Family Court Dispositions of Juvenile Traffic and Drug Cases, for Selected Years	168
5.3	Correctional Approaches to Juvenile and Adult Traffic and Drug Offenders, 1970–90	175
5.4	Admissions to Juvenile Probation for Traffic and Drug Offenses, 1969–93	178
5.5	Admissions to Juvenile Training Schools for Traffic and Drug Offenses, 1969–94	180

TABLES

6.1	Foreigners' Share of All Inmates in Year-End Prison Population, 1983–94	186
6.2	Class-F Inmates' Share of Year-End Prison Population, 1983–94	187
6.3	Distribution of Prison Admissions for Nonforeign, Foreign, and Class-F Offenders, 1993	195
6.4	Offenses of Probationers and Parolees Not Permanent Residents of Japan, 1994	197
6.5	Nationality of Probationers and Parolees Not Permanent Residents of Japan, 1994	198
7.1	Male Population Distribution and Rate of Prison Admissions, 1966–92	218
7.2	Male Admissions to Prison by Age, 1966–92	226
7.3	Estimates of Future Number of Men Aged 65 Years and Over Admitted to Prison	231
7.4	Distribution of Prison Admissions of Men Aged 60 Years and Over, 1970–94	239
7.5	Number of Men Aged 60 Years and Over per 100 Men Aged 18–49 Admitted to Prison, 1970–94	242
7.6	Hospitalizations of Male Prisoners, 1987–94	245
8.1	Public Prosecutors' Dispositions of Yakuza Cases, 1983–93	255
8.2	Public Prosecutors' Referrals of Yakuza Defendants for Formal Trial, 1983 and 1992 Compared	258
8.3	Police Referrals to Public Prosecutors of Female Drug Defendants among Female Special-Law Defendants, 1979–91	261
8.4	Juvenile Traffic Defendants Adjudicated by Family Courts, 1980–90	264
8.5	Juvenile Drug Defendants Adjudicated by Family Courts, 1982–92	266

Preface

The unique features of Japanese corrections first impressed me favorably in 1970, when I attended the United Nations Congress on the Prevention of Crime and Treatment of Offenders in Kyoto. Later opportunities to inspect prisons in other countries added to my appreciation of a basic principle of comparative criminology: the history and sociocultural nature of a people shape the style and intensity of their reactions to crime, as well as the prevalence and characteristics of their crimes. The remarkably low and declining imprisonment rate of Japan invited careful examination.

Contemplating my retirement from the Center for the Study of Crime, Delinquency, and Corrections, Southern Illinois University at Carbondale, in 1987, I decided to seek an opportunity for an extensive examination of the operations of Japanese corrections. I proposed to Minoru Shikita, then director general of the Japanese Correction Bureau, that a book be prepared on the workings of the Correction Bureau. Later Keiji Kurita, the director general of the Japanese Rehabilitation Bureau, agreed to broaden the coverage. Director General Shikita accepted the proposal with enthusiasm and arranged for a grant from the Takeuchi Foundation of Hitachi, Ltd., in 1988 for preliminary research in

Japan. A Fulbright award supported nine months of research in 1990–91. I returned to Japan in 1992 to complete the investigation.

The results of the project, as originally planned, are reported in *Japanese Corrections: Managing Convicted Criminals in an Orderly Society* (Carbondale: Southern Illinois University Press, 1996). The materials and ideas seeped beyond the scope of the original plan and constitute this second book.

For both books, I would prefer that the research had been undertaken by a full-fledged expert, especially a Japanese criminologist well acquainted with the practical and theoretical issues of correctional agencies and their variety about the world. Since such a well-qualified expert has lacked my opportunity, I seized this unusual opening for research that fitted my near four decades of serious examination of corrections in the United States and abroad. My practical experiences in those decades have stimulated and shaped my curiosity about Japanese corrections. A combination of practical observations and theoretical insights has guided my examination of an extensive literature on Japanese history, social institutions, and beliefs. My unfamiliarity with the language and the specifics of correctional practice of Japan has been partially remedied by English-speaking officials, especially those who have studied at the center in Carbondale and are familiar with my research purposes.

Over recent years, other persons who assumed the responsibilities of directors general have continued the unconditional support essential to the project. Kazuyoshi Imaoka, Kazuo Kawakami, Kiyohiro Tobita, Noboru Matsuda, and Sinichiro Tojo have headed the Correction Bureau in turn. Keiji Kurita, Kunpei Satoh, Tsuneo Furuhata, Hiroyasu Sugihara, and Tatuzo Honma have held the position in the Rehabilitation Bureau. They made my investigation feasible without reservations, but the two bureaus and their officials are not responsible for my findings and conclusions.

PREFACE

Many staff members from the bureaus contributed their time and knowledge, including those who joined in a frank appraisal of their work and experiences. To name all would add another chapter to the book, but several have earned special mention (in alphabetical order): Ko Akatsuka, Takehisa Kihara, Masaru Matsumoto, Keisei Miyamoto, Akira Murata, Satoru Ohashi, Yoshiaki Okumura, Masaharu Ozawa, Keiichi Sawada, Kenji Teramura, Hiroshi Tsutomi, Kioichi Watanabe, and Mitsuyo Yoshitake.

The staff of Southern Illinois University Press has confirmed my belief that preparation of a worthy book is a joint effort. For several years, Darrell L. Jenkins and his Social Studies staff at Morris Library of Southern Illinois University at Carbondale were indispensable in giving me access to the diverse literature explored for this book.

Carol Holmes Johnson shared two of my tours to Japan and my appreciation of the attractive features of Japan and its people. She has created a small museum of Japanese artifacts in our home, has retained good humor in the half-century of our marriage, and serves as my companion, my constructive critic, and the diligent operator of our computer.

Criminalization

and

Prisoners

in

Japan

1

Introduction: Exceptions to an Exceptional Reluctance to Imprison Offenders

An outstanding feature of Japanese corrections is the very limited reliance on imprisonment, but despite the general trend of fewer and fewer convicted criminals entering Japanese prisons, at least six kinds of inmates (I will call them "cohorts") have assumed greater numbers in recent decades: offenders among the *yakuza* (members of crime syndicates), women offenders, traffic offenders, juvenile drug abusers and traffic offenders, offenders among foreigners (aliens convicted in Japan), and elderly offenders. The number and quality of probationers and parolees also have been affected. The six cohorts differ in absolute numbers, with only marginal impact on prison administration, but all mirror developments in society at large.

Originally, the word *cohort* referred to a unit of the military legion of ancient Rome. More recently, demographers have used the term to denote a subpopulation of a society distinguishable from other subpopulations by age, gender, or other status attribute. Age-cohorts have been employed in criminological research to trace the effects on crime rates over time of changes in social and political conditions (see, for example, O'Brien 1989; Menard 1992; Steffensmeier, Streifel, and Shihadeh 1992). This book extends the term *cohort* to cover the six status groups (or prisoner subpopulations) because they too reflect the effect over time of changes in social and political conditions.

The respective cohort has been drawn, through criminal justice processing, from a subpopulation in the Japanese society that includes both criminals and noncriminals. The selective process—that which determines which members and how many members of the larger cohort are treated as criminals—has brought a greater absolute number of persons to the prisons or juvenile training schools of Japan.

Admissions of the yakuza accelerated after unprecedented violence and the nationwide consolidation of gangs weakened the usual ambivalent attitudes toward them. The campaign against stimulant drugs undermined the tolerance of female offenses that has in the past limited the admissions to women's prisons. Drug and traffic offenses have assumed greater shares of teenagers. Skyrocketing traffic accidents and deaths stimulated a multifaceted campaign including imprisonment for gross traffic violations. Although only a small proportion commit crimes, the increased volume of visitors has resulted in a greater absolute number of imprisoned foreigners. Because the number of Japanese over sixty-five years of age has grown rapidly, their representation among prisoners has risen without necessarily mirroring any possibility of their greater inclination to commit crimes.

Agenda for the Study of Cohorts

In tracing statistics for prison admissions over the decades, I became aware that the six cohorts were entering prison in increasing numbers. Why were greater numbers of these people joining the march in lockstep toward imprisonment? In addition to any greater inclination of individuals toward criminality, the factors influencing the de-

INTRODUCTION

clining admissions to prison must have lost at least some of their potency.

Haley (1991, 13) summarizes a key point for explaining the Japanese preference for avoiding imprisonment: "No characteristic of Japanese political life seems more remarkable or intrinsic than the separation of authority from power." In his view, when Japanese people and their criminal justice system contemplate what to do about nonconformists, they rely heavily on the willing obedience, obligation, and legitimacy that is the essence of authority.

As measured by mastery of the passions and corporate loyalty in accord with group expectations, rectitude stems mostly from the conscience of the individuals, not from any external pressure. The family and school are building blocks of the social order; they develop the individual's conscience in the course of transmitting norms from one generation to the next. Authority takes on moral dimensions by linking commitment to traditions, one's sense of identity, and emotional allegiance to the behavioral standards supporting the social order.

Power, says Haley (1991, 13), is "the capacity to coerce others to do something they would not otherwise do." Imprisonment is an instrument of coercion; as an arm of the criminal law, it expresses the threat of punishment to deter the potential law violators and to persuade criminals to abandon their depravity.

Criminalization refers to the assignment of criminal status to individuals. The ideas associated with the concept are fundamental in explaining why the correctional institutions of Japan have experienced an increase in the number of arrivals among the yakuza, women drug offenders, violators of traffic laws, and juveniles involved in drug and traffic offenses. The prisons and juvenile training schools of Japan received a greater volume of admissions not because of any actions on their part but because they are dependent on developments in society at large. Changes in public policy have followed the perception of a major crisis. Rulebreakers were previously regarded with only moderate suspicion. Even if their misconduct was prohibited by law, it was rather tolerated as only minor rulebreaking. But in the more recent attitudinal climate, in which society claims that something has to be done quickly to end the crime crisis, these rulebreakers have been singled out as targets for imprisonment.

In turning to criminalization, lawmakers and policymakers have signaled a reduced reliance on authority in managing the cohorts and a substitution of the sanctions of the criminal law. The switch in emphasis implies—but does not justify as a final conclusion—a Japanese movement toward the American faith in imprisonment as a major solution to the threats of crime.

Accommodating Factors External to Corrections

Japan's low imprisonment rate illustrates the two interrelated implications of a comment by Rose (1970, 366): "Presumably the object of a penal system is not necessarily to reduce the total incidence of crime, since this may depend primarily upon factors outside the control of the system, and any positive effects the penal system produces may be marginal and swallowed up in the results of other factors concerned." Since the penal system cannot reduce the extent of criminality, alternatives to imprisonment—including simple return to the community—have their proper place and function in responsible criminal justice policy. Also, among "other factors concerned" is that Japanese culture lends credibility to the official faith that leniency will return most offenders to the "straight life" with little or no agency intervention.

The second and more direct implication of Rose's statement is that, instead of being masters of their own destiny,

INTRODUCTION

correctional agencies must accommodate themselves to circumstances shaped and determined elsewhere. The goals set for corrections, whether attainable or illusionary, are imposed in the contests among proponents of opposing ideas of how criminals should be handled. The nature and magnitude of prison admissions are due to factors outside the control of correctional agencies. Even the level of crime, as Christie (1993, 12) has concluded, has no direct relation with the number of prisoners per one hundred thousand inhabitants at any particular time. The criminal law defines the potential clientele. The police "recruit" for the pipeline of criminal justice administration. The public prosecutors and judges shape the number and kinds of offenders making up the clientele of the correctional agencies. Developments in the community have vital effects on the ultimate outcome of agency intervention.

The impact of external events is illustrated by the fluctuations in the number of convicted offenders entering Japanese prisons (see table 1.1). The number rose from 1926 through 1935 and dropped sharply during wartime. The postwar chaos inflated prison admissions. Since then the trend has been generally downward.

Japanese public policy lacks the American faith in imprisonment as the answer to criminality. Since 1926, when comparable data were first available, Japan has trailed the United States in absolute number of prisoners. In 1994 Japan had fewer prisoners than in 1926, but in the United States the number of inmates in the prisons of all states and the national government has increased from almost 98,000 in 1926 to over a million in 1994.[1] Since Japan's population is about half that of the United States, the rates per one hundred thousand population provide a more valid comparison (see table 1.1).[2] From the ratio of 1.12 in 1950 (a ratio indicating relative approximation of the two rates), the discrepancy broadened progressively to reach in 1994 an American rate 13.41 times greater than the Japanese rate.

INTRODUCTION

Table 1.1
Prisoners Present at Year-End, Japan and U.S., 1926–94

	Japanese Prisoners		U.S. Prisoners		
Year	No.	Rate per 100,000 Population[a] (A)	No.	Rate per 100,000 Population[a] (B)	Ratio B/A
1926	39,513	65.1	97,991	83	1.27
1930	41,188	63.9	129,453	104	1.63
1935	51,094	73.7	144,180	113	1.53
1940	38,599	53.7	173,706	131	2.44
1945	36,824	51.1	133,649	98	1.92
1950	80,589	96.9	166,123	109	1.12
1955	67,813	76.0	185,780	112	1.47
1960	61,100	65.4	212,953	117	1.79
1965	52,657	53.6	210,895	108	2.01
1970	39,724	38.3	196,429	96	2.51
1975	37,744	33.7	240,593	111	3.29
1980	41,835	35.7	315,974	138	3.86
1985	46,105	38.3	480,568	200	5.22
1990	39,892	32.3	739,980	292	9.04
1993	37,164	29.8[b]	909,000	344	11.54
1994	37,425	29.9[b]	1,004,608	401	13.41

Sources: Data from the Correction Bureau; Maguire and Pastore 1995, 540.

[a] Equals the number of prisoners (as counted on 31 December of the given year) divided by the number of persons in the country's total population that year and multiplied by 100.

[b] Based on estimated population of Japan.

INTRODUCTION

The Organization of Japan's Correctional Bureaus

The impact of external events on correctional agencies is illustrated by the fluctuations in the number of convicted defendants entering Japanese prisons—a downward trend for Japan's imprisonment rate and an escalating pattern for the six cohorts. In either situation the agencies must adjust to changing circumstances. All correctional functions are concentrated in Japan's Correction Bureau and its Rehabilitation Bureau, twin subunits of the Ministry of Justice in the national government.[3] The headquarters of the bureaus are in one of the two twenty-story skyscrapers in central Tokyo, overlooking the emperor's palace. The Rehabilitation Bureau administers probation, parole, and aftercare for inmates of prisons and juvenile training schools. The Correction Bureau manages all prisons, detention facilities, and juvenile training schools.

Fifty probation offices, thirty branch probation offices, and eight regional parole boards disperse the operations of the Rehabilitation Bureau throughout the nation. The probation offices are responsible for supervising those convicted adults whom the courts grant probationary supervision, juveniles placed on probation by the family courts, and inmates paroled from prisons and training schools. The probationers and parolees supervised by the probation offices are mostly supervised by some fifty thousand unsalaried volunteer probation officers.

Among fifty-nine prisons, the Correction Bureau manages six prisons for women, four others that are hospitals for adults, eight for young adults under twenty-six years of age, and four that receive foreigners along with Japanese offenders. The fifty-four juvenile training schools are of four types (primary, middle, special, or medical) according to age, physical or mental difficulties, and criminalistic tendencies. The Correction Bureau has fifty-two juvenile classification homes and one branch that diagnose juveniles referred by family courts.

Criminalization: A Break from the Usual Legal Approach

The six cohorts personify a distinct approach that, unlike reduced use of imprisonment in general, has brought more of their members to prison or juvenile training schools. Among the explanations for the increased resort to imprisonment is the revision of public policy for coping with criminality.

A search for means of easing the impact of the law's sanctions on defendants has been replaced by greater enlistment of penal sanctions to deal with a public issue. In the atmosphere of social crisis, the policymakers reduce their heavy reliance on the citizens' self-discipline and turn to the coercion of the criminal law. New legislation may be enacted, existing law changed, or criminal policy revised. The enacted law or new policy supplies standards for the apprehension, prosecution, and punishment of individuals whose conduct has been redefined from tolerable marginality to outright criminality. The agents of criminal justice are authorized to recognize officially this "movement across moral boundaries," as Lauderdale (1976) puts it. They gain the means and authority either (a) to take unprecedented suppression of marginal conduct now included among crimes or (b) to increase the severity of responses to misconduct previously defined as a crime.

The Japanese rejection of the "excessively bad person" is consistent with the interpretation of criminalization by the labeling theorists, who invite study of the *group's negative evaluation* of the persons considered to be criminal, instead of only studying the persons who have been called criminals. The "audience" (the group doing the evaluation) judges the behavior of "criminals" to be so dangerous that

INTRODUCTION

the criminal law should be brought against them. Deviance is not a quality of the actor (the characteristics of the "criminal") but a result of the imposition of the audience's evaluation of the actor. "Social groups create deviance by making the rules whose infractions constitute deviance," argues Becker (1963, 9), "and by applying these rules to particular people and labeling them as outsiders." The criminal status is *conferred* on the person. The *imposed* status (the position or social ranking given the individual) is that of an "excessively bad person."

"Deviance can be thought of as a product of the movement of moral boundaries," hypothesizes Lauderdale (1976, 660–61), "rather than as a product of the movement of actors across those boundaries." Groups of contemporary "criminals" may have been subjected to a modification of previous tolerance and to the strengthening of criminal justice measures taken against them. The movement of moral boundaries, as opposed to the movement of criminals across the boundaries, can be described in terms of the "tolerance quotient" (Lemert 1951). The numerator of the quotient is a measure of the amount of some disapproved conduct in a community. The denominator is a measure of the tolerance the residents have for the misconduct. The higher the quotient is, the greater is the likelihood of criminalization of the misconduct. The value of the quotient can be raised either by an increased amount of flagrant misconduct (the numerator) or by a decreased tolerance of that misconduct (the denominator).

The cohorts have been among the members of a group of "marginal deviants" who have been singled out as not conforming to the dominant sociocultural norms. The marginality exists in two senses: first, these deviants stand between complete conformity to and flagrant rejection of the dominant norms; second, usually the evaluation by the "audience" of deviant conduct has been ambivalent. Through criminalization select members of the marginal-deviant group are denounced officially as violators of the criminal law. Also, through revision of the criminal law and modification of criminal justice policy, the moral boundaries are shifted because of the increased amount of misconduct believed to be flagrant or because changing conditions have reduced the previous tolerance of marginal deviance.

Among automobile drivers there are those who speed excessively or engage in "aerobatic" competition for priority on the streets and highways. The Japanese public joins Americans in regarding that misconduct as "minor" rulebreaking. Japanese gangsters have enjoyed a degree of tolerance, perhaps because the yakuza resemble conventional Japanese society in paternalistic structure, fictive family values, and ritualistic rules of conduct. Japanese women do not necessarily accept the subordinate and passive position demanded in the course of their socialization. Their elders often criticize Japanese adolescents for an easygoing manner, a tendency to undermine traditional values and to extol individualism.

From those more inclusive areas of marginal deviance, the process of criminalization selects out particular forms of misconduct to become targets of the criminal justice system. Conditions are changed for the decisions of public prosecutors and judges about the fate of offenders. Criminalization of previously tolerated misconduct must attract the moral authority of the Japanese people if the legalized restrictions are to have lasting effect. In other words, the shifting of moral boundaries must extend beyond the sphere of written law.

Criminalization as a Political Process

Criminalization is a political process whereby constituencies possessing power use the criminal law to deal with what they perceive to be a major public issue, but they disagree on the specifics of the public issue and the proposed

INTRODUCTION

criminal law or its amendment. "Traditional crimes" have already been incorporated in the criminal law. Threats to human life—such as murder—were criminalized decades or centuries ago. The values of capitalism have favored protection of private property from ordinary theft and larceny. Sociocultural change may stimulate controversy about unprecedented expansion of the scope of traditional crimes. (Is the physician performing abortions another kind of murderer? Should the businessperson selling shoddy or dangerous goods be considered another criminal against property?) But traditional crimes not exposed to unprecedented interpretations do not draw widespread controversy.

"New crimes"—nontraditional crimes—represent the broadening of the scope of the criminal law and the responsibilities of the criminal justice agencies. Criminalization is undertaken among the political reactions to a public issue. The expanded reach of "new crimes" gives them a potential for political controversy beyond that of "traditional crimes" that are likely to be accepted as part of living routines. Controversy is endemic because influential constituencies have differing self-interests in whether or not the conduct is to be criminalized or in how that conduct is to be penalized. The interest groups disagree on the specifics of the public issue and on what should be done to deal with it.

The six cohorts analyzed in this book differ broadly, first, in whether or not they are examples of either "traditional crimes" or "new crimes"; second, as peculiar settings for criminalization; and third, in whether or not the process of criminalization is relevant to explaining each cohort's greater prison admissions. The first two aspects differentiate two versions of criminalization: accelerated criminalization and extended criminalization.

Two cohorts—foreigners and the elderly—are exceptions to criminalization (the third aspect) as the source of greater use of imprisonment. Instead, their increasing prison admissions are due to the great number of foreign or elderly persons in Japan. In that sense, the term *responsive incarcera-*

tion will be used to highlight the spontaneous nature of the higher imprisonment rates as a reaction to developments in society. The foreign and elderly offenders have become an issue for criminal justice agencies because of the unprecedented increase in their numbers in Japanese society, rather than because of any qualitative change in their conduct.

Demographic trends in Japan are increasing the proportion of Japan's total population held by persons over sixty years of age (see chapter 7) and are bringing more and more foreigners to Japan (see chapter 6). The rather small proportion of criminals among members of either cohort is producing a progressively greater number of their members arriving at prison gates. The relevant crimes are "traditional," rather than "new," because new laws have not been enacted to expand the scope of criminalization.

In accelerated criminalization the usual tolerance of misconduct is replaced by modification of existing criminal laws and by tightening of the administration of criminal laws. The use of the word *accelerated* here denotes not only an expanded scope of criminalization but also the previous existence of criminal sanctions against the particular kind of misconduct. Some developments in society at large have raised the level of general concern about that misconduct. In the attitudinal climate of a public crisis, the conduct of the particular cohort of criminals is being reevaluated. In contrast to usual tolerance, progressively greater admission of these criminals to prisons mirrors sterner reactions to their activities.

The yakuza, the criminal syndicates in Japan, have enjoyed remarkable tolerance, some acceptance by legitimate social institutions, and even popular esteem as though they are contemporary examples of ancient heroes. These criminal organizations try to avoid violence against other persons and groups. Usually, aggressive suppression of the yakuza would not attract universal support, but the gangs have changed their operations in ways reducing public tolerance. Their violence has increased, and they have ex-

INTRODUCTION

panded their operations into other kinds of offenses (Katoh 1991). Chapter 2 describes how those changes in yakuza activities aroused public concern and stimulated the national Diet to enact the Antiboryokudan Law in 1991 (amended in 1993) to authorize unprecedented action against the crime syndicates.

In extended criminalization the emphasis is placed on broadened criminalization and the creation of "new crimes" in official efforts to cope with a perceived social crisis. The perceived threat to social stability is crucial to the case for the passage of new anticrime legislation and the modification of criminal justice policy as elements of criminalization. Here, too, the possibility of conflicts among political constituencies is magnified. Three cohorts qualify: traffic offenders, women drug-law violators, and juveniles involved in either drug or traffic offenses.

Since World War II, car ownership in Japan expanded at a remarkable rate exceeding the capacity of urban streets and rural highways. The government initiated a multifaceted program to deal with the traffic crisis, including unprecedented use of criminal sanctions (see chapter 4). Because of public doubts about treating traffic offenders as criminals, the legislators and criminal justice officials had to be discriminant in this field of extended criminalization.

Abuse of stimulant drugs escalated after World War II and brought forth the Stimulant Drug Control Law of 1951 and later amendments. Violators of the law added significantly to prison admissions in subsequent years, especially among women. As a "new crime," drug offenses attract controversy when criminalistic. The population of women's prisons continues to be only a small fraction of that of male prisons. As an exception to the usual preferential treatment of female offenders, the rate of admissions to women prisons for drug offenses has been greater than that for male prisons (see chapter 3).

The juvenile justice system frequently expresses its commitment to "protective measures," and family courts have preferred dismissals of juvenile cases over referrals to training schools. Despite this relative leniency, for both traffic offenses and abuse of drugs (especially violations of the Poisonous and Hazardous Substances Control Law) juveniles have arrived at training schools in increasing numbers and probation offices have had growing clienteles (see chapter 5). The juvenile traffic offenders were identified with the *bosozoku* in the mass media; these groups of adolescents and young adults rallied on the streets and modified their vehicles to the discomfort of most Japanese. Although efforts to control them assumed the dimensions of a public crisis, the family courts continued to minimize referrals to the training schools, but they acknowledged the demand for sterner measures by greater use of probation (see table 5.2). The family courts have regarded juvenile stimulant drug offenses more seriously than poisonous substance offenses among juveniles. Dismissals of cases (85.53 percent in 1990) are predominant in dispositions of poisonous substance cases. Stimulant drug cases received relatively sterner dispositions in 1990: 34.26 percent for training schools and 44.81 percent for probation (see table 5.2).

The Low Profile of Formal Law in Japan

The process of criminalization involves the application of the criminal law for Japan in some unprecedented way, especially in supplementing customs and other means of inducing self-discipline. To make clear that the creation of the six cohorts has been very remarkable, I here examine the place of criminal law in the history and current nature of Japanese society.

Early Japan had a collection of feudal domains. "The whole of Japan was torn by fractions and plagued by incessant civil war," summarizes Sansom (1963b, v), "until late

INTRODUCTION

in the sixteenth century, when a process of national unification by force of arms was begun." Shogun Ieyasu Tokugawa ushered in the Tokugawa Era (1603–1867) and moved feudal Japan toward a centralized government through clever military leadership, skillful political treatment of defeated adversaries, and binding feudal lords (*daimyo*) to him by awarding fiefs.

As an island society Japan did not suffer threats from foreign countries until Commodore Matthew C. Perry entered Edo Bay in February 1854, and after that not until occupation by the Allied forces after World War II. The few outsiders who otherwise came had to adapt themselves to the Japanese ways rather than presenting alternative customs and norms. A full-fledged body of written law was not framed until the Meiji Restoration, when a group of feudal lords took control of the imperial court in Kyoto on 3 January 1868, terminated the Tokugawa regime, proclaimed the emperor's direct responsibility for government, and began a series of reforms that established the institutional structure of a "new" Japan (Beasley 1972, 1–2).

A full-fledged body of written law was not framed until 1868. Based on Chinese concepts but impregnated with Japanese customs and morality,[4] a partial code developed about A.D. 800; it had an administrative and civil part (the *ryo*) and another part (the *ritsu*) including provisions for arrest and imprisonment. The Joei-shikomoku in 1232 was the closest Japan had to formal law in feudal times until the nineteenth century. (Joei was the era name given the year 1232; rather than a legal code, the Joei-shikomoku was a set of practical rules to guide the shogun's court and the provincial constables.) After 1483 several feudal lords issued "house laws" that set forth rules of conduct for members of the lord's family in administration of the domain. The people were to be benefited by good government and moral scriptures, but punishment of offenders was harsh. Later the Tokugawa regime issued a statement of principles for government of the feudal domains (the Buke Sho-hatto) that did not constitute a code of law (Sansom 1963a, 111, 394–99; 1963b, 251–55, 405).

Modern Japanese law largely has been imported from the West, declares Noda (1976, 39), who comments: "There may be a marked difference between modern and the old law at the level of state [formal] law, but at the level of living law (that of tradition and custom) there was no break in the continuity. The latter evolved spontaneously and unconsciously plays an important role in the social life of the Japanese people today." Outside the sphere of written, formal law and criminal justice agencies, Japanese traditions and customs lend order to behaviors within families, communities, work groups, and other recurrent organized activities. Despite the importation of ideas from the West, the Meiji reformers preserved the earlier sources of social discipline. Tightly organized all-embracing groups continued to hold the complete loyalty of their members, argues Bellah (1971, 382). "The substance of Japanese legal thought—not what was written in law books but what people thought and felt about law—resisted rapid transformation," explains Ozaki (1978, 123).

"The Japanese manner of thinking clearly favors neither the formation nor the functioning of [formal] law as a conceptually arranged system of rights and duties," says Noda (1976, 174). He finds "a great gulf" between the rationalism presupposed by Western law and the Japanese, who are "imbued with mystic sentimentalism." Similarly, Singer (1981, 72) notes: "The Japanese are adverse to committing themselves to rules that, though beautiful and reasonable in themselves, may prove harmful to the peaceful flow of social life by introducing into this ever-changing element factors of excessive intellectual rigidity and harshness." The Japanese, comments Van Wolferen (1989, 10, 327), have "situational instead of general moral rules and hold particularistic values rather than universalistic ones." Rather than coming from immutable principles, Van

Wolferen believes, good behavior for the Japanese "is constantly determined by individuals' views of how others expect them to behave . . . in which conformity to social expectations is . . . the only possible way to live."

Informal Mechanisms for Diversion from Correctional Institutions

Only a fraction of the accused persons, and even only a substantial portion of convicted felony defendants, end up in Japanese prisons or juvenile training schools. The procedures for diverting suspects and defendants from the correctional institutions are embedded now in the legal codes and the philosophy of the procuracy and judiciary, as I will explain shortly. The philosophy of those functionaries and the structure of their offices are crucial to the implementation of official leniency. Haley (1991, 125-29) sees the policy as the "second track" of two parallel systems. The first track, already discussed in this chapter, is the "formal institutional process similar to most contemporary legal systems derived from continental European models." The second track channels the "extraordinarily lenient" processing by the police, prosecutor, and judge when offenders acknowledge guilt, express remorse, and compensate their victims.

"Perhaps one of the most significant factors for the low incidence of criminality," contends Suzuki (1979, 142-44), "may be found in the informal mechanisms in which small but intimate groups effectively control the behavior of their members." He refers to the effects of what I will shortly consider as the cultural foundations of official leniency. In Japan the contemporary influence of "informal mechanisms" stems from elements of Japan's earlier history.

In the Tokugawa system of rule, the samurai (retainers of the daimyo) were forced to either live in a castle town and serve as salaried bureaucrats or surrender their aristocratic status. "While the physical distance of the samurai from the farming land enhanced their bureaucratic character," says Tonomura (1992, 169–74), "it also restricted them from direct intervention in village affairs. With minimal involvement of the urban bureaucrats, the primary producers paid taxes and kept the local peace and order."

The village's headman, appointed by the government from among the local people, represented them in contacts with the government but also was held responsible for the village in satisfying the tax assessment calculated in units of rice, in overseeing the registration of members of households (in itself, a means of Tokugawa control), and in disseminating the rulers' orders. The Tokugawa system of social control accorded autonomy to the feudal villagers as long as the rulers' political purposes were served. "Although it [the system of feudal villages] was used principally as a political tool," summarizes Masland (1946, 355–56), "it did nevertheless develop an autonomous body of neighborhood families for the handling of community problems."

"Most Japanese scholars find that the traditional rural community provided the prototype of conformity which characterizes Japanese society," declares Ishida (1983, 35). In addition to the effect of the Tokugawa system of control, the rice agriculture and the isolation of rural communities from one another by mountains created social cohesion of the feudal villagers and great pressure for conformity with local expectations. Rice growing was a group endeavor; the entire village worked so closely that cooperation was second nature. Tasks were not specialized; everyone performed all chores. The work was repetitive from year to year; perseverance, more than innovation, was required. The operations could be conducted through consensus, without strong individual leadership (Smith 1961, 522–25; Steiner 1965, 210–12; Hayashi 1988, 87–92).

The transition from the Tokugawa Era to the Meiji Era was revolutionary in the sense of profound change, but once military opposition was overcome, the violence that generally accompanies a revolution did not occur. The new forces did not undercut the major source of social discipline. "By continued emphasis on the Japanese way," comments Levy (1970, 264), "they [the reformers] were able to get individuals to adapt quickly to new ways in spheres in which they were essential and retain the old, at least long enough for a more gradual transition in other spheres of life." The Meiji government attempted to extend the villagers' strong sense of conformity to the national level (Ishida 1983, 25-26).

The Cultural Foundation for Official Leniency in Japan

The officials' reluctance to use imprisonment rests fundamentally on the popular and official faith in the customary ways of influencing conduct. Koichi Miyazawa and Cook (1990) point to the combination of traditional Eastern ethics and the priorities of a modern industrial state. They see this combination as permitting Japan to avoid the "inefficiencies and high crime rates" of other industrial and developing nations (55).

"We hate crimes but not criminals" is a saying in Japan that, according to Nagashima (1990, 4-6), has a double meaning. First, unlike the Western concentration on legal responsibility, the folk belief of the Japanese is that the moral responsibility of the offender also must be considered. Second, it is emphasized in Japan that criminals are "fellow countrymen" and deserve to be accepted back into society "when they purify themselves from the tainted past" (6). Offenders are believed to be capable of self-correction if they accept the moral responsibility as given priority over more limited legal responsibility. Offenders are expected to be strongly motivated to restore social harmony.

Japanese culture places heavy emphasis on the subordination of self to the group. In group relationships, personal attachments are to people of superior rank (parent, boss, elder, and so on). The vertical dimension strengthens cohesion among group members; the leader feels a paternalistic appreciation of subordinates. "A junior takes care to avoid any open confrontation with his superior," says Nakane (1984, 36–37), who explains that "avoidance of such open and bald negative expression is rooted in the fear that it might disrupt the harmony and order of the group, that it might hurt the feelings of the superior and that, in extreme circumstances, it could involve the risk of being cast out of the group as an undesirable member."

Setsuo Miyazawa (1994) argues that acknowledging such "risk" corrects any impression that Japanese management of deviance is purely benign: "It is more accurate to say that Japanese people conform because they know that conformity will be highly rewarded while non-conformity costs enormously." Companies and schools can apply "extremely harsh treatment," he notes, to "members who defy the existing power structure and social methods" (89).

The word *giri* (duty) is basic to Japanese social psychology: Noda (1976) isolates several of its elements. Duty locates the individual in relationships with others according to the status of the respective parties; the principles of the hierarchical order of feudal Japan persist in a contemporary form. The person benefiting from another person's observation of duty cannot demand the observance but must wait for voluntary dutiful performance. Giri obligations are perpetual; they cannot be extinguished even when they have been fulfilled. Although selfish gain may be involved, the relationships carry feelings of affection. The obligations are made binding on the Japanese person by a sense of honor, not simply by the threat of punishment.

A series of letters to the editor published in the *Japan Times* provides practical insights into Japanese social psychology. On 14 October 1990, a Japanese woman described

INTRODUCTION

her surprise about the attitude of the American who managed the office where she was employed. A Japanese employee was forging taxi receipts; the manager was determined to fire him. The woman wrote in part:

> Suffering from a serious labor shortage, (the Japanese middle managers) apparently did not like to lose even one body from their section, even if it was a man whose moral standards were incredibly low and did not mind cheating the company. Anyway... he agreed to turn in a letter of apology.... Not only did he admit his guilt, but he also entreated the company for merciful punishment, which was, to be brief, 'let me stay in your company.' The American manager simply asked, 'Is this a joke?' I was stunned. My question is whether this is a typical response of American people, or he is an exception in dealing with this kind of situation.

On 28 October 1990 another writer expressed the bewilderment of many foreigners about Japanese social psychology.

> I'm an American, employed by an electronics company to teach employees English. After several months of being put off by an 'I'm busy' manager, who really had no interest in studying English, I was confronted by my boss as to why I wasn't teaching. I told him the truth, that the manager said he was busy. In the meantime, the manager had already told the boss I refused to teach him in the hours he had available... a blatant lie. However, rather than his being discredited I was left in a bad light, as if I had done something wrong. That manager is still a highly respected and trusted employee. In America, lying, stealing, cheating the company you work for are immediate grounds for dismissal, not to mention loss of respect one would receive from fellow employees. So my reaction is the same as the manager's. Is this a joke?... In the case of taxi tickets, what is to keep this guy from graduating from small-time thievery to big-time embezzlement?

Two other writers appeared to have a better grasp of the Japanese emphasis on acceptance of "purified" offenders, on the offender's fear of being cast out from the group, on the expectation that executives will have paternalistic concern for employees, and on avoidance of conflict. On 28 October 1990, one writer explained in part: "The American manager didn't realize that in Japanese culture, the rest of the Japanese managers should also feel responsible for the act of one of their group (company), especially a lower rank member, and that they are bound to resolve the problem within the confines of the group."

Another writer whose letter was published on 28 October viewed the situation from the perspective of a Japanese employee: "It is unlikely the American comprehended the gravity of the employee's apology. It represented a total surrender, self-prostration and a vow of indebtedness that should far exceed the debt of pilfered fares.... [The American] does not perceive how drastic firing is ... from the Japanese point of view ... or that honesty is less important than debt within a Japanese organization. Whereas the Japanese might see this as an opportunity to gain a devoted employee, the American sees a crook being let off the hook."

Unlike many Americans apprehended for a crime, Japanese offenders tend to be anxious to maintain or restore a positive relationship with another person they have harmed. A Japanese offender is likely to respond positively to the public prosecutor and sentencing judge, who expect the offender to express regret and make restitution to the victim. When forgiven by the victim and the officials, the offender is expected (and often expects) to undertake the limitless obligation of abandoning criminal ways. Giri presses the "other persons" to accept as sincere the offender's expression of the wish to adhere to conventional mores. "Japanese not only believe that human character is mutable," declare Wagatsuma and Rosett (1986, 477), "but view an excessively bad person as 'non-human.' When such persons reform, they are seen as 'returning to being a real human being.' "

The Structure for Administering Leniency in Japan

When defendants are believed to be repentant and capable of self-corrections, the public prosecutors and sentencing judges are likely to return them to the community without penal incarceration. Those agents of criminal justice are, of course, also socialized to forgive the deserving offenders and penalize the "excessively bad person as nonhuman." The offenders also are likely to subordinate self-interests to those of the group.

In addition, the official policy of leniency is built into the offices of the public prosecutors and judges within the administrative structure of the criminal law. Their actions are authorized by the Japanese Penal Code and the Japanese Code of Criminal Procedure, which, in turn, are products of events some century and a quarter earlier, when Japan began its rapid modernization of its institutional structure.

While the Meiji government was dealing with the samurai who had been defeated, the number of prisoners surged from thirty-two thousand in 1882 to sixty-five thousand in 1885. Suspended prosecution emerged as an immediate and practical solution, says Nishikawa (1990), without incorporation at that time in the legal code. Public prosecutors seized opportunities to avoid prosecution of minor offenses if reasonable grounds existed. The present Code of Criminal Procedure offers general criteria and leaves the concrete rationale to the prosecutors' discretion. Article 248 states: "If after considering the character, age and situation of the offender, the gravity of the offense, the circumstances under which the offense was committed, and the conditions subsequent to the offense, prosecution is deemed unnecessary, prosecution need not be instituted" (UNAFEI n.d., 127).

Thereby, Japan has embraced the principle of discretionary prosecution, says George (1988). As opposed to the principle of mandatory prosecution, under which the prosecutor must pass on for trial every case involving a suspicion of guilt, the courts accept and adjudicate cases instituted by the public prosecutors and decide whether or not the evidence warrants formal action.

Even if the case has been convicted in court and a prison sentence ordered, the judge in Japan may suspend that sentence; the defendant may be returned to the community with or without probationary supervision. Article 25 of the Penal Code authorizes the court's action for persons who are sentenced for no more than three years and, if previously imprisoned, have not been sent to prison again within five years of a previous prison sentence.

Judges are reluctant to attach probationary supervision to the suspension when there are extenuating circumstances. They see supervision as an additional burden and prefer to return the more worthy recipients of suspension to the streets without supervision. Furthermore, another suspension would be denied if the individual commits a new crime. The net effect is that probationary supervision signals the judge's belief that probationers are the least favorable of the successful candidates for suspended prison sentences (Kouhashi 1985; Nishikawa 1990). The proportion of suspensions requiring probationary supervision has dropped from 18.5 percent in 1981 to 14.3 percent in 1993 (Research and Training Institute 1984, 106; 1987, 98; 1994, 62).

Turning Over Functions to the Private Sector

From a pragmatic perspective, nonprosecution and use of suspended sentences were introduced to alleviate the

INTRODUCTION

financial burden on the government during the Meiji Restoration, when it was engaged in modernization to prevent colonization by the imperialist nations of the West (S. Miyazawa 1991). A precedent was set for turning over to the private sector some of the functions usually handled by the government. The growth of the national bureaucracy was inhibited by the National Personnel Authorization Law (May 1960), which fixed the number of officials; and simultaneously the cabinet required every ministry to reduce its personnel by 5 percent (Pempel 1982). Until the 1970s the government preferred a "welfare society" to a "welfare state"; social services were expected to be assumed by the family, community, and private employers (Watanuki 1986).

In Japan the private sector is enlisted in reducing the costs for the correctional agencies. Subcontracting binds small and large companies and gives the industrial prison a place in the scheme. By gaining access to the free market, the prisons keep some two-thirds of the inmates in a forty-hour workweek. When the contemporary system of probation and parole was being introduced in 1949, the shortage of funds favored reliance on unsalaried volunteer probation officers (VPOs) for supervision (Rehabilitation Bureau 1990). The Volunteer Probation Officer Law sets the maximum number of VPOs at 52,500 for two-year terms subject to reappointment. No salary or allowance is paid, but expenses in performing duties are paid "within the limit laid down by the national budget."

For most released prisoners, the family is the primary buffering agency; for those without family support or other resources, the rehabilitation aid hostels are expected to cushion any shock. The hostels (halfway houses) also are operated by volunteers; their finances are partially subsidized by the government.[5] The probation offices are responsible for supervising private associations that operate the hostels. The hostels have difficulties in meeting their expenses, comments the Rehabilitation Bureau (1990), when they lack sufficient funds other than the government subsidy.

Antiprostitution Law: An Example Case

With the enactment of the Antiprostitution Law in 1956 and its amendment in 1958, street prostitution became subject to criminal sanctions. The Diet's action qualifies as "extended criminalization" in that the scope of the criminal law was broadened to cover conduct not previously so penalized. The issues raised illustrate the impact of external events on criminal justice practice and the dependence of criminal justice reform on more general public issues.

Hobson (1987, 4–5) identifies three elements of the "politics of prostitution": the historical and cultural traditions that frame its discourse and guide the search for alternatives, a body of laws and legal practices, and a reform movement linked to other movements. Those components are satisfied by the framing and enactment of the Antiprostitution Law after World War II. The enfranchisement of women at that time provided a window of opportunity for political action against prostitution among women's issues.

Passage of the law was a remarkable political achievement, overturning the institutionalization of prostitution. Shogun Yoritomo Minamoto established brothels in the twelfth century to prevent army desertions. In the Edo period (1600–1867), prostitution was legal if licensed, subject to police registration and control, and limited to designated red-light districts, such as Yoshiwara District in Tokyo, Shinmachi in Osaka, and Shimabara in Kyoto (Buruma 1984; O'Callaghan 1968; Bayley 1976).

Grounded in traditions shaping conventional relations between men and women, Japanese prostitution is evaluated from a different cultural perspective than that used to evaluate prostitution in America.[6] Traditions do not imbue Japanese males with taboos on erotic pleasure (Benedict 1967). Sex is not a moral issue in Japan, but, Christopher (1987) says, men, whether married or single, are still accorded far more sexual freedom than women—particularly more than married women.

Early reform efforts were directed against prostitution. In 1842 the Tempo Reform heavily censored pornography and instructed "ladies of pleasure" to find other employment. In 1872 the Meiji government canceled debts of geisha and prostitutes to houses of pleasure, limited contracts for apprentices to seven years, and required the prostitutes to register with city governments (Dalby 1983). Founded in 1886, the Kyofu Society of Japanese Christian Women petitioned the national government to forbid the export of Japanese women for prostitution in foreign countries and to abolish concubinage. In 1890 the Salvation Army marched into red-light districts to call on prostitutes to give up their trade. Existing until World War II, the Kakusei Society was instrumental in closing brothels in twenty-two prefectures (Yokoyama 1991).

In the late nineteenth and early twentieth centuries, pioneer feminists raised the issues of suffrage, arranged marriages, literary outlets for women, legal rights, birth control, and the abolition of licensed prostitution. The movement literally disappeared with mobilization of women's groups for the World War II effort (Pharr 1981; Robins-Mowry 1983).

During the postwar occupation, the Supreme Commander for Allied Powers (SCAP) issued on 21 January 1946 a memorandum recommending the abolition of licensed prostitution. SCAP policy was to rule through the Japanese government (Fukutake 1989). On 15 January 1947 the government stipulated penalties for persuading women to perform prostitution or to obligate a woman to engage in prostitution. In 1948 the legal basis for police regulation was eliminated. Public opinion increasingly called for maintenance of public morals and the protection of women (Shikita and Tsuchiya 1990).

A postwar reform gave women the right to vote and to hold electoral office. Perry (1980) describes as almost an accident its inclusion among the SCAP directives. A young woman among the twenty-one Americans drafting the directives prepared the clauses on civil rights, he says, and the draft drew little attention in the flurry of activities.[7] After the election law was revised by the Diet, thirty-nine of the seventy-nine female candidates were elected to the House of Representatives. Their presence gave new impetus to women's issues, including opposition to prostitution (Fujita 1968, 94).

Provisions of the Antiprostitution Law, passed in 1956 after several sessions of the Diet, mirror the political bargaining that narrowed the victory. Persons who profited from the trade exerted heavy pressure on male members of the Diet. Prostitutes held a national convention to create a labor union and to campaign against enactment of the law (Yokoyama 1991). The law had been framed to avoid abolishing all commercial sex and singling out patrons for prosecution. "It is not commercial sex that the law enjoins," notes Bayley (1976, 113), "but public display and knowing facilitation by third parties." The law defines prostitution as engaging in sex relations with an indefinite number of partners, for pay or promise of pay. Under the law the partner is not subject to punishment. The law prohibits solicitation, loitering and following a prospective partner in public places, waiting for a partner in public, and calling attention to the service. The law prohibits recruiting a girl by force, intimidation, trickery, falsehood, or other influences; procuring customers; providing a place for prostitution; entering into a contract for prostitution; or living off a prostitute's earnings (Koshi 1970).

From 1960 through 1985, the number of violations of the Antiprostitution Law dropped sharply (Shikita and

Tsuchiya 1990, 197–98). In 1960 the police cleared 17,045 violators. Thereafter, referrals to the public prosecutors were reported: 11,385 in 1965, 6,711 in 1970, 2,938 in 1975, and 3,617 in 1985.

The Rise and Decline of Guidance Homes

In 1958 the Antiprostitution Law was amended, and the Women's Guidance Home Law was enacted. "The revision made it possible to place women aged 20 or older under guidance," say Shikita and Tsuchiya (1990, 197), "if they are indicted and convicted of soliciting or awaiting men in public, and when the court suspends the execution of their sentence of imprisonment." Article 25 of the Penal Code authorized diversion of convicted prostitutes from penal punishment to women's guidance homes. The law targeted two groups: the entrepreneurs profiting from prostitution and street prostitutes. The leniency of the courts reduced the number of entrepreneurs in illicit sex who were sent to prison; at the end of 1994, prisons held only sixty-eight men and eight women who had been convicted under the Antiprostitution Law (Research and Statistics Section 1995a, 23).

The Antiprostitution Law implies a desire to protect women from exploitation and corruption. "Since 'guidance disposition' aims at facilitating women's real resocialization by correcting their habit of prostitution," says the Correction Bureau (1967, 55), "the treatment at women's guidance home centers on (1) social education, (2) vocational guidance and (3) medical care for mental or physical handicaps which may obstruct their rehabilitation." Social education was to be "moral training and cultivation of finer sentiments."[8] Departure from the accepted female role was to be corrected. Vocational training consisted of needlework, handicrafts, and vocational guidance in lieu of instruction in specific occupations. A gratuity of eight thou-

Table 1.2
Distribution of Violations of the Antiprostitution Law, 1960–85

Violations	% Distribution				
	1960	1965	1970	1975	1985
Solicitation and Similar Acts	73.2	67.9	60.3	51.8	18.6
Arrangement and Similar Acts	12.3	14.2	18.6	26.1	45.5
Contract for Prostitution	1.0	0.9	1.8	2.9	16.2
Offering of Places	9.1	8.9	12.5	13.0	11.2
Employment for Prostitution	4.2	7.5	6.0	5.2	7.7
Other	0.2	0.6	0.8	1.0	0.8
Total %	100.0	100.0	100.0	100.0	100.0

Source: Adapted from Shikita and Tsuchiya 1990, 198.

Note: The figures in 1960 represent police clearances; thereafter, the figures represent offenders referred to the public prosecutors' offices.

sand yen was received at release. Medical treatment emphasized eradication of venereal disease and improvement of the inmate's physical condition (Correction Bureau 1967, 55–56).

Admissions to the homes peaked at 408 in 1960 and dropped to 253 in 1965, 49 in 1970, 20 in 1980, and 7 in 1988 (Correction Bureau 1990, 74). When I visited the only remaining women's guidance home in 1991, no residents were present. The sharp decline suggests either an increasing disinterest in enforcement of the law or a shift of commercial sex away from street prostitution.[9] Shikita and Tsuchiya (1990, 198) prefer the latter explanation: "A decline in the number of those referred to prosecutors and a change in the rates of types indicate that the tricks used for prostitution have become so elusive that investigations into it

INTRODUCTION

have become difficult. The major type of prostitution has been shifting from 'street prostitution,' exemplified by solicitation on the streets, to other forms."

The shift of offenses supports that conclusion (see table 1.2). Solicitation was dominant initially; employment for prostitution held a minor share, and solicitation declined consistently. The management of prostitution assumed greater shares in the form of arrangement, contracts for prostitution, and offering of places. The nature of commercial sex seems to have changed. The idea of call girls has been imported from the West; sexual services are offered by bar girls, sensuous nightclubs, and massage parlors (Longstreet and Longstreet 1970; Buruma 1984). Relatively few prostitutes operate on the streets independently of the entertainment enterprises where other forms of commercial sex operate.

2

The Yakuza and Accelerated Criminalization

"Most of those prisoners are yakuza," the warden of a class-B prison told me in an industrial workshop. A couple hundred men bent their heads in dedicated attention to work tasks. Only the whir of machinery broke a silence that might be attributed to a church. Three unarmed prison officers and representatives of private contractors were the only supervisors.

Weakened Tolerance of the Yakuza

For Japan and its declining imprisonment rate, the progressively greater incarceration of the yakuza is remarkable. The criminalization of yakuza offenses is not a recent development; rather, their situation is a prime example of the accelerated criminalization. Despite the long-term public tolerance of the yakuza as folk heroes, new developments have made their suppression a political issue. These developments include the unprecedented level of gang violence, gang efforts to exploit legitimate businesses, and consolidation of gangs into seven nationwide "families."[1] The gangs had enjoyed some tolerance because of their strikebreaking and because their ultraconservative politics had opposed postwar Marxism. Van Wolferen (1989, 103) observes that

"Japan's low crime statistics would probably rise if the police had to cope unaided with a chaos of criminals operating individually or in small groups." Huang and Vaughn (1992) summarize arguments that "a symbiotic relationship" has existed between organized crime and the police in Japan.

The attitudes of gangsters also have changed. More gangsters place illicit economic gains over respect for the yakuza traditions. A police official told Buruma (1984–85, 47): "They won't listen to us any more. If the boss fails to generate enough money, his men will no longer be loyal." The gangs are more business-oriented, Buruma says, and less like protection societies for social outcasts; their right-wing politics often have become only a front for illicit activities.

New legislation gave the police, prosecutors, and courts new means of controlling the gangs. In 1958 legislation was aimed against the intimidation of witnesses and against the intensified intergang warfare. The Code of Criminal Procedure was modified to authorize denial of bail to gang-associated persons, unless specifically granted by a court, when they were expected to retaliate against a witness. Legislation specifically targeted unlawful assembly of two or more persons with dangerous weapons for the joint purpose of killing or bodily injury of another person. Intensified intergang conflict also brought strengthening in 1964 and 1987 of the Law for Punishment of Acts of Violence, along with the penalty against habitual acts of violence (Shikita and Tsuchiya 1990).

The Elements and History of the Yakuza

The term *organized crime* usually denotes certain analytical dimensions: a hierarchical organizational structure, restricted membership, a criminal subculture of violence or threats of violence, a drive for maximum profit at minimum risk, traffic in illicit goods or services that are in public demand, an effort to mesh illegal activities with legal enterprises, and immunity ordinarily from law enforcement (Hagan 1983; Albini 1975; Abadinsky 1981; Herbert and Tritt 1984; Albanese 1985; Bynum 1987; Schneider 1993). Although absolute transfer of the Western model is not appropriate, yakuza activities share those general characteristics. Social chaos after World War II lent impetus to the growth of the yakuza. The National Police Agency speaks of *boryokudan* members because of their violence; the Japanese word *boryoku* means "violent" in English. Recruitment criteria and socialization of new members favor organizational continuity and internal discipline. Illicit transactions can be systematic because the gangs enjoy a degree of public tolerance and are usually insulated from vigorous suppression. Regardless of cultural and structural differences between societies, all crime syndicates are subject to economic principles affecting both legitimate and criminal enterprises. Illicit businesses provide services prohibited by law: drugs, gambling, prostitution, or "protection." Criminals gain impressive incomes because citizens, otherwise respectable, demand the services. Differences among the illegal markets affect their relative importance.

Despite general similarities with the Western model, the yakuza comes in a peculiarly Japanese version. A typical gang, say Shikita and Tsuchiya (1990, 77), "includes the categories of professional gamblers, street peddlers, delinquent youth groups, stevedore gangs and unscrupulous constructors." These subverse subgroups, "true antisocial and malignant elements of a society," emerged "under the influence of the socioeconomic conditions of the time."

Takeuchi (1986–87) analyzes the cross-national economic factors affecting the income-producing operations of Japanese crime syndicates. Smuggling of drugs risks police reactions, competition of foreign outlaws, and difficulties of subterranean distribution. Users demand drugs regardless of price; high profits entice the gangsters despite

THE YAKUZA

the risks. Demand for prostitution also is high, but the yakuza's domination of the market seems to be declining. Before World War II, young girls could be enticed from villages by promises of legitimate employment and forced into the sex trade; now, better chances for legitimate employment undermine any female interest in the trade unless earnings are very high. Demand drops as the price of a "trick" rises; yakuza sex entrepreneurs are facing increased domestic and foreign competition. The syndicates are striving to sustain protection rackets in street vending and the entertainment businesses but have become more active in use of force to mediate financial and corporate disputes.

The yakuza have been creatures of the socioeconomic conditions for some 250 years. Before the Tokugawa period (1603–1868), feudal lords, or daimyo, warred among themselves. Ieyasu Tokugawa brought stability by consolidating political power through clever military leadership, skillful treatment of defeated adversaries, and hierarchical control of individuals and groups, and by requiring possible opponents to send hostages to Edo (now Tokyo) (Sansom 1963c; Duus 1969). The Tokugawa system of rule was designed to maintain law and order, to enforce official programs of frugality and morality, to collect taxes, and to suppress any resistance. Only one castle town was permitted in each domain; all other strongholds were dismantled. The samurai were forced to either live in a castle town and serve as salaried bureaucrats or surrender their aristocratic status (Tonomura 1992; T. Sato 1990).

Some samurai failed to find a secure place in Tokugawa society in the 1644–51 period or in the social system after the Meiji Restoration, when the modernization was launched (Ino 1974). Some unemployed samurai turned to banditry in the Tokugawa Era and, in a phenomenon similar to the folklore of Robin Hood in the West, became idealized as though they were legendary defenders of the underprivileged, despite their violence and looting.

Among the samurai lacking bureaucratic skills and sufficient income, some became members of the Hatamoto-yakko, a group who adopted a life of dissipation. They were loyal to one another, avenging the killing of their fellows, and spreading terror. They would cut down any passerby who displeased them, and they refused to pay for meals or service. At last, in 1686, the government stamped out the Hatamoto-yakko (Ino 1974). Other unemployed samurai became members of the Machi-yakko, a group who worked for the Yorioya, brokers supplying construction labor for the shogun. The term *yorioya* means "fictive parent" and their laborers were the Yoriko (fictive children). This relationship is similar to the *oyabun-kobun* relationship found in the contemporary yakuza, which is a relationship roughly equivalent to that of a father and son (Ino 1974).

Some contemporary gangs resemble feudal gambling gangs, such as the *bakuto*, and street traders, such as the *tekiya* or *yashi*, who sold, among other items, incense, drugs, and other pharmaceutical products. These groups were tightly knit in the oyabun-kobun fashion, behavioral codes, and a specialized argot. Constant conflicts over economic territory resulted in brawls and sometimes deaths. The Tokugawa police often forced gang members to be informants, to escape punishment for their own crimes or protect other gang members from arrest (DeVos with Mizushima 1973).[2]

The Social Psychology of Gangs

Today the yakuza organization resembles conventional Japanese society, summarizes Raz (1992, 221), in "the paternalistic structure, the surrogate family, the badges bearing the gang logo, the system of ranking, the business cards, and numerous other signs of belonging." The leader is in the oyabun status, receiving the absolute obedience of the subordinate, who is in the kobun status. The "apprentice"

THE YAKUZA

learns basic criminal practices and is tested before gaining full membership. Admission of recruits through sponsors has required a loyalty oath symbolized by the "rite of exchanging cups" (Iwai 1986; Kaplan and Dubro 1986). In the usual ceremony, explains Iwai (1966), the new member is told: "Having drunk from the *oyabun's* cup and he from yours, you now owe loyalty to the *ikka* (the fictive 'family') and devotion to your *oyabun*. Even should your wife and children starve, even at the cost of your life, your duty is now to the *ikka* and *oyabun*."

To insulate themselves from successful prosecution, the yakuza have relied on witnesses' fears of reprisal,[3] on witnesses' and victims' doubts that the police can help, on victims' belief that the losses are too small to justify reports to the police, and on choosing victims already vulnerable to arrest. Gang leaders tend to be protected by their followers' acceptance of responsibility for gang offenses and the bosses' avoidance of direct involvement (Iwai 1986).

The yakuza draw on traditions in their peculiar way. For example, they follow the bakuto custom of ceremoniously severing the end joint of the little finger to erase doubts about their loyalty to the leader. The *demukai* ritual is another demonstration of fidelity. Colleagues come to the prison gate to welcome the released yakuza inmate. If he is a boss, the welcoming party comes in scores of large and expensive foreign automobiles, dressed in dark suits, and wearing sunglasses, to flaunt yakuza power. Fuchu Prison usually times the release in very early morning to avoid traffic congestion (Johnson and Hasegawa 1992; Kaplan and Dubro 1986; Rome 1975).

Tattooing was a protection against witchcraft in feudal Japan; it became a symbol of manliness and resistance to political despotism. Its symbolism was muddled in the Nara Era (710–84) and later in the Tokugawa period, when officials used tattoos to make criminals publicly visible. Contemporary yakuza mark their membership with tattoos from shoulder to knee (DeVos with Mizushima 1973; Rome 1975). Prison staffs see massive tattooing as evidence of yakuza affiliation.

The openness of their operations is striking; Kersten (1993, 278) finds not only that the yakuza are "more visible than some of their counterparts in Western societies, but also that they are numerically more significant as far as crime control efforts are concerned." Brass plates proclaim the gang headquarters in the neighborhood; public advertising invites recruits; business cards name the organization and gang rank of the member; videotapes record the installation ceremony of a new chief.[4]

The mass media exploit their popular acceptance as a modern version of the romanticized outlaw samurai. The *New York Times* reported on 22 January 1995 that the Yamaguchi-gumi was handing out food, water, and diapers to victims of the paralyzing earthquake at Kobe. A gang official told the reporter by telephone that goods were being transported by motor scooters, boats, and a helicopter. "The yakuza have a sense of chivalry, of public spiritedness," the official insisted.

The ritualism of the yakuza rules of behavior squares with Japanese conventions and, along with folk myth, is a favorite theme for Japanese motion pictures, says Buruma (1984). The typical film begins with a scene of peace and security in medieval Japan. The horn of a large foreign automobile (usually an American luxury vehicle) disturbs the scene; the occupant is a fat man smoking a cigar. A gang of "noble" yakuza, in happi coats (Japanese-style jackets) and displaying a gang insignia, is setting up a street market for a neighborhood festival. Men in flashy Western dress kick over the market stalls, but the "heroic" yakuza beat the bullies and send them off running.

To obtain information on self-blame of gangsters versus nongangsters in their victimization of others, researchers for the Research and Training Institute (1992b) questioned 4,376 persons (including 1,109 juveniles) who entered adult or juvenile institutions in the final quarter of 1985. Gangsters were less inclined than nongangsters to "feel sorry for the victim" or to believe their crime was "wrong." In bodily injury and assault cases, 68 percent of the nongangsters, but only 23.9 percent of the yakuza, said: "I am worse than the victim." In extortion cases, that reply was given by 90.2 percent of the nongangsters and 65 percent of the gangsters, but only 22.2 percent of the gangsters gave that reply when the victim was also a gangster.

Most juvenile offenders do not become involved directly with adult gangsters, although, as Kersten (1993) points out, some authors see a "somewhat systematic" recruitment. When there are linkages, according to Iwai (1966) they are through the *chimpira*, a term applied to older delinquents who avoid punishment by greater leniency accorded juvenile offenders. Some of them mature into yakuza or express acceptance of their values.[5]

The Rising of Gangs and Police Responses

The postwar chaos (1945–49) brought the gangs to the fore. Sometimes they would serve as contractors to the American military, who were not aware of their background (DeVos with Mizushima 1973). New gangster groups, composed of former soldiers, engaged in black-marketing, gambling, being bodyguards for wealthy persons, or robbery. Sometimes they used World War II weapons in competition for territory. When the occupation authorities returned law enforcement to the Japanese, social order was restored and crimes of the yakuza declined.[6]

From 1950 to 1964, the economy recovered, and the yakuza profited from construction, labor for seaports, gambling, prostitution, liquor bars, and illicit drugs. The membership rose from 92,860 in 1958 to 184,091 in 1964 and dropped consistently to 86,287 in 1988. Seven "families" (Yamaguchi, Honda, Sumiyoshi, Inagawa, Kobusai, Kyokutou, and Matsuba) absorbed minor gangs into nationwide organizations (Yokoo 1986).

The gangs have been heavily involved in the stimulant drug trade. In 1974 the police cleared 5,919 such offenders, of whom 63 percent were gangsters. The number of offenders escalated to 24,022 in 1984, but the representation of the yakuza eased to 47 percent. The number of cleared stimulant drug offenders dropped to 16,093 in 1991, and the involvement of gangsters to 43 percent (Research and Training Institute 1984, 81; 1987, 74; 1991, 74).

In 1965–69 the enforcement of the laws reduced gang membership by direct control operations and attempts to isolate the yakuza from ordinary citizens. Because attacks by rivals on gang headquarters imperil the neighbors, the police closed many highly visible gang offices. Mass arrests and imprisonment at this time, especially of bosses and their lieutenants, were intended to weaken criminal organizations. Gang revenues were curtailed by cutting their supply lines for illicit drugs, interrupting gambling operations, reporting to tax authorities the gang's failure to report illicit income, and controlling the importation of guns. The police publicized their activities to arouse public opposition. The public was offered police assistance in coping with the gangsters' efforts to intimidate individuals and communities (Miyawaki 1979; National Police Agency 1991).

The police label the 1970s as the "Period of Oligopoly of Three Major Groups." Many medium and minor gangs lost illegal income because of the police campaign and were hard hit by the stagnation of the economy when the Organization of Petroleum Exporting Countries (OPEC) abruptly raised the price of oil. Those gangs were absorbed by three major families: Yamaguchi, Sumiyoshi, and Inagawa. These families introduced modern management methods, such as computerized information. Gang membership dropped from 138,506 in 1970 to 103,955 in 1980. In

1970 the three families controlled 26 percent of all gangs; in 1980, 39 percent. Since 1980 the death or retirement of aged leaders stimulated struggles for dominant positions. The number of intergang wars with firearms were 54 in 1975, 27 in 1980, 246 in 1985, 118 in 1990, and 75 in 1993 (Research and Training Institute 1979, 59; 1985, 49; 1987, 65; 1994, 91).[7] The unsavory reputation and severe discipline of the yakuza have deterred younger men from joining. In 1966 persons under thirty years of age made up 56.1 percent of the 147,171 members. In 1987 only 30.4 percent of the 86,287 members were under age thirty.

The gangsters have expanded their pursuit of greater profits. "Their traditional fund-raising activities such as stimulant drug trafficking, gambling and demand for 'muscleman's charge' are still active," report the police (National Police Agency 1992, 49–50). "However," the report continues, "recently they have been trying to make money through new types of fund-raising activities including intervention in civil affairs and company racketeering." The threat of violence is applied in disputes in traffic accidents, collection of debts, loan negotiations, and real estate transactions. "Company racketeering" covers manipulation of stockholders' meetings, disguising extortion under a political movement, exacting compensation for the noise of construction, selling an organizational newspaper at a high price, or investing criminal profits in legitimate businesses.

After 1970 the crime syndicates became highly active in the trade of stimulant drugs;[8] Tamura (1992) offers four reasons gang leaders—many released from prison in the early 1970s—turned to stimulants as the economic base for reorganizing their illicit businesses. The gangs were capable of coordinating the illicit and covert transactions. At that time no equally lucrative source of income was available. The profits strengthened influence over local gangs. The gang members also were habitual users of stimulants.

Tamura (1992) speculates that gang members are reluctant to deal with narcotics and hallucinogens because consumer demand for them would be weak compared with that for stimulants. Narcotics are expected to undermine nationhood, and the effect of stimulants, as opposed to the relaxing effect of narcotics and hallucinogenics, may suit the Japanese workaholics.

The yakuza have built relationships with criminal groups in other countries for traffic in drugs, illegal immigration, and forging international driver's licenses, passports, and visas. "Crime groups also earn big money by intervening in illegal employment of foreigners, raking off part of their wages," report the police (National Police Agency 1992, 50–51), "and by forcing foreign women called 'Japayukisan' to prostitute themselves, causing an international problem."

Unprecedented Actions Against Gangs

The crime syndicates stirred unprecedented official concern because of aggravated intergang violence, nationwide integration of yakuza organizations, and gang movement into new income-producing activities. New legislation aimed at gang violence dealt with assault and unlawful assembly of two or more persons with dangerous weapons and with punishment of acts of violence. Because of the intergang violence, the police became especially concerned about the availability of firearms, despite their longstanding control of firearms and swords. Their confiscation of weapons was handicapped by more sophisticated techniques in smuggling and concealment (National Police Agency 1991).

In 1991 the national Diet took the unprecedented action to authorize the definition of yakuza groups as antisocial organizations. Law No. 77 (1991), the Law Concerning Prevention of Unjust Acts of Boryokudan Members, (simply called the Antiboryokudan Law), was revised in April 1993 by Law No. 41 and broadened the scope of the efforts to suppress the illegal activities. The two laws introduced the concept of "designated boryokudan members" in singling out the gangsters and their organizations who (a) engaged in "unjust acts" related to demanding tribute from legitimate businesses and private persons and (b) comprise nationwide crime syndicates. Public safety commissions are created in the prefectures to assist victims, to prevent intergang violence, to obstruct the recruitment of gangsters, to encourage the withdrawal of members from the gangs, and to facilitate community opposition to the yakuza. My abridgement of the English translation of the law and its revision follows.[9]

> Public safety commissions (PSCs) of prefectural governments are authorized to designate those boryokudan organizations (a) that use undue influence for acquiring funds, accumulating assets, or carrying out the organization's activities and (b) that are controlled by representatives of a stratified configuration of many subordinate boryokudan groups.
> Before making such designations, the PSC will announce publicly the name of the boryokudan being considered, will conduct a public hearing, and will receive confirmation of the National Public Safety Commission (NPSC) that the above conditions for designation are satisfied. The NPSC will form a Panel Commission of Experts (composed of "persons of learning and experience" and of "noble-minded character"). Any person protesting a designation shall be able to demand review by the NPSC; such review must precede any appeal to a court. The designation will be valid for three years. If the designated boryokudan disbands during that period, the PSC must cancel the designation.
> The law prohibits extortion in illegally demanding (a) the purchase of goods, (b) vacating of land or houses against the will of legitimate residents, (c) the "contribution" of monies or goods, (d) unlawful loans, (e) sub-

contracting of civil engineering or construction, and (f) indemnification of damages in traffic accident cases. The PSC is authorized to order that such illegal acts be ceased and to issue orders (valid for up to a year) against repetition of such acts. If they so desire, aggrieved parties will be assisted by the PSC to recover any losses suffered at the hands of designated boryokudan members.

The PSC will assist operators of businesses (through information, material, or instruction of implementing employees) in preventing losses and in methods of coping with unjust demands.

The PSC is authorized to order restrictions on the use of offices in administering the prohibited activities or causing undue concern of neighbors or passersby. The PSC may prohibit the use of gang offices for assemblage, conspiring, issuing commands, or conducting liaison in conflicts between designated boryokudans. The PSC may post notices of such orders at readily visible places at points of access to the offices. The PSC may prohibit coercion or enticement of juveniles to recruit them for designated gangs or to prevent their resignation of membership.

The PSC may designate prefectural centers composed of citizens who counter violence and unlawful acts of boryokudan members by disseminating knowledge of preventive measures, by offering advice in "situations of distress related to unjust acts," by eliminating gang influence on juveniles, and by helping persons wanting to resign from the boryokudan. The NPSC may designate "public-interest, juridical persons" to serve in national centers dedicated to coordinating the operations of prefectural centers.

To implement the law's provisions, the PSC may request reports from members of the designated boryokudan and their associates. The PSC shall be able to have the police enter the offices of the designated boryokudan and carry out such activities as questioning the members and associates. In urgent situations, the PSC may issue provisional orders without a hearing but will hold a hearing as soon as possible after issuing the order. Violators of PSC orders may be imprisoned for not more than a year or may be fined not more than one million yen ($7,692 at 130 yen to a $1 U.S.) or both.

An Early Review of the New Law's Effects

What were the consequences of the Antiboryokudan Law? Eighteen organizations were defined as "designated boryokudan" from June 1992 to early March 1993. The Yamaguchi-gumi of Kobe was the largest, with 23,100 members (National Police Agency 1994). More time will pass before a conclusive evaluation of the consequences will be available, but the National Research Institute of Police Science (a unit of the National Police Agency) has sampled attitudes of gangsters as preliminary evidence of results. The following review draws selectively on two reports, summarized in English in Tamura et al. 1993 and Uchiyama et al. 1993.[10]

A sample was drawn of 1,440 gang members who were arrested or detained as crime suspects from January to February 1993. The research subjects completed questionnaires and were interrogated afterward. The statuses of respondents were bosses (78); leaders, or "middle managers" (641); and members, or "soldiers" (692). The gang status was uncertain for 29. Motives for having joined the yakuza varied among status levels, because average age and length of membership was greater as the level was raised. Persons less than twenty years of age frequently said they had been attracted by the image of a "suave lifestyle" and expectation of a "hedonistic life." Men in their forties were more inclined to identify gang membership with responsibility and "human feelings," advantages for "my business," and means of "eking out a living."

Whether bosses, leaders, or members, the respondents have changed the "life targets" they expect yakuza membership to serve. The responses in a 1987 survey were compared with those of the 1993 survey. In the interim, the arrested gangsters claimed an attitude swing toward the practical purposes of building wealth, operating a business, or earning a day-to-day living. The 1993 survey found less interest in gaining stature in a "lawless society," faithfully observing its strictures, or living an aimless lifestyle.

The respondents were most likely to recognize that police control had tightened, that the people had become more critical of the gangs, and that the gangs were more cautious about attracting police actions. To a more moderate degree, they acknowledged that intergang conflict had diminished, recruitment had been handicapped, and more members had withdrawn from the gangs. Even lower priority was given to the citizens' fear of the yakuza, weakened citizen readiness to seek illicit services, or willingness of corporations to pay tribute. Regardless of status level in the gang membership, one-third of the respondents reported either a total loss or a decrease in their own legal income and a heavier loss from illegal sources.

In trying to cope with the effects of the Antiboryokudan Law, the arrested gangsters said, the gangs were most likely to reduce their visibility to the general public. Signs, emblems, and member nameplates were removed from the offices. Members were instructed to avoid actions that victimized citizens or stimulated intergang conflict. To a moderate extent, formal conferences were held to mobilize efforts for reducing the impact of the law; some members were expelled. To the least extent, basic changes in the crime syndicate's public identity were attempted by changing its name to appear as a business corporation or a political organization.

Were the arrested gangsters prepared to sever their affiliation with the crime syndicates? The distribution of their replies were as follows: "no intention," 26.5 percent; "will quit immediately," 23.3 percent; "will quit one or more years from now," 9.9 percent; "don't know," 36.3 percent; and "no response," 4.1 percent. Those expressing a desire to withdraw from the gangs were most likely to present socially approved motives: "for sake of my family," "to earn an honest living," or "persuaded by kin and friends." Also important were the immediate experience of being arrested and persuasion by the police. Of intermediate priority were the mounting public rejection of gangs, poor health or the approaching age for retirement, and difficulty of acquiring income through the gang's operations. Least attention was devoted to disbanding or weakening of a gang and to unfair treatment by the leaders or other members of the gangs.

Respondents who were not motivated to quit tended to cite the strength of linkages to bosses or friendships with the members. Other frequent reasons were the practical considerations of "no place where I can live," "too late in life for a fresh start," "can't make a living otherwise," or "need money to quit." Little attention was given to possible gang retaliation for trying to quit.

What forms of help would encourage withdrawals? The respondents emphasized provision of legitimate income and financial assistance, in addition to "severance pay." Of intermediate priority were availability of counseling, immediate living expenses, and a loan to start a business. Availability of housing and vocational training drew least concern.

The Yakuza's Share of Prison Admissions

The campaign raised the number of yakuza arriving at prison gates from 1970 to 1985. The number hovered in the seven thousands through 1988 and then began a decline (see table 2.1). Because very few women prisoners are identified with the yakuza, only male admissions appear in table 2.1. The yakuza and nonyakuza admissions are distinguished in the table. With the gangsters removed, the general but irregular decline in the admissions over the years

THE YAKUZA

Table 2.1
Admissions of Male Yakuza to Prison, 1970–94

Year	Yakuza Admissions	% Yakuza of Total Admissions	Yakuza Admission Rate per 100,000 Population[a]	Nonyakuza Admission Rate per 100,000 Population[a]
1970	4,147	16.4	12.32	62.92
1975	5,477	21.3	14.77	54.44
1980	6,898	25.0	17.59	52.61
1985	7,967	26.3	19.18	53.76
1986	7,576	25.8	18.08	51.98
1987	7,750	27.2	18.26	48.78
1988	7,418	27.4	17.26	45.67
1989	6,261	26.6	14.38	39.74
1990	5,622	25.8	12.83	36.78
1991	5,031	24.9	11.28	34.50
1992	4,564	22.9	10.10	34.04
1993	4,074	20.0	8.89	35.45
1994	3,811	18.8	8.19	35.48

Sources: Research and Statistics Section 1971a, 1981a, 1986a, 1991a, 1994a.
[a]Equals rate per 100,000 Japanese males aged 20 years and over in Japan's total population.

is strengthened. The effect is highlighted by the column of admissions percentage shares held by the gangsters. From 16.4 percent in 1970, the irregular but long-term trend was upward and peaked at 27.4 percent in 1988. Thereafter, the percentages dropped consistently.

The absolute number of yakuza opposed the general decline of prison admissions through 1985; they assumed a greater percentage share of all admissions. In the following years, the share fluctuated but continued to be impressive until beginning a consistent decline in 1989. Their imprisonment rates followed a similar trend. After 1985 the yakuza rates joined the nonyakuza males in the decline.

Convicted offenders headed for prison are classified in detention centers according to gender, nationality, kind of penalty, age, length of sentence, and existence of a physical or mental disability. The bulk of them (18,827 of 21,953 in 1993) are classified generally as either class-A or class-B offenders.

During processing, the detention houses distinguish whether or not new adult inmates possess "advanced criminal tendencies" (and should be designated class-B offenders) according to four criteria: previous imprisonment, association with the yakuza, nature of the offense, and other antisocial conduct. Previous incarceration brings assignment to class B when the newcomer (a) has been in a juvenile training school or child-care institution more than twice as a delinquent; (b) has been imprisoned within the last five years; or (c) has committed serious crimes after release from previous imprisonment, although more than five years have passed. Persistent departures from rectitude—such as drug abuse, alcohol addiction, or vagrancy—are seen as a class-B lifestyle. Association with the yakuza for more than a year draws class-B designation. Certain crimes, especially when repeated, are considered characteristic of gangsters. These are violations of the law against violence, extortion, intimidation, unlawful possession of firearms and swords, assault and unlawful assembly with weapons, prostitution, and gambling. Habitual or intentional criminal acts call for class-B designation; situational or accidental crimes for class A.

Over the years the gangsters have taken up greater shares of those prisoners classified as possessing advanced criminal tendencies (class B). In 1975 there were 24,040 total prisoners classified as class B. The numbers ranged from 28,469 to 29,449 between 1981 and 1990 and then declined

Table 2.2
Representation of Male Yakuza among
All Class-B Prisoners at Year-End, 1975–91

Year	Class-B Yakuza	% Yakuza of Class-B	% Class-B of Yakuza	% Class-B of Nonyakuza
1975	6,775	28.2	85.4	57.9
1981	10,802	38.2	92.1	55.6
1982	11,096	37.2	91.9	57.0
1983	11,315	39.2	91.8	52.7
1984	11,907	41.3	91.8	52.2
1985	12,317	42.9	89.3	50.8
1986	12,583	43.2	90.6	51.5
1987	12,788	43.4	90.8	52.3
1988	12,828	43.8	91.9	51.9
1989	12,505	45.0	92.5	52.5
1990	11,259	43.2	92.8	53.4
1991	10,469	41.7	93.1	55.2

Sources: Research and Training Institute 1985, 54; 1989, 80; 1992a, 70.

to 25,111 in 1991. Meanwhile, the class-B yakuza rose consistently from 6,775 in 1975 to 12,505 in 1989, thereafter dropping to 10,469 in 1991. The percentages in table 2.2 relate the two arrays of absolute numbers. The yakuza have taken up progressively greater shares of all class-B prisoners, from 28.2 percent in 1975 to 45 percent in 1989. Their shares dropped to 43.2 percent in 1990 and 41.7 percent in 1991.

The vast majority of the yakuza prisoners, of course, have been assigned to class-B prisons. The classification criteria would have that result. In 1975 those prisons held 85.4 percent of the gangster-inmates. Since 1980 the percentages have hovered around 90 percent. Of the remaining male prisoners (the nonyakuza), their referrals to class-B prisons have ranged from 50.8 to 57.9 percent, a high figure, but short of the classification of the gangsters.

Tracing Trends in Crimes among Admissions

Among the offenses for which individuals are imprisoned, the percentage share of gangsters varies, and it suggests how the campaign against crime syndicates has affected prison admissions. The absolute number of prison admissions gained initially, from 4,147 in 1970 to 5,477 in 1975, 5,898 in 1980, and 7,959 in 1985, and then declined thereafter to 5,622 in 1990 and 3,811 in 1994. Table 2.3 presents three major groups of crimes according to percentage share of all yakuza crimes: (1) yakuza-operation crimes (those in which gangsters were heavily involved); (2) drug crimes, involving both drug traffickers and drug abusers; and (3) "conventional crimes" (crimes of violence, crimes against property, sex offenses, and traffic violations that are characteristic of individuals usually populating prisons). Gangsters do not necessarily commit conventional crimes in direct relationship to their pursuit of illicit economic gain. With the information available to me, it is not feasible to identify which of the gangsters' conventional crimes served yakuza purposes.

The first group (yakuza-operation crimes) further differentiates offenses by those typical of the crime syndicates' pursuit of illicit profits versus those offenses defined in the course of an official campaign to control the syndicates.

Yakuza-operation crimes have lost their share of total admissions, mostly because of a decrease in typical crimes. Extortion, gambling, and lottery activities were predominant in 1970, but they lost their position over the years. Traffic in pornography, intimidation, and prostitution have

THE YAKUZA

Table 2.3
Distribution of Offenses for Male Yakuza
Admitted to Prison, 1970–94

Offenses	% Distribution					
	1970	1975	1980	1985	1990	1994

First Group: Yakuza-Operation Crimes

Typical	27.8	17.9	12.3	12.6	13.0	11.8
Extortion	(14.6)	(11.6)	(8.8)	(9.7)	(10.0)	(9.5)
Gambling	(10.1)	(5.0)	(2.3)	(1.9)	(1.7)	(1.2)
Other[a]	(3.1)	(1.3)	(1.2)	(1.0)	(1.3)	(1.0)
Control Law	17.1	15.8	11.2	9.7	10.1	11.3
Firearms	(2.3)	(4.3)	(2.4)	(3.3)	(4.6)	(6.0)
Assault	(2.0)	(1.6)	(1.3)	(1.1)	(0.8)	(1.0)
Violence	(12.7)	(9.9)	(7.5)	(5.3)	(4.7)	(4.3)
Total	44.9	33.7	23.5	22.3	23.1	23.1

Second Group: Drug Crimes

Total	1.5	17.5	35.6	39.2	35.2	35.9

Third Group: Conventional Crimes

Violent	27.3	23.0	18.0	17.6	19.3	18.4
Bodily Injury	(21.2)	(18.6)	(14.6)	(14.2)	(15.5)	(14.9)
Homicide	(3.9)	(2.5)	(2.5)	(2.6)	(2.6)	(2.0)
Robbery	(1.6)	(1.5)	(0.8)	(0.7)	(1.2)	(1.4)
Other[b]	(0.6)	(0.4)	(0.1)	(0.1)	(0.0)	(0.0)
Property	18.4	14.5	11.7	11.0	11.5	12.0
Larceny	(13.0)	(10.2)	(8.2)	(7.0)	(7.8)	(7.2)
Fraud	(3.3)	(2.6)	(2.2)	(3.1)	(2.6)	(3.5)
Other[c]	(2.1)	(1.7)	(1.3)	(0.9)	(1.1)	(1.3)
Sex[d]	2.6	2.5	1.0	0.7	1.1	0.7

Table 2.3 cont. on next page

THE YAKUZA

Table 2.3 continued

Offenses	% Distribution					
	1970	1975	1980	1985	1990	1994
Third Group: Conventional Crimes
Traffic	2.2	4.9	6.3	5.5	4.4	3.7
Total	50.5	44.9	37.0	34.8	36.3	34.8
Fourth Group: Other Crimes[e]
Total	3.1	3.9	3.9	3.7	5.4	6.2
Total %	100.0	100.0	100.0	100.0	100.0	100.0

Sources: Research and Statistics Section 1971a, 1976a, 1981a, 1986a, 1991a, 1995a.

[a] Pornography, intimidation, and prostitution.

[b] Kidnapping, violations of explosives control law, gross negligence, and prison escape.

[c] Forgery, intrusion, arson, embezzlement, counterfeiting, and stealing property.

[d] Rape and indecent assault.

[e] Violations of public order, other penal laws, and other special laws.

a regular place in yakuza operations but have held a minor position among prison admissions.

Admissions for drug offenses are especially difficult to separate into yakuza and nonyakuza crimes, because drug abusers involve both gangsters and other offenders. This category is treated separately and shows a significant fluctuating increase over the years.

Intended to strengthen efforts to control the crime syndicates, three laws have had impact on prison admissions, although they have brought fewer gangsters to prison than the typical yakuza crimes. The three control laws are aimed, respectively, toward sharply restricting the possession of firearms and swords, inhibiting assault and unlawful assembly of two or more persons with dangerous weapons, and punishing acts of violence. The latter two laws were directed also against mass disturbances by groups other than the gangsters. The effect of the Law for Punishment of Acts of Violence was considerable in 1970 but tapered off. Police campaigns against possession of guns have had significant effect in sending the yakuza to prison. The Assault with Unlawful Assembly Law has had modest and declining effect.

The third major group of yakuza crimes is comprised of conventional crimes that bring to prison offenders other than gangsters. In the percentage distributions of their prison admissions, the yakuza are represented less and less over the years. Largely for bodily injury and homicide, crimes of violence are especially influential in the decline. Larceny is dominant among crimes against property. Fraud holds only a minor position; its persistence suggests involvement in questionable business practices. Sex crimes, primarily rape, have declined, but their numbers have always been relatively few.

Imprisonment of the yakuza for traffic offenses has been uncommon, but it gained importance until 1980 and then tapered off. Imprisonment for traffic offenses has become more frequent in absolute numbers; chapter 4 concentrates on that development. Traffic offenses held only a modest place among the prison admissions of the yakuza, but since none of the other offense categories consistently increased their share, the traffic offenses were especially influential in replacing the share lost by typical yakuza crimes.

Ratios: Measuring the Yakuza Presence

Yakuza members and persons closely associated with the criminal organizations are more likely to be prosecuted. For cases other than traffic offenses in 1992, public prosecutors sent 77.2 percent of the yakuza cases and 61.9 percent of the nonyakuza cases to the courts for trial (Research and Training Institute 1993, 15). When convicted, the yakuza are less likely to be granted probation in lieu of a prison sentence. The Rehabilitation Bureau reports that, of probationers terminated in 1993, only 11.2 percent were gangsters. Their revocation rate was 36.4 percent, compared with 25.9 percent of other probationers. Yakuza prisoners are unlikely to be recommended by wardens for parole; those prisoners also prefer release on completion of their sentence, over the supervision that goes with parole. Nevertheless, yakuza composed 17.5 percent of the parole terminations in 1993. Their revocation rate was 5.3 percent, compared with 7.5 percent for other parolees; perhaps the yakuza lived up to the official experience that, when selected properly, they are compliant parolees (Research and Statistics Section 1994b).

The yakuza attract the attention of penologists because of their high proportion among all Japanese prisoners. They do occupy a significant share of the prisoners, and the size of the shares varies according to the crimes that brought them to penal institutions. Ratios enable us to examine in more detail the second of these two conclusions (see table 2.4). The ratio is computed by dividing the number of yakuza inmates by the number of nonyakuza inmates. As the ratio drops below 100, the advantage of nongangster admissions increases. The ratios are artificially inflated and should be regarded with caution when the numbers are few.

The gangsters gained greater shares in prison admissions over the years but lost shares in 1994. For all crimes one in five newly arrived prisoners were gangsters in 1970; the proportion was greater than one in three in 1985 and 1990. The ratios rose from 0.20 in 1970 to 0.36 in 1985 and 0.35 in 1990 but dropped to 0.23 in 1994. The trend was established despite lower ratios of gangster admissions after 1975 for crimes typical of yakuza operations.

Admissions for crimes typical of yakuza operations gained ratios as the years unfolded; typical crimes were

THE YAKUZA

Table 2.4
Ratios of Yakuza to Nonyakuza Male Admissions to Prison, 1970–94

Offenses	1970	1975	1980	1985	1990	1994
First Group: Yakuza-Operation Crimes						
Typical	1.36	1.38	1.47	1.79	1.52	1.04
Extortion	(1.03)	(1.18)	(1.26)	(1.89)	(1.68)	(1.13)
Gambling	(3.18)	(3.02)	(4.02)	(4.84)	(3.06)	(2.04)
Other[a]	(1.01)	(0.83)	(1.43)	(0.66)	(0.63)	(0.43)
Control Law	1.50	1.86	1.62	1.96	2.02	1.37
Firearms	(2.20)	(2.90)	(1.81)	(3.00)	(4.09)	(1.80)
Assault	(2.05)	(1.87)	(1.31)	(2.15)	(1.15)	(0.95)
Violence	(1.36)	(1.60)	(1.63)	(1.59)	(1.48)	(1.12)
Total	1.41	1.57	1.54	1.86	1.70	1.18
Second Group: Drug Crimes						
Total	0.90	1.37	0.71	0.66	0.59	0.39
Third Group: Conventional Crimes						
Violent	0.41	0.51	0.60	0.66	0.77	0.41
Bodily Injury	(0.63)	(0.78)	(0.94)	(1.08)	(1.14)	(0.72)
Homicide	(0.30)	(0.28)	(0.38)	(0.41)	(0.48)	(0.23)
Robbery	(0.10)	(0.14)	(0.11)	(0.11)	(0.21)	(0.09)
Other[b]	(0.19)	(0.40)	(0.24)	(0.29)	(0.02)	(0.13)
Property	0.07	0.07	0.08	0.08	0.08	0.06
Larceny	(0.06)	(0.06)	(0.08)	(0.07)	(0.08)	(0.05)
Fraud	(0.08)	(0.08)	(0.09)	(0.12)	(0.12)	(0.11)
Other[c]	(0.09)	(0.11)	(0.10)	(0.08)	(0.11)	(0.08)
Sex[d]	0.09	0.14	0.12	0.11	0.14	0.05

Table 2.4 cont. on next page

THE YAKUZA

Table 2.4 continued

Offenses	Ratios					
	1970	1975	1980	1985	1990	1994
Third Group: Conventional Crimes						
Traffic	0.02	0.07	0.13	0.14	0.10	0.08
Total	0.11	0.14	0.16	0.17	0.18	0.11
Fourth Group: Other Crimes[e]						
Total	0.57	0.76	0.82	0.63	0.55	0.38
Total Crimes	0.20	0.27	0.33	0.36	0.35	0.23

Sources: Research and Statistics Section 1971a, 1976a, 1981a, 1986a, 1991a, 1995a.

[a] Pornography, intimidation, and prostitution.

[b] Kidnapping, violations of explosives control law, gross negligence, and prison escape.

[c] Forgery, intrusion, arson, embezzlement, counterfeiting, and stealing property.

[d] Rape and indecent assault.

[e] Violations of public order, other penal laws, and other special laws.

influential in the gain, especially for the crimes of gambling, lottery activities, and extortion. The three control laws, especially control of firearms and swords, heavily involved the crime syndicates. The gangster-inmates were underrepresented among drug offenses because of the data mingling "customers" and traffickers.

Overall, the ratios were very low for gangster participation in conventional crimes. Involvement in bodily injury offenses was noteworthy in both comparatively higher and increasing ratios as the years proceeded. Probably that offense was associated with extortion among crimes typical of the crime syndicates. Homicide and robbery drew enough gangsters for imprisonment that they were specified as violent crimes of the yakuza. Other violent crimes were not exceptional, except for a few instances of kidnapping. Other than bodily injury, the admissions for violent crimes failed to lend support to any expectation that gangsters are prone to apprehension for crimes of violence. The yakuza are more likely to be imprisoned for sex crimes—and in the 1980s for traffic violations—than for property crimes. Among other crimes against property, forgery and embezzlement cases have been few but of increasing absolute numbers. Added to crimes of fraud, they suggest the greater invasion of the business sector for illicit economic gain. Sex offenses have been rape to the greatest extent, rather than indecent assault; pornography is usually listed as a sex crime, but for the crime syndicates, traffic in pornography is among the sources of illicit income. Prison admissions of yakuza for traffic law violations have been few when compared with the corresponding admissions of nonyakuza inmates.

Putting the Leadership in Prison

Among the police strategies, the top bosses and their lieutenants were targeted in "large-scale roundups of the bosses, leaders and members of crime groups who constitute the core" of syndicate organizations (National Police Agency 1992). The top and middle levels of the leadership gained higher percentages (bosses' admissions to prison divided by total admissions of gang members), rising steadily from 13.7 percent in 1970 to 20.2 percent in 1975, 29.2 percent in 1980, 31.6 percent in 1985, 32.9 percent in 1990, and 37.3 percent in 1994 (see table 2.5).

The progressively higher representation of the bosses among yakuza prison admissions attests to the rigor of the campaign against executives of the crime syndicates. In addition to the trend for the percentages listed in table 2.5, both bosses and total yakuza members were present in greater absolute numbers for crimes in yakuza operations than for conventional crimes.

Table 2.5 is dedicated to the propositions, first, that the bosses were more heavily represented in prison admissions than their hirelings as the years proceeded and, second, that the gains differed among the crimes. As an example, of the second proposition, the gang leaders were not represented among yakuza admissions for sex crimes (rape and indecent assault) in 1970, but by 1994 they held 32.1 percent of the yakuza admissions for sex crimes. The nature of the comparison must be kept in mind if that percentage is not to be misinterpreted as evidence of a very heightened sex drive among imprisoned bosses. Actually, only 9 of the 1,420 bosses and 28 of all 3,811 yakuza admissions had been imprisoned for sex crimes in 1970—9 of 28 equals 32.1 percent.

In 1970 bosses held 19.5 percent of the prison admissions for yakuza operations; by 1994 the percentage had risen to 49.5 percent. The bosses' share of the yakuza conventional crimes increased at a higher rate from 8.2 percent in 1970 to 33.5 percent in 1994, but for all years it trailed the percentage for yakuza operations.

For violation of the control laws, the executives became increasingly vulnerable for imprisonment, particularly for violations of gun control, but they also were imprisoned especially for participation in gambling and lottery activities. Whether for typical crimes or violations of control laws, the bosses were highly represented in prison admissions. Among the typical crimes not specified, the bosses had high ratios for prostitution and pornography in the early years, while intimidation became more noteworthy in the 1990s.

Imprisonment of bosses for conventional crimes increased at a noteworthy rate for all subcategories. Unlike the trend for all yakuza, the prison admissions of bosses rose sharply for all versions of violence. Perhaps the campaign against the gang leaders especially targeted violent

Table 2.5
Share of Bosses among Yakuza Admitted to Prison, 1970–94

Offenses	% Share of Bosses					
	1970	1975	1980	1985	1990	1994

First Group: Yakuza-Operation Crimes

Typical	20.8	25.0	37.5	42.6	45.3	47.9
Extortion	(14.3)	(20.6)	(33.8)	(30.8)	(41.4)	(45.4)
Gambling	(32.4)	(36.4)	(51.5)	(59.3)	(68.4)	(70.2)
Other[a]	(15.7)	(16.2)	(37.5)	(53.2)	(45.1)	(43.6)
Control Law	16.9	25.0	37.9	46.6	45.5	51.3
Firearms	(26.8)	(30.6)	(51.5)	(55.8)	(52.3)	(61.7)
Assault	(16.7)	(27.3)	(36.4)	(32.9)	(41.3)	(21.0)
Violence	(15.1)	(22.2)	(33.8)	(43.7)	(39.5)	(44.0)
Total	19.5	25.0	37.7	44.4	45.4	49.5

Second Group: Drug Crimes

Total	27.9	22.5	27.5	27.1	27.1	32.3

Third Group: Conventional Crimes

Violent	10.3	20.0	32.9	33.7	35.5	38.7
Bodily Injury	(9.9)	(20.2)	(32.6)	(33.5)	(35.3)	(38.8)
Homicide	(13.0)	(22.6)	(37.2)	(40.2)	(44.8)	(42.9)
Robbery	(2.9)	(8.2)	(20.3)	(17.7)	(16.2)	(30.8)
Other[b]	(29.2)	(47.4)	(50.0)	(16.7)	(100.0)	(50.0)
Property	5.4	9.6	13.8	18.2	18.7	24.8
Fraud	(8.7)	(13.5)	(25.3)	(26.6)	(29.9)	(35.6)
Larceny	(3.1)	(7.0)	(8.5)	(11.9)	(13.3)	(17.7)
Other[c]	(14.3)	(18.7)	(27.5)	(39.4)	(30.6)	(35.3)
Sex[d]	—	8.0	16.9	22.8	17.5	32.1

Table 2.5 cont. on next page

Table 2.5 continued

Offenses	% Share of Bosses					
	1970	1975	1980	1985	1990	1994
Third Group: Conventional Crimes						
Traffic	14.6	15.1	23.0	28.7	34.0	36.2
Total	8.2	15.4	24.7	35.9	29.4	33.5
Fourth Group: Other Crimes[e]						
Total	13.8	22.2	34.4	38.9	39.8	41.3
All Crimes	13.7	20.2	29.2	31.6	32.9	37.3

Sources: Research and Statistics Section 1971a, 1976a, 1981a, 1986a, 1991a, 1995a.

[a]Pornography, intimidation, and prostitution.

[b]Kidnapping, violations of explosives control law, gross negligence, and prison escape.

[c]Forgery, intrusion, arson, embezzlement, counterfeiting, and stealing property.

[d]Rape and indecent assault.

[e]Violations of public order, other penal laws, and other special laws.

incidents. Except for larceny and fraud, few gang leaders were involved in imprisonment for property offenses. Bosses had increased admissions to prison for traffic offenses.

Managing the Gangster-Inmates

The numbers of yakuza have been a problem for the prison administration; their potential conduct raises qualitative problems. The underground values and intergang rivalries of yakuza inmates hold possibilities for violence and strong resistance to the prison's controls. Their menu of crimes suggests commitment to criminal careers and a dedication to illicit economic gain. They try to continue intergang conflicts, prefer to be with other members of their gang, and strive to recruit nongang members. If prisoner A belongs to X gangster group and has a fight with prisoner B belonging to Y gangster group, their fellows will try to help their colleague. The yakuza try to bribe or intimidate prison officers to gain advantages. They have a disproportionate share of disciplinary violations; Warden Hisashi Hasegawa noted that they were responsible for over 90 percent of the violations at Fuchu Prison, primarily for disobedience, violence against inmates, and fighting.

Gang bosses have been found more committed to the crime syndicates, whether free or imprisoned, than ordinary members, possibly because, as expected, they averaged more years of affiliation with their gang (12.3 versus 7.1 years) and a greater proportion of their income from yakuza operations (59.4 versus 34.6 percent). A Ministry of Justice research project in 1963 traced participation in organized crime of 6,527 yakuza inmates (Research and Training Institute 1965). Legitimate income made up 24.5 percent of the leaders' income, the remainder being unstable or nonexistent; for gang members (*kumiin*) the equivalent percentages were 19.3 and 46.1. Bosses were more likely to claim they had initially craved membership because of their commitment to yakuza values, 49.4 percent versus 10.1 percent of the kumiin. Other motives attracted the members: temptation of anticipated profits (34.8 percent versus 19.3 percent for the bosses);[11] satisfaction of personal needs (10.6 versus 7.4 percent); and recruitment by a yakuza member (14.3 versus 5.4 percent).

The researchers concluded that those gangster-inmates who had initially craved yakuza membership because of yakuza values, individuals alienated from conventional Japanese society, were more likely to resist the prison staffs' efforts toward rehabilitation. The individuals who had much legitimate income were less resistant than those receiving major income from gangs and those with largely unstable income. Opposition rose with extended duration of gang membership.

Another survey distinguished gangsters, former gangsters, and nongangsters among 996 prisoners who were considered to be dangerous and habitual criminals and who were housed in thirty-seven class-B prisons. Prison officers were asked to rate their conduct in prison. The nongangsters drew the most favorable assessment, the yakuza the least favorable, and the former gangsters an assessment in between. The former gangsters somehow linked abandonment of yakuza membership with more positive prison conduct. Gang bosses and members were given higher ratings if at least thirty years of age (Research and Training Institute 1980, 76–77).

The same study measured the fluctuations in prison conduct, attitudes toward prison, and number of changes in work positions. The nongangsters were the most consistently "good," the conduct of former gangsters was erratic but approaching "good," and the conduct of gangsters was the most erratic. The evaluations of the three groups were similar in attitude toward work and in the average number of changes in work allocation. Concentration of yakuza in certain prisons seems to dampen their rule violations. Custodial density was the percentage of yakuza among inmates. Rule-violation rates per one hundred inmates dropped in accord with higher density: at high density (15 percent yakuza population or more) the rule-violation rate was 64.6 percent; at intermediate density (10 to 15 percent) the rate was 72.7 percent; and at low density (less than 10 percent) the rate was 74.1 percent.

The yakuza are managed within the prison's general control system. The newly arrived gangsters are greeted by an ongoing system of routinized regimentation that envelops them in routinized activities. On weekdays, after breakfast in their cells, most inmates march to the workshops, their arms swinging in British military style, and begin work at 7:20 A.M.. (Military marching, taught on entering prison, is among the compliance-inducing rituals.) In midmorning there is a fifteen-minute tea break in the workshop. Lunch is served there at noon, and work resumes at 12:40. After the midafternoon tea break, work ends at 4:30 for the march to the cells, where dinner is distributed at 5 P.M.. Lights are out at 9:00 P.M. The behavioral regulations are sternly administered. Surveillance is supplemented by shakedowns of the inmates and their possessions. Good food, proper medical care, athletics, and recreation forestall the buildup of frustration. Modest sums of money can be earned through diligent work. Japanese prisons employ a progressive grade system whereby conformity with official expectations earns promotion to a higher grade and to the greater privileges associated with each successive grade. Housing in single-person or seven-person cells permits selective dispersion. Dispersion among cells dampens intragang conflict. Gang members not in conflict may be in the same workshop and cell. Usually, a warden is expected to manage his own problematic individuals. To separate notorious criminals, rare transfers can be arranged when the receiving warden and the regional headquarters approve. The Tokyo headquarters must approve transfers between correction regions.

Gangsters try to do "easy time," a reaction common among professional criminals. Their accommodation is pragmatic rather than a surrender of yakuza values. As recidivists, experienced with penal life, they set out to minimize the discomforts and to maximize possibilities of early release. Yakuza values emphasize subordination of the gang member in the kobun status to the boss in the oyabun status. Their socialization within the gang prepares them to be outwardly compliant to the instructions of the prison officers in the oyabun status.

3

Women Drug Offenders and Extended Criminalization

The sociocultural system and traditions of Japan influence the salience of gender roles to criminality and responses to it. This chapter focuses on the rising prison admissions of women, in contrast to the general decline of the Japanese imprisonment rate. The paradox suggests that criminalization of previously tolerated misconduct has been a crucial process here as for other cohorts.

Women Prisoners Go Their Own Way

Women prisoners in Japan are only a small fraction of the inmates, but their share of all inmates doubled between 1926 and 1994 (see table 3.1). The number of males present on an average day more than doubled by 1950, when the postwar chaos peaked their numbers. Since then their number declined in an irregular trend. Women prisoners had about the same trend until 1980, when their number followed a separate pattern.

Three statistics measure the women's separate pattern. The first is the share of all prisoners that were represented by women, which was 2.06 percent in 1926 and 4.12 percent in 1994. In the intervening years the percentage fluctuated,

Table 3.1
Average Daily Prison Population of Men and Women, 1926–94

Year	Average Daily Population Men	Average Daily Population Women	% Share of Women	No. of Women per 100 Men[a]
1926	38,713	816	2.06	2.11
1930	38,409	621	1.59	1.62
1935	49,062	763	1.53	1.55
1940	38,277	560	1.44	1.46
1945	47,808	1,169	2.39	2.44
1950	83,492	1,762	2.07	2.11
1955	65,129	1,376	2.07	2.11
1960	61,998	1,332	2.10	2.15
1965	51,548	1,265	2.39	2.45
1970	40,064	853	2.08	2.13
1975	37,038	812	2.14	2.19
1980	40,842	1,300	3.08	3.18
1985	43,977	1,828	3.99	4.16
1990	39,434	1,707	4.15	4.33
1991	37,034	1,623	4.20	4.38
1992	35,951	1,571	4.19	4.37
1993	35,697	1,512	4.06	4.24
1994	35,780	1,538	4.12	4.30

Source: Data from the Correction Bureau.

[a]Equals the number of women in each year divided by the number of men and multiplied by 100.

reaching its bottom in 1940. Then the general trend was upward; the greatest increase came after 1975.

The second statistic—the number of women present per one hundred male inmates—rises as the average population of women inmates narrows its difference from the average population of men. Again the women reduced their percentage share until 1940; the share rose abruptly in 1945 and then settled down to a more modest rate of increase until 1970. From 1970 through 1991, drug offenses fueled a major and consistent rise in percentage share.

The third statistic—the age-specific imprisonment rate per one hundred thousand Japanese—relates the number of prisoners to the number of persons of that gender in the society (see table 3.2). The statistic cancels the possibility that the increased number of prisoners merely reflects a larger population from which the offenders are drawn. Ideally, in that respect, age-specific rates are the superior barometer of changes in the size of the population of prisoners. The number of adult prisoners (ages twenty years and over) is divided by the number of Japanese aged twenty years or more who theoretically could be imprisoned. The decreasing age-specific rates after 1950 have not kept pace with the general population growth, and the probability of imprisonment has been reduced. As the ratios in table 3.2 show, the female rate has declined less than the male rate. The trend for the ratios was erratic until 1975, although tending to increase in the long term. After 1975 the ratios reflect a strong gain of women's rates relative to male rates.

Drug Admissions: A Key Factor in Representation of Women

The upsurge of women prisoners is largely the result of the increasing prosecution of women using methamphetamines and amphetamines in violation of the Stimulant Drug Control Law of 1951. As an example of extended

Table 3.2
Imprisonment Rate per 100,000 Population, Ages 20 Years and Over, 1945–94

Year	Rate[a] Male (A)	Female (B)	Ratio[b] B/A
1945	287.0	5.5	0.0192
1950	387.4	7.4	0.0191
1955	267.6	5.2	0.0194
1960	231.8	4.6	0.0198
1965	172.1	3.9	0.0227
1970	119.0	2.4	0.0202
1975	99.5	2.0	0.0201
1980	104.1	3.1	0.0298
1985	105.9	4.1	0.0387
1990	90.0	3.6	0.0400
1991	83.0	3.4	0.0410
1992	79.5	3.2	0.0402
1993	77.9	3.1	0.0398
1994	76.9	3.1	0.0403

Source: Demographic data from the Correction Bureau.

[a] Equals the average number of prisoners (ages 20 years and over) present each day divided by Japan's total population (ages 20 years and over) and multiplied by 100,000.

[b] As the ratios increase, the female rate is approaching the value of the male rate.

criminalization, female users of stimulant drugs were caught up in the tightening of the previous prohibition in an atmosphere of crisis.[1] The preferential treatment of women defendants was suspended. Penal sanctions already existing were giving unprecedented salience against what was politically conceived as a threat to the social order.[2]

WOMEN DRUG OFFENDERS

Drug abuse had been limited to a few opium and cocaine addicts, but abuse of stimulant drugs (amphetamines) grew during the chaos after World War II, when the public gained access to the stimulant drugs produced for the military during the war (National Police Agency 1992). The Stimulant Drug Control Law of 1951 strengthened penalties, and it was amended in 1954 and 1955. The Mental Health Law was amended to compel hospitalization. By 1958 the drug crisis seemed to have been overcome, but arrests escalated in 1970-74 (Ministry of Health and Welfare 1979). In 1980 the police reported 20,200 cases cleared for violation of the Stimulant Drug Control Law: 28.1 percent for possession, 34.1 percent for selling or buying, 37.3 percent for use, 0.4 percent for smuggling, three cases for illicit production, and seven cases for other violations (Research and Training Institute 1985, 60). By 1990 police clearances had dropped to 15,267: 30.2 percent for possession, 19.9 percent for selling or buying, 49 percent for use, 0.8 percent for smuggling, and eight cases for other violations (Research and Training Institute 1992a, 74).

A survey tapped public attitudes about stimulant drug users. Commissioned by the National Police Agency, a private institute mailed questionnaires to two thousand people randomly selected in Tokyo, Nagoya, Osaka, and Fukuoka in 1991 (National Police Agency 1992). In the 1,060 responses, the drug problem was described as very serious by 35.6 percent and rather serious by another 45.9 percent. In explaining stimulant drug abuse, 96.2 percent linked it with gangsters, 77.1 percent with crime, 72.3 percent with pathological conditions due to a poison, 67.7 percent with ruin and bankruptcy, and 44.2 percent with disreputable persons.

The pivotal importance of drug admissions is further demonstrated in table 3.3. First, from only 7 in 1968, those admissions rose to 785 in 1985 and gradually tailed off to 501 by 1993 and 1994. Second, those numbers are of greater consequence because they represented at least half of all ad-

Table 3.3
Drug and Nondrug Admissions to Women's Prisons, 1968–94

Year	Total Admissions	Drug Admissions	Drug % of Admissions	Drug (A) Rate per 100,000 Population[a]	Nondrug (B)	Ratio A/B
1968	776	7	0.9	0.02	2.22	0.009
1969	648	7	1.1	0.02	1.81	0.011
1870	568	7	1.2	0.02	1.55	0.013
1971	513	11	2.1	0.03	1.36	0.022
1972	568	13	2.3	0.03	1.46	0.020
1973	549	39	7.1	0.10	1.33	0.075
1974	467	52	11.1	0.13	1.06	0.123
1975	517	58	11.2	0.15	1.16	0.129
1976	570	74	13.0	0.18	1.23	0.146
1977	616	141	22.9	0.35	1.17	0.299
1978	707	248	35.1	0.60	1.12	0.536
1979	847	357	42.1	0.86	1.18	0.729
1980	843	384	45.5	0.91	1.09	0.835
1981	996	507	50.9	1.19	1.15	1.035
1982	1,121	588	52.4	1.37	1.24	1.105
1983	1,157	603	52.1	1.39	1.28	1.086
1984	1,298	728	56.1	1.66	1.30	1.277
1985	1,363	785	57.6	1.76	1.30	1.354
1986	1,299	708	54.5	1.58	1.32	1.197
1987	1,272	701	55.1	1.54	1.26	1.222
1988	1,193	658	55.1	1.43	1.16	1.233
1989	1,039	536	51.6	1.15	1.08	1.065

Table 3.3 cont. on next page

WOMEN DRUG OFFENDERS

Table 3.3 continued

Year	Total Admissions	Drug Admissions	Drug % of Admissions	Drug (A)	Nondrug (B)	Ratio A/B
1990	999	560	56.1	1.19	0.93	1.280
1991	914	518	56.7	1.09	0.83	1.313
1992	914	510	55.8	1.03	0.82	1.256
1993	919	501	54.5	1.00	0.83	1.205
1994	955	501	52.5	0.98	0.89	1.101

Rate per 100,000 Population[a]

Source: Statistics from the Correction Bureau.

[a] Rates are per 100,000 Japanese women in Japan's total population.

missions to women's prisons after 1980 (note the percentages in column 4 of table 3.3). Third, both total admissions and drug admissions declined after 1985. Fourth, drug offenses played the key role in raising the number of women entering prisons while the general trend was toward reducing the imprisonment rate in Japan. The rates per one hundred thousand Japanese women are very low because admissions to women's prisons are in the hundreds. Table 3.3 distinguishes between the admissions for drugs and those for offenses other than drugs. The rates for drug offenses opposed the general decline until 1985, increasing progressively from 0.02 per one hundred thousand Japanese women in 1968–70 to 1.76 in 1985. In the following years, the rates for drug offenses tailed off. Meanwhile, the rates for nondrug offenses followed the progressive decline of the general imprisonment rate.

After 1968 the imprisonment rates for drug offenses gradually moved closer to the nondrug rates, and they surpassed the latter after 1980. Ratios in the far right column of table 3.3 represent the drug rate divided by the nondrug rate. The increase of the ratios is not fully consistent, but the ratios reflect the widening differences between the two rates, in keeping with my hypothesis that drug admissions have been identified with the increased use of imprisonment. After 1985 the differences between the two rates roughly stabilized.

Social Changes and Women's Roles

The history and contemporary nature of Japanese society underline the definition and operation of the roles of women. Within that universe, Japanese women differ from men in the chances that they will violate law, whether or not their misconduct will be criminalized, and whether or not they become prisoners.

Japan was essentially an agricultural country during the Tokugawa period (1603–68), when modernization began. Most workers in cotton spinning and silk reeling were young women from rural areas that suffered poverty and a surplus of labor. The father or brother signed a contract for the girl's employment to obtain cash for the family. The "factory girls" worked under appalling conditions: low pay, inadequate nutrition, dangerous machinery, and sexual harassment. Fences prevented escapes (Hazama 1976; Clark 1979; Sievers 1983; Tsurumi 1990; Kondo 1990; Saso 1990).[3]

"For the sake of the *ie*," writes Fukutake (1967, 39–44), "the personal wishes and desires of individuals had to be ignored or sacrificed." The ie was the agricultural or family business. Outsiders (especially sons-in-law) could become members. The ie held land, a reputation, or specialized skills in perpetuity (Nakane 1984; Kondo 1990). The "bride of the house" was added to the family labor force and expected to provide an heir. Marrying off daughters was expensive, but a poor family could supplement income when daughters earned low wages in cotton mills, through domestic service, or by "selling themselves" into indentured prostitution (Fukutake 1989).

The Meiji Civil Code resurrected the patriarchical ie with the notion of "good wives and wise mothers." The family patriarch had absolute authority and could dispose of his wife's property as he liked. Only for wives was adultery a punishable offense. Each prefecture was required to support at least one high school for young women, as described by an official of the Ministry of Education: "Since the family is the root of the nation, it is the vocation of women who become housewives to be good wives and wise mothers, and girls' high schools are necessary to provide appropriate education enabling girls from middle and upper-middle-class families to carry out this vocation" (Sievers 1983, 112; see also Smith 1987, 9; Kondo 1990, 265–68).

Middle- and upper-status women and their families have looked on higher education as a means of marrying a future company executive. "The aspiring executive," says Saso (1990, 35–38), "would prefer to wed a better-educated woman who would then be expected to devote herself to furthering the education of their children." Now, she continues, social perceptions encourage such women to seek a professional career. Professional women enjoy higher status, Saso argues, less discrimination, and less pressure on newly wed women to quit paid employment. During the high economic growth from 1960 until 1973, many males continued to high school and universities. The shortage of unskilled labor created a demand for women in their midthirties and forties who, because they had left the labor force to raise children, had little work experience (Brinton 1993). Holden (1983) reports that the female workers have moved from farming to other industries, especially women older than thirty-five years.

However, the job opportunities available to women, says Saso (1990), are obscured by women's substantial employment as unpaid family workers and the self-employed.

Many women work in their own homes as instructors in music, English, mathematics, and flower arranging. Those who seek jobs after bearing children usually must accept the inferior wages of small companies. Women in clerical positions are expected to serve tea and perform routine tasks without training and promotions for career advancement.

Usui (1994) acknowledges that Japan falls short on gender equality in pay and access to managerial positions, but she insists that Japanese see gender differences where Americans point to gender inequality, since a large proportion of the Japanese, including younger women, see home and family as the primary career for women. Surveys by the prime minister's office, she reports, showed female respondents increasing their approval of temporary withdrawal from employment but objecting to complete withdrawal. "Women were also substantially benefited by the enactment of a new constitution," asserts Sievers (1983, 191), "which became operative in 1947 and gave them important protections under law," and "by a revised civil code emphasizing equality and the importance of the individual." A new Equal Employment Law in 1986 requires employers to treat the sexes equally in recruitment, training, promotion, dismissal, and retirement, but the law does not penalize violators (Carney and O'Kelly 1987).

Changes in family law and shifts in the labor market, says Smith (1987, 12), have improved immeasurably the position of women; nevertheless, he continues, "I think it would be a grave error to overestimate the degree of improvement." The family is still considered the fundamental unit of society and "the product of the wife's investment of her adult life in her husband and their children." Many Japanese worry about a growth of single-parent families and other "social ills." Smith explains: "A young Japanese friend of mine said: 'We are desperately trying to avoid catching the American disease.'"[4]

Why Have Attitudes Toward Female Offenders Shifted?

Japanese lend a special flavor to the influence of gender on pretrial and sentencing decisions. Parisi (1982) mentions three models Western criminologists follow: the preferential or paternalistic, the punitive, and the equal treatment models. The equal treatment model denies any gender-related differences in dispositions. Nagel and Hagan (1983) summarize the "chivalry-paternalism thesis," which resembles Parisi's first model, and the "evil woman thesis," which shares some elements of Parisi's punitive model.

The preferential model contends that the decision makers assume female offenders are inherently submissive creatures, lacking power, not being dangerous to others, especially prone to becoming involved in crimes under the influence of male associates, but also more susceptible to rehabilitative appeals. The public prosecutors and judges would be expected to believe women especially unlikely to be positively changed by imprisonment. The Confucian philosophy favors the preferential model by demanding that subordinates be dutiful and that superiors care for their people. The preferential model draws some support from the erosion of female rates from police clearances to prison admissions. For all penal offenses in 1991, women were 19.3 percent of all police clearances in Japan but 4.3 percent of prison admissions (Research and Training Institute 1992a, 87, 113).

Advocates of the punitive or "evil woman" perspective argue that women offenders receive more harsh treatment than men either because their misconduct is considered "unladylike" or because their susceptivity to negative influences demands firmer control for "their own protection" (Parisi 1982). "It follows that if women accrue benefits from a presumption that they cannot commit wrongdoings," comment Nagel and Hagan (1983, 115–116), "then, if the presumption is shown to be false, the benefits will now be lost." Their point is consistent with the Japanese interpretation that when defendants show no repentance or effort to make restitution to their victims, they are "nonhuman" violators of giri principles and should suffer the full penalties of the law.

Some female criminologists in the West note the distinction between the "good" and "evil" women. "Historically, researchers and writers in the field of criminology have seen criminality as the result of individual characteristics that," contend Fletcher and Moon (1993, 9), "are only peripherally affected by economic, social, and political forces." In that vein, they continue, the physical and psychological nature of women is believed to impel them to be either "good girls," who are not criminals, or "bad girls," who are criminals. Speaking of "the madonna-whore duality," Feinman (1986, 25) argues that any deviation from the "wife-mother role" is seen to be "a disruption of the social order," because "the traditional woman becomes a source of stability in an otherwise chaotic world."

A Japanese anthropologist notes a folk belief in Japan that, because of their menstruation and childbearing, women were too impure to enter religious places (Befu 1971, 105-6). An American recounts an incident on a tour bus in Kyushu in the 1950s. The teenage guide called attention to a shrine for a local deity on Amadake Island off the coastal highway. Until about ten years earlier, she said, women could not set foot on the island because of "their inherently polluting nature." She concluded: "Nothing untoward seems to have occurred as a consequence of the lifting of the ban" (Smith 1987, 5)

Crimes Associated with Female Gains

Western criminologists debate a number of issues about criminality and gender (see, for example, Adler 1975; Steffensmeier 1978; Hartz-Karp 1981; Wilson 1983). Has the feminist movement in itself increased chances of participation in crimes? Have economic and technological changes led to new female roles that converge with traditional male roles sufficiently to increase the involvement of women in offenses previously believed to be exclusively those of males?

The debate has raised doubts about the use of the feminist movement as a convenient monocausal account for explaining the complex set of factors producing the criminality of women in the West. Smart (1982) questions that use of the feminist movement. First, the official statistics do not support the premise. Second, expanded economic opportunity is expected to offer unprecedented opportunities for crime by women in general, but the labor market has chiefly improved for middle-class women only and denies other women access to illegitimate opportunities. Simon and Sharma (1976, 400) note that the case of Japan raises doubts about the universality of Western relationships between female status indicators and the changing patterns of female criminality. "Could it be that different forces are at work in different countries," they ask. "We need to reassess notions of the relationship between industrialization, modernization, and crime."

"Far-reaching postwar changes in women's social position in Japanese society seem," concludes Kinko Saito Sato (1981, 263), "to have had little influence upon the criminality of women in both qualitative and quantitative perspectives." She describes infanticide, participation in a suicide or murder, professional negligence causing death, and accidental fire as "female offenses" in Japan. Arrest statistics illustrate that Japan has not experienced the full force of the feminist movement, but the involvement of women differs from that of men. The overwhelming proportion of arrested women are accused of theft. Of the Penal Code offenses cleared by the police in 1991, females held these percentages: homicide 19.7 (infanticide 95.7), larceny 25.8 (shoplifting 54.3, bicycle theft 6.1, motorbike theft 4.3, housebreaking 2.9), arson 16.7, fraud 16, embezzlement 12.7, extortion 8.2, bodily injury 7.3, assault 4.8, and robbery 4.7 (Research and Training Institute 1992a, 88).

Example Cases of Women Inmates

At a women's prison in 1992, I obtained three women's case histories and details of the events that brought those women to prison. The case histories lend substance to the official statistics on qualities of women inmates.

The first woman, twenty-three years of age on entering prison, had been in a training school for stimulant drug abuse and in 1992 was serving her first prison sentence for that offense. Soon after her birth, her parents were divorced; she was reared by her mother's parents. She never met her father and believes her mother does not understand her. She has seldom visited her mother, because the mother lives with a lover and has had a child by him. After her grandfather died, the inmate continued to live with her grandmother, who worked nights as a restaurant hostess. Alone at night, the girl had friends of doubtful reputation and attended junior high school irregularly. Because the grandmother did not control the girl, a child guidance center decided she should live with an uncle. She did not like being with the uncle. After graduation from junior high school, she failed to obtain employment and resumed contacts with disreputable persons. She found part-time work as a nightclub hostess, where a yakuza member supplied her with stimulant drugs and forced her to work in a "soapland." (Turkey had formally protested use of the term *Turkish bath* for a Japanese massage parlor. The Japanese authorities substituted the term *soapland*.) She turned herself in to the police for stimulant drug offenses and was sentenced to a year in prison.

Entering prison two years ago for habitual theft (picking pockets), the second woman is the oldest person at a women's prison, at age eighty. She is serving her twelfth prison sentence; the first was for shoplifting at age forty-seven. Now she is serving a three-year sentence for seizing a shoulder bag from a woman in a department store. She explains the crime as an attempt to release emotions aroused by a quarrel with the eldest of her two sons with whom she is living. The store security officer witnessed the crime and called the police.

The third woman entered prison at age thirty without previous offenses; she was 45 years of age in 1992. Reared in a rural area, she sought work in Tokyo after high school graduation. First working in a factory, she became a clerk at a department store, where her boss became her first lover. She quit to become a cabaret hostess and had another lover. Her third lover, aged 71 years, was wealthy and had several women as lovers at the same time. The inmate insists she loved him, but she became acquainted with a younger man who might become her husband. She entered the home of her 71-year-old lover and stabbed to death him and his 61-year-old wife. Her explanation for the crime is unclear, but she realized vaguely that the marriage would be impossible if the older man were alive. She stole jewelry in an attempt to make the crime appear to be a burglary. Although she moved away with another man, the police apprehended her; she was given a life sentence.

Crime Patterns of Women Entering Prison

Although only a small minority when compared with the absolute number of male prisoners, women inmates have scored remarkable gains in imprisonment rates and relative share of all prisoners (see tables 3.1 and 3.2). The absolute number of admissions to women's prisons have been less regular, changing from 568 in 1970 to 517 in 1975, 843 in 1980, 1,363 in 1985, 999 in 1994, and 955 in 1994. How have women's crimes differed over the years, in delivering

WOMEN DRUG OFFENDERS

Table 3.4
Distribution of Prison Admissions for Women,
With and Without Drug Crimes, 1970–94

Offenses	1970	1975	1980	1985	1990	1994
% Distribution: Drug Crimes Included						
Violent	8.1	12.6	7.6	7.6	5.0	8.6
Homicide	(6.0)	(8.9)	(5.7)	(5.5)	(3.5)	(5.5)
Bodily Injury	(0.5)	(1.5)	(1.2)	(0.4)	(0.3)	(1.0)
Robbery	(0.9)	(0.8)	(0.2)	(0.9)	(0.4)	(1.3)
Other[a]	(0.7)	(1.4)	(0.5)	(0.8)	(0.8)	(0.8)
Property	64.8	64.0	40.9	31.5	33.3	33.9
Larceny	(49.3)	(47.6)	(29.2)	(20.8)	(22.3)	(22.3)
Fraud	(11.1)	(12.6)	(7.6)	(7.5)	(6.8)	(7.6)
Arson	(1.4)	(1.9)	(2.0)	(1.4)	(2.7)	(1.6)
Forgery	(1.4)	(1.0)	(1.1)	(0.6)	(1.5)	(1.0)
Embezzlement	(1.2)	(0.8)	(0.8)	(1.2)	(0.9)	(1.3)
Other[b]	(0.4)	(0.2)	(0.2)	(0.1)	(0.6)	(0.1)
Drug	1.2	11.2	45.6	57.6	56.1	52.5
Prostitution	23.9	9.3	4.0	1.0	1.2	0.8
Traffic	1.2	0.8	0.9	0.9	2.6	2.9
Gambling	0.2	0.4	0.1	0.3	0.0	0.0
Sex	0.3	0.6	0.3	0.3	0.0	0.1
Other[c]	0.3	1.1	0.6	0.8	1.8	1.2
Total %	100.0	100.0	100.0	100.0	100.0	100.0
% Distribution: Drug Crimes Eliminated						
Violent	8.2	14.2	14.0	18.0	11.4	18.0
Property	65.6	72.1	75.2	74.4	75.9	71.4
Prostitution	24.2	10.5	7.4	2.2	2.7	1.8

Table 3.4 cont. on next page

Table 3.4 continued

Offenses	1970	1975	1980	1985	1990	1994
% Distribution: Drug Crimes Eliminated						
Traffic	1.1	0.9	1.7	2.1	5.9	6.2
Gambling	0.2	0.4	0.2	0.7	0.0	0.0
Sex	0.3	0.6	0.6	0.7	0.0	0.2
Other	0.3	1.3	0.9	1.9	4.1	2.4
Total %	100.0	100.0	100.0	100.0	100.0	100.0

Sources: Research and Statistics Section 1971a, 1976a, 1981a, 1986a, 1991a, 1995a.

[a] Kidnapping, extortion, violations of the violence law, illegal possession of firearms or explosives, and gross negligence.

[b] Intrusion, stealing property.

[c] Violations of public order, other penal laws, and other special laws.

women to prison gates? Despite the effects of case processing by the procuracy and judiciary, prison admissions generally resemble arrest statistics (see table 3.4). Property offenses occupy a major share of admissions to women's prisons. Larceny is dominant, and fraud and arson hold secondary positions. Homicide is most prominent among crimes of violence.

From 1970 to 1994, the most noteworthy trend has been the increased incarceration of women for drug offenses. That dominant trend was considered earlier in this chapter. The other offenses presented trends also worthy of attention.

Although larceny has clung to a high share of all prison admissions, property offenses have lost their share of prison admissions of women. Fraud and arson also are worthy of recognition. Forgery and embezzlement are specified in table 3.4, but they and other property crimes fail to support any claim that female prisoners have expanded significantly the variety of their offenses against property.

The Antiprostitution Law sent a large number of women to prison in 1970, but the share dropped sharply in recent years. As explained in chapter 1, the target of that law has been the managers of commercial sex, not the prostitutes. Men have assumed increasingly the dominant share of persons imprisoned under the Antiprostitution Law.

Homicide is an offense especially common among female inmates; it dominates the number of violent offenses in absolute numbers and in the erratic trend over the years. Bodily injury and robbery are in minor positions, and other violent offenses have been few and of wide variety.

Few women are imprisoned for traffic offenses, but their increasing use of motor vehicles is reflected in the consistently greater share traffic violators hold of all admissions to women's prisons from 1975 to 1994. Sex offenses include traffic in obscene literature as well as indecent assault and rape. A few women have been imprisoned for the illicit trade and for rape. I lack the information on specific cases to explain their convictions for rape; possibly they had been convicted either for participation in recruitment of prostitutes or for affairs with underage males.

Chapter 23 of the Penal Code has been instrumental in the imprisonment of a limited number of women. The Penal Code prohibits gambling (other than for "monetary entertainment"), habitual gambling, operating a place of gambling, and sale of lottery tickets. The latter two forms of illicit trade have had a modest and declining effect on admissions to women's prisons.

To demonstrate the profound effect of the rising tide of admissions for drug offenses, in the second portion of table 3.4 I removed those admissions from the percentage distribution of the crimes sending women to prison. As the years unfolded, the number of drug admissions rose sharply, to have increasing impact on the relative proportionate importance of the other crime categories. Removing the admissions for drug offenses decreased the total absolute number of admissions from 568 to 561 in 1970, from 517 to 459 in

1975, from 843 to 459 in 1980, from 1,363 to 578 in 1985, from 999 to 439 in 1990, and from 955 to 454 in 1994.

As expected, property offenses gained the greatest advantage, from 65.6 percent in 1970 to between 71.4 and 75.9 percent in the following years. Larceny was the chief motor in this change, with fraud (an offense also characteristic of women) in the secondary position. Together embezzlement and forgery had doubled their representation by 1994, but the increase was insufficient to attest to a feminine invasion of white-collar offenses.

The violent offenses recorded an impressive increase, with homicide (another crime characteristic of imprisoned women) the chief instrument. Bodily injury and robbery joined the trend toward higher percentages, and the other violent offenses continued to be greatly scattered. Except for the continued importance of homicide, violent crimes held a minor place in the imprisonment of women.

Other remaining crime categories gained proportionate stature but clung to the trends recorded with drug offenses included in the first part of table 3.4. Incarceration for prostitution declined from a high percentage in 1970; traffic offenses were exceptional but increased over the years; gambling and sex offenses were very few among prison admissions of women.

Comparing Admitted Inmates by Gender

As found in other countries, fewer Japanese women than men are imprisoned. In addition to that quantitative difference, how are the imprisoned sexes qualitatively dissimilar? Ministry of Justice statistics make possible certain general answers, but the relatively small number for female admissions to prison restrict reliable conclusions. First, drugs and two offenses characteristic of women (larceny and homicide) compose a large portion of all admissions to women's prisons: 56.5 percent in 1970, 67.7 percent in 1975,

Table 3.5
Female Prison Admissions per 100 Male Admissions, 1970–94

Offenses	1970	1975	1980	1985	1990	1994
All						
Ratio	2.2	2.0	3.1	4.5	4.6	4.7
No. of Women	568	517	843	1,363	999	955
Drug						
Ratio	5.4	3.5	6.5	10.0	10.5	10.3
No. of Women	7	58	384	785	560	501
Property						
All						
Ratio	3.0	2.8	3.2	3.8	4.2	4.0
No. of Women	368	331	345	430	333	324
Larceny						
Ratio	2.9	2.7	3.1	3.4	3.7	3.5
No. of Women	280	246	246	283	223	213
Fraud						
Ratio	3.6	3.5	3.5	4.6	5.1	5.3
No. of Women	63	65	64	68	68	73
Arson						
Ratio	5.3	6.0	7.6	7.8	13.5	7.8
No. of Women	8	10	17	20	27	15
Violent						
All						
Ratio	0.7	1.0	1.1	1.8	1.2	2.1
No. of Women	46	65	64	104	50	82

Table 3.5 cont. on next page

WOMEN DRUG OFFENDERS

Table 3.5 continued

Offenses	1970	1975	1890	1985	1990	1994
Violent						
Homicide						
Ratio	4.9	7.2	7.7	10.7	7.8	12.7
No. of Women	34	46	48	75	35	52
Traffic						
Ratio	0.1	0.1	0.2	0.3	1.0	1.4
No. of Women	6	4	8	12	26	28
Prostitution						
Ratio	188.9	106.7	57.6	11.5	11.4	13.3
No. of Women	136	48	34	13	12	8

Sources: Research and Statistics Section 1971a, 1976a, 1981a, 1986a, 1991a, 1995a.

80.5 percent in 1980, 83.9 percent in 1985, 81.9 percent in 1990, and 80.3 percent in 1994. Second, the remaining offenses are scattered and usually in small number in the respective years. The small numbers exaggerate the percentage changes over the years. To avoid unreliable conclusions, I limited tables 3.5 through 3.8 to those crimes that for at least a single year hold at least 2 percent of all admissions to women's prisons.

Imprisonment differs between the sexes according to the crimes. Already we have considered the great impact of drug offenses on admissions to women's prisons. Table 3.5 measures the extent of that impact compared to the imprisonment of men. In 1970 2.2 women entered prison for every 100 men, but despite only 7 female admissions for drugs, there were 5.4 women entering prison for every 100 men imprisoned in 1970 for drug offenses. The few women renders suspect the rate for 1970. For the following years, we may have more faith in the increase of ratios from 3.5 per 100 male drug offenders in 1975 to 10.5 in 1990.

Altogether, female admissions gained on male admissions consistently from 1975 to 1994. The total number of women per 100 men was few (2 in 1975 and 4.7 in 1994), but there was a relative increase in number of women entering prisons. The ratios measure the greater effect of drug offenses on the inmate population of women's prisons, showing an increase from 3.5 women per 100 men imprisoned in 1975 to 10.5 in 1990. The impact widened as the years proceeded. In number of admissions, the impact for women's prisons was greater for drugs than for all offenses of women arriving at the prisons.

Property offenses are most numerous for women's prisons. Despite high ratios for all property crimes, women had less advantages over men for larceny than for other property offenses, especially in 1985, 1990, and 1994. Larceny, of course, is the most numerous property offense, but less numerous offenses (such as fraud and arson) had greater influence in sustaining the ratio for all property offenses. Arson and fraud are common offenses for women's prisons, and the offenses had high ratios. Embezzlement and forgery are not represented on the table because of their few numbers, but they too had high ratios, suggesting increasing and still minimal representation of women among those prisoners.

Except for homicide, women continued to be underrepresented in the ratios for violent offenses when compared with the ratios for all crimes. Admissions to women's prisons for bodily injury and robbery were few in number and produced very low ratios. Prostitution sent decreasing numbers of women to prison; although the ratios show high representation of women in the management of commercialized sex, the women lost representation as the years passed. More women have been imprisoned for traffic crimes, but the ratios attest to the continued predominance of males.

The lengths of sentences are among the factors influencing the size of prison populations and, thereby, the imprisonment rate. A sentence of less than a year usually adds a person to the prisoner count for a single calendar year. Longer terms will add her or him to the prison population for two or more calendar years. Although the trend has been irregular, women's sentences have increased and become longer on average from 16.4 months in 1970 to 24.3 months in 1994 (see table 3.6).

The averages for women generally exceed those for men, but the distribution of crimes has penalized the women unduly. For example, proportionately women are more likely to enter prison for homicide than are men. The longer average sentences for homicide have greater influence on the total sentences of women than on those of men. To rule out that effect, in table 3.6 I list standardized means of sentence lengths for men. With the female distributions of crimes applied to male admissions, the standardized average lengths of sentence either approach the female average (for 1975) or exceed them (for the other years).

Sentences tend to lengthen with the years, but the trend is inconsistent. Sentences for homicide, of course, are highest, with male sentences exceeding those of women. Arson occupies second place, with women drawing the highest averages in two of the six years listed. Other property offenses result in sentences longer than those for traffic and prostitution crimes.

For specific crimes, the sexes usually switch their position in length of sentences as the years proceed. Men usually have received longer sentences than women for drugs, homicide, and robbery but not for violent crimes in general. Women had higher averages for bodily injury and the other violent crimes for which they were imprisoned, but the numbers of such admissions were so low that the mean lengths of sentence were inflated. Embezzlement, forgery, and a scattering of other offenses presented the same situation. Women had longer sentences than men for traffic

Table 3.6
Mean Length of Prison Sentence, 1970–94

	Mean Length of Sentence (in months)					
Offenses	1970	1975	1980	1985	1990	1994
All						
Women	16.4	22.3	18.4	20.5	22.2	24.3
Men	17.5	17.3	17.4	19.2	20.9	25.5
Men, Std.[a]	18.3	21.0	19.9	21.0	22.3	25.5
Drug						
Women	7.9	13.1	14.8	16.4	19.3	20.8
Men	15.1	13.2	15.2	17.8	20.4	22.1
Property						
All						
Women	17.0	19.4	19.4	20.8	23.7	22.9
Men	16.7	17.1	18.4	19.3	21.7	21.4
Larceny						
Women	15.9	17.5	17.1	19.3	22.2	21.2
Men	16.7	17.2	18.6	19.3	21.4	21.4
Fraud						
Women	18.1	21.8	19.4	20.7	22.8	23.6
Men	14.9	14.6	15.4	17.4	20.3	19.8
Arson						
Women	31.5	54.0	50.3	42.0	42.9	39.2
Men	45.6	47.2	45.1	46.0	51.1	49.0
Violent						
All						
Women	50.1	53.0	42.1	54.1	57.5	58.3
Men	24.2	23.7	24.2	28.1	28.5	32.4

Table 3.6 cont. on next page

Table 3.6 continued

	\multicolumn{6}{c}{Mean Length of Sentence (in months)}
Offenses	1970	1975	1980	1985	1990	1994
Violent						
Homicide						
Women	58.3	60.3	47.7	60.9	70.4	70.3
Men	70.7	69.7	71.6	80.9	84.3	87.6
Traffic						
Women	9.2	6.7	7.9	9.9	9.5	8.6
Men	8.0	6.9	6.9	7.0	7.7	7.6
Prostitution						
Women	6.5	6.5	6.7	11.1	10.5	21.6
Men	9.3	8.9	11.0	13.7	14.4	14.6

Sources: Research and Statistics Section 1971a, 1976a, 1981a, 1986a, 1991a, 1995a.

[a] Equals standardized mean length of sentence for males. The total number of males is adjusted to accord with the percentage distribution of female prison admissions by crimes. The theoretical absolute number of men for each crime is multiplied by the actual mean length of male sentences for the respective crime.

offenses; their offenses are fewer when compared to men's, perhaps because only the more grave women traffic offenders were sent to prison. Only in 1994, when few women were imprisoned for that crime, did women draw longer sentences under the Antiprostitution Law than men.

In deciding that a suspect should be released without trial, the public prosecutors are likely to prefer the person who has not been imprisoned for a previous offense. Similarly, the sentencing judges employ previous imprisonment as one of the criteria for deciding whether or not a prison sentence should be suspended. For prison admissions in

Table 3.7
Share of First Admissions among Prison Admissions, 1970–94

	\% Share of First Admissions					
Offenses	1970	1975	1980	1985	1990	1994
All						
Women	43.1	53.4	65.1	57.4	50.3	55.7
Men	47.4	42.5	40.9	38.9	37.1	37.8
Drug						
Women	28.6	82.8	77.3	56.7	47.9	51.9
Men	31.0	40.1	42.8	32.8	26.5	29.1
Property						
Women	41.6	42.6	47.5	48.6	43.5	47.2
Men	32.5	29.5	31.0	34.0	30.9	31.6
Larceny						
Women	33.9	31.3	35.0	33.9	34.5	35.2
Men	31.1	27.2	28.4	30.8	27.7	29.3
Fraud						
Women	66.7	72.3	75.0	71.6	45.6	63.0
Men	30.2	32.8	32.5	37.6	35.7	32.4
Arson						
Women	62.5	100.0	82.3	95.0	96.3	86.7
Men	69.3	65.1	69.2	68.7	68.5	67.0
Violent						
Women	90.2	90.8	98.4	94.2	92.0	97.5
Men	49.2	44.5	39.1	40.2	40.9	43.2
Homicide						
Women	94.1	100.0	100.0	96.0	97.1	98.1
Men	71.2	68.0	66.8	64.2	65.5	68.6

Table 3.7 cont. on next page

WOMEN DRUG OFFENDERS

Table 3.7 continued

Offenses	% Share of First Admissions					
	1970	1975	1980	1985	1990	1994
Traffic						
Women	100.0	100.0	100.0	91.7	88.5	92.9
Men	89.6	76.4	65.2	60.6	64.6	63.3
Prostitution						
Women	27.9	29.2	29.4	23.1	58.3	75.0
Men	15.3	20.0	44.1	50.4	49.5	40.0

Sources: Research and Statistics Section 1971a, 1976a, 1981a, 1986a, 1991a, 1995a.

general, women not previously exposed to incarceration are more vulnerable than men to becoming prisoners (see table 3.7). Except in 1970, first offenders took up a higher percentage of admissions among women entering prison than among men. The percentage shares of all admissions represented by first termers were 43.1 for women and 47.4 for men in 1970, 53.4 and 42.5 in 1975, 65.1 and 40.9 in 1980, 57.4 and 38.9 in 1985, 50.3 and 37.1 in 1990, and 55.7 and 37.8 in 1994. That higher vulnerability has added to the number of women being imprisoned.

In the standardization procedure, we may apply the male percentage of first offenders to the actual total number of female admissions for each year. The actual and theoretical numbers, respectively, of female first-time inmates would be 245 and 269 in 1970, 276 and 220 in 1975, 549 and 345 in 1980, 782 and 530 in 1985, 503 and 371 in 1990, and 532 and 361 in 1994. The actual numbers of female first offenders are listed in table 3.3. The differences in numbers of first termers suggest that the greater imprisonment of first-term women has inflated the prison admissions of women after 1970 by 56 in 1975, 204 in 1980, 252 in 1985, 132 in 1990, and 171 in 1994.

With few women imprisoned for drug offenses in 1970, the initial impact on first offenders of the criminalization of stimulants was about the same for the sexes, but thereafter the vulnerability of women was boosted. The differences between the sexes persisted in subsequent years, but the singling out of first offenders declined for both sexes. Since the numbers of imprisonment for drug offenses were considerable, I suggest that the criminalization of drug offenses has persisted for both sexes, and especially for women.

The vulnerability of female first offenders also applied to other crime categories. For property offenses, larceny has high priority for both sexes, but arson and fraud were more instrumental in raising the level of the female first offenders' susceptibility to incarceration. Homicide, an offense especially characteristic of women prisoners, was responsible for the heavy representation of female first offenders. That phenomenon is to be expected, but the relatively lower percentage for male homicides may be attributed to their earlier greater involvement in other crimes.

The remarkable presence of female first offenders is to be expected for traffic and prostitution offenses. The few women involved—except for in prostitution in 1970—would unduly raise the percentages, although perhaps the few women may reflect the limiting of imprisonment to the most flagrant female offenders, including first offenders.

Whereas table 3.7 deals only with those inmates behind bars for the first time, the mean numbers of prison admissions given in table 3.8 measure total exposure to incarceration. In this broader scope of recidivism, the women continue to have the least exposure to imprisonment. The difference is at least partially due to two factors already discussed: the women's greater representation in offenses characteristic of first offenders, such as homicide; and the artificial boosting of averages by the few female admissions for some other offenses.

Except for the few cases in 1970, we again find women with fewer average prison admissions than men for drug offenses. The differences between the sexes widens as the years proceed. Women drug offenders are less benefited by the tolerance usually accorded first offenders. Imprisonment rates are high for prostitution cases, but the relatively few offenders artificially boost the rates for both sexes.

For homicide and traffic offenses, crimes usually bring first offenders to prison, the differences between the sexes narrows, but men persist in the higher average prison admissions. Property offenders are particularly prone to multiple incarcerations, especially among the variety of crimes grouped as larceny. Fraud and arson counter the influence of larceny by drawing more female than male first offenders in most years.

Opening Another Women's Prison

Adult female offenders in Japan are housed in five independent prisons and one branch prison. Tochigi Women's Prison, located north of Tokyo, serves the Kanto Plain in Honshu.[5] Wakayama Women's Prison, on the coast of Honshu, south of Osaka, is part of the Osaka Correction Region but also receives women from Tokyo. Kasamatsu Women's Prison, in central Honshu, serves the Nagoya Correction Region but also has individuals from Tokyo. Fumoto Women's Prison is part of the Fukuoka Correction Region and is on the southern island of Kyushu; some inmates also come from the Hiroshima and Takamatsu Correction Regions. Sapporo is an auxiliary branch to a main male prison and serves Sapporo Island north of Honshu. Iwakuni Women's Prison in the Hiroshima Correction Region became in 1989 the fifth independent prison.

Table 3.8
Mean Number of Exposures to Imprisonment among Prison Admissions, 1970–94

Offenses	1970	1975	1980	1985	1990	1994
All						
Women	3.31	2.83	2.13	2.05	2.42	2.40
Men	2.80	3.02	3.06	3.19	3.44	3.54
Men, Std.[a]	3.48	3.66	3.05	3.17	3.60	3.38
Drug						
Women	3.86	1.34	1.38	1.72	2.11	2.04
Men	3.11	2.60	2.52	2.95	3.47	3.52
Property						
All						
Women	3.18	3.19	3.07	2.82	3.24	3.22
Men	3.62	3.88	3.94	3.98	4.26	4.31
Larceny						
Women	3.55	3.76	3.59	3.41	3.89	4.00
Men	3.63	3.90	3.95	3.96	4.32	3.41
Fraud						
Women	2.04	1.64	1.62	1.85	2.36	1.74
Men	4.12	4.28	4.46	4.38	4.50	4.67
Arson						
Women	2.12	1.00	2.41	1.32	1.04	1.83
Men	2.07	2.33	2.08	2.18	1.99	2.13
Violent						
All						
Women	1.24	1.49	1.02	1.13	1.20	1.28
Men	2.42	2.69	2.97	2.97	3.12	3.09

Table 3.8 cont. on next page

Table 3.8 continued

	\multicolumn{6}{c}{Mean No. of Exposures to Imprisonment}
Offenses	1970	1975	1980	1985	1990	1994
Violent						
Homicide						
Women	1.06	1.00	1.00	1.08	1.09	1.06
Men	1.75	1.91	1.90	2.08	2.08	2.02
Traffic						
Women	1.00	1.00	1.00	1.08	1.11	1.07
Men	1.20	1.49	1.83	2.00	1.94	2.04
Prostitution						
Women	4.59	4.41	3.35	6.50	2.62	1.94
Men	3.79	4.80	2.66	2.61	2.30	3.13

Sources: Research and Statistics Section 1971a, 1976a, 1981a, 1986a, 1991a, 1995a.

[a]Equals standardized mean length of sentence for males. The total number of males is adjusted to accord with the percentage distribution of female prison admissions by crimes. The theoretical absolute number of men for each crime is multiplied by the actual mean length of male sentences for the respective crime.

Prison overcrowding stimulated penal reform in America that affected women inmates either directly by an increase in their numbers or indirectly as a ricocheting effect of an unprecedented multiplication of male prisoners (McKelvey 1977). Japan differs in that only women's prisons have been overcrowded recently. The movement has been from branch units to an increasing number of independent women's prisons: Tochigi (1906), Wakayama (1949), Kasamatsu (1949), Fumoto (1950), and Iwakuni (1989).

Iwakuni was originally a juvenile prison for males less than twenty years of age who had been sentenced to adult prisons. Juvenile training schools, also administered by the

Correction Bureau, are distinct from the nine juvenile prisons. Since 1965 fewer persons of that age category have been sent to adult prisons. From 1965 to 1975, the relative proportion of serious offenders among juveniles declined. Fewer family court referrals to public prosecutors resulted in the drastic decrease (Yokoyama 1980, 16). The family courts are authorized to refer certain offenders aged 16–20 years to public prosecutors for processing under special protective procedures. For those few juveniles, the public prosecutors decide whether or not prosecution in adult courts is appropriate.

Iwakuni became available and was completely reconstructed to become a woman's prison. Reconstruction illustrates some of the problems the Correction Bureau faces in the thorough renovation of major prisons. Iwakuni's reconstruction was stimulated by the serious difficulties of finding an alternative site because of local resistance to any new prison and because of the high cost of land. The building of private residences around the juvenile prison necessitated reconstruction within a limited space.

In keeping with the standard plans for all modern prisons, Iwakuni has four-floor cell blocks with large congregate sleeping rooms that have ordinary windows on two floors, similar single-person rooms on the other two floors, western toilets in each sleeping room, a large room for personal laundry on each floor, and brightly colored hallways and staircases. Bathing facilities are centralized in a special building.

Administering Women's Prisons

Administrators running a women's prison encounter unusual conditions. Women's prisons in Japan differ from male institutions in that women's prisons receive all classes of inmates whereas detention centers group classes to go to particular male prisons according to length of sentence, possession of "advanced criminal tendencies," and age. Housing assignment within the women's prisons distinguishes the types of prisoners.

Japanese women prisoners are on average older than Japanese male prisoners. In 1970 the women admitted to prison had a mean age of 39.1 years, the men a mean age of 31.9 years. For the following years, the women continued to be older than the men: 40 years versus 34.3 in 1975, 40 versus 36.4 in 1980, 40.2 versus 38.1 in 1985, and 40.5 versus 39.9 in 1990 (Research and Statistics Section 1971a, 1976a, 1981a, 1986a, 1991a, 1995a).

Meanwhile, the average age of female correctional officers is declining. Warden Hisashi Hasegawa of Fuchu Prison told me that in women's prisons "prison officers are like granddaughters dealing with grandmothers." After World War II, recruitment of female officers was heavy; socioeconomic chaos greatly increased the number of prisoners, and many male officers had been killed in military actions. The earlier female cadres have been retiring at age sixty; older officers have been promoted. Turnover is aggravated by resignation of young female officers when they marry, reflecting the cultural opposition to working wives. In a conversation with me, the warden of Tochigi Women's Prison observed: "We must become more tolerant to meet this difficulty."

The Correction Bureau's recruitment policy was changed in 1981 to add more women to staffs. Some women already were on staffs; for example, Saga Branch Prison, a predecessor of Fumoto Women's Prison, had fourteen female officers in 1931. A special examination of female applicants by the National Personnel Authority accelerated recruitment. The effects are mirrored at Wakayama, where the percentage of women on the staff is greatest at the lowest level: 84.4 percent of ordinary officers, 63.6 percent of senior officers, and 37.5 percent of section chiefs are women.

Although infrequent, the admission of a pregnant inmate is of course exceptional to women's prisons. In his survey of fifty-five state and two federal prisons for women in the United States, Boudouris (1985) found few institutions with nurseries, and infants born to inmates are housed temporarily in the prison infirmary until they are placed elsewhere.[6] He describes Bedford Hills Correctional Facility for women in New York as having the only prison nursery where infants may stay longer, usually up to one year. Existing for more than sixty years, the program includes a children's playroom, a parenting center, and a furlough house in Brooklyn where the inmate mother may spend a week with her children.

In 1990, the Correction Bureau of Japan reports, fifteen babies were born to inmate mothers in community hospitals; twelve of these were given initial care in the prisons. Later all babies were cared for either by the inmate's family (2) or by a child-care agency in the community (13). Now babies born to imprisoned mothers are less stigmatized than before, because of Japan's declining birthrate and the increased value given infants. As the warden of a women's prison commented, the elderly inmates have become a bigger problem than the very young.

Twelve babies were born in 1988 to inmates of five women's facilities operating in Japan: five at Tochigi, three at Wakayama, three at Kasamatsu, one at Fumoto, and none at Sapporo. For lack of facilities, the infants, with the exception of one at Tochigi, were placed immediately either with the mother's family or in an infant-care facility in the community. Tochigi referred two babies to the mother's family and two to a community facility. Because of a short sentence, the fifth baby was cared for by her mother.

Rule Violations and Prison Administration

The exercise of official authority exemplifies the special features of administering a women's prison. In conversations with staff of women's prisons in Japan, I became aware of myths I have encountered in the United States and Europe about women inmates. "Nasty" female prisoners engage in more flagrant misconduct than "nasty" male prisoners. Among the women there is a greater proportion of moody, temperamental, and complaining individuals. The women entering prisons today have less respect for themselves and for the interests of other persons than the female offenders entering prisons a decade ago. Ambivalence colors attitudes toward inmates, vacillating among personnel from perceptions of viciousness to the other extreme of sympathy for "victims of poverty and childhood neglect."

Whether only overly simplistic stereotypes or generalizations based on extreme conduct among women inmates, myths about women inmates illustrate, first, that the attitudes of keepers around the world are similar in reflecting the conditions they encounter in their work and, second, that the characteristics of arriving inmates mirror the changes underway in society at large. The keepers are assigned the responsibility of applying official rules (framed in abstraction apart from the dynamics of human interaction) to persons deprived of personal freedom without their willing consent. The relationships between the keepers and the kept operate within a dictatorship, despite the good intentions of either party.

Despite the similarities in prison work among economically advanced societies, prisons in Japan are different in the relationships between prison officers and inmates. They are relatively free of violence because of Japanese emphasis on duty (a cultural theme shared by prisoners in varying degrees), stern supervision of inmates that permits no doubt about the power of the officials, the relative brevity of most sentences, and the paternalistic ties accepted by prison officers and most inmates. Officers are expected by supervisors, colleagues, and most inmates to serve concurrently as enforcers of official standards and lay counselors to inmates.

As I already discussed in this chapter, Japan falls short

in eliminating the gender inequality fathered and maintained by traditions, although changes underway in its economy and in other elements of its infrastructure are moving the Japanese in that direction. As an arm of the law's fundamental conservatism, the prison is a social institution usually isolated from the rest of the social structure. It responds eventually to changes in the society it serves, but the pace of response is slow.

Rule violations of inmates may be interpreted as their failure to adjust to the realities of the prison world, but the infractions are also effects of the official dominance of the inmates. Isolation from the free community demands that the person new to prisoner status adjust to unfamiliar traditions, values, and relationships of penal confinement as a human experience. The violations may be those of a rebellious personality ready to reject the power of the keepers; the rebel does not accept the authority the prison administration assumes the keepers possess. Especially during the early stage of penal confinement, the infractions demonstrate the new inmate's tardiness in learning the "rules of the game." Incidents may mirror the emotional upheavals stimulated by news from home or troublesome experiences in the prison.

I was told by security officials that the officers in Japan are expected to report even the most trivial violations, to convince inmates that they receive equal treatment and protection from possible predators. If the rule is in writing and based on Prison Law, violations must be reported, but, if the situation involves "guidance," the incident need not be reported. Examples of the latter would be a "messy room" or failure to fold clothing or store a futon.

Official Data on Prisoner Infractions

The Ministry of Justice publishes annually several statistical tables on rule violations of prisoners. Publication of such data is at least unusual among prison systems of the world. The Japanese data are a genuine contribution to reliable and objective assessment of prison operations, but the lack of similar information from other countries prevents cross-national comparisons.

Analysis of statistics for women's prisons around the world is handicapped by their relatively small population when compared with male prisons. Differences of rates for women from those for men are exaggerated when less than a half dozen violations are reported for women. The small number of women inmates favor aberrations that confuse the search for recurrent patterns. For example, table 3.9 records an aberration among women discharged from prison in 1993; one woman was punished for thirty-five incidents involving damage to the physical structure of the prison during her incarceration. At first glance, it appears that a wave of property destruction had struck women's prisons.

Such cases reveal one of the faults of statistical analysis, but the analysis of prison data also reveals opportunities for case studies and other research methods. In that spirit, I am taking advantage of the statistics on rule violations to reveal possibilities for qualitative investigation.

In 1993 women averaged 2.14 rule violations per inmate; the men averaged 2.38 violations per inmate. The 282 women punished that year represented 18.6 percent of the 1,514 women in prison on the last day of 1993. The comparable percentage for men (with a total of 8,704 incidents) was 24.4 percent of the 35,723 men present on the last day of 1993 (Research and Statistics Section 1994a).

Violence against staff is most characteristic of women. Physical confrontation was involved, but none of the female incidents resulted in sufficient injury to require major medical care. Almost all of the most serious male violence against staff entailed serious injury. Less serious assaults held the overwhelming shares of incidents for both sexes. Improper inmate relations required officer intervention in "quarrels" but without actual physical confrontation.

Table 3.9
Rule Violations of Inmates Discharged, 1993

Rule Violations	No. of Rule Violators Women	Men	% Distribution Women	Men	Violation Rate[a] Women	Men
Violence Against Staff	18	232	6.4	2.7	1.33	1.48
Violence Against Inmates	34	1,989	12.0	22.8	1.71	1.42
Reactions Against Prison Control	28	1,575	9.9	18.0	3.82	3.30
Disobedience	(9)	(779)	(3.2)	(9.0)	(4.11)	(2.81)
Insult, Disrespect	(7)	(91)	(2.5)	(1.1)	(1.86)	(4.65)
Manipulation	(5)	(30)	(1.8)	(0.3)	(1.00)	(3.07)
Illicit Communication	(3)	(184)	(1.1)	(2.1)	(2.67)	(4.58)
Refusal to Work	(3)	(462)	(1.1)	(5.3)	(3.67)	(3.11)
Damage to Building	(1)	(21)	(0.3)	(0.2)	(35.00)	(8.90)
Improper Inmate Relations	14	1,045	5.0	12.0	2.57	2.18
Quarrels	(11)	(945)	(3.9)	(10.8)	(2.73)	(2.26)
Extorting Food	(3)	(100)	(1.1)	(1.2)	(2.00)	(1.44)
Participation in Sub-Rosa Economy	93	1,096	33.0	12.6	1.63	1.89
Prohibited Trade	(82)	(846)	(29.1)	(9.7)	(1.58)	(1.80)
Possession of Articles	(8)	(1.63)	(2.8)	(1.9)	(1.62)	(2.42)
Production of Articles	(3)	(87)	(1.1)	(1.0)	(3.00)	(1.69)
Deviant Conduct	11	270	3.9	3.1	1.27	1.80
Self-Injury	(9)	(99)	(3.2)	(1.1)	(1.11)	(2.52)
Other[b]	(2)	(171)	(0.7)	(2.0)	(2.00)	(1.51)
Miscellaneous	84	2,506	29.0	28.8	2.54	3.00
All	282	8,704	100.0	100.0	2.14	2.38

Source: Research and Statistics Section 1994a.

[a] Average number of violations per number of inmates who were punished for violation of the particular rule.

[b] Women: gambling 1, indecent conduct 1; men: gambling 125, smoking 27, indecent conduct 19.

Reactions against prison controls include various forms of relatively latent opposition to the keepers by the kept. Women became involved to the lesser extent, and then in marginal situations described as "insult and disrespect" and "manipulation." Disobedience was the chief infraction for both sexes, but women had the greater rate for it as well as for refusal to work.

As a social institution, the prison is obligated to protect the community and also to provide inmates with the basic necessities, such as food, shelter, and medical care. The official economy of the prison is supposed to monopolize the transfer of consumer goods and professional services. The prison is also engaged in production, especially in Japan, where two-thirds of the inmates spend forty hours in prison shops making articles for contracts with private firms. Some production directly meets needs of the prisoners.

As private citizens, the inmates had developed various preferences that are socially accepted, merely tolerated, or specifically prohibited by law. As prisoners subject to the restrictions accompanying penal confinement, these persons inevitably find many of their preferences—even some of those socially accepted—denied in the anonymity and cost-consciousness of the prison. A sub-rosa economy among inmates emerged as an array of attempts to satisfy preferences either overlooked or specifically denied by the prison's management. Within such an economy, inmates may trade prohibited articles, ranging from food to illicit drugs or beverages. They may fashion prohibited articles or change equipment to serve purposes other than officially intended. As consumers or sub-rosa entrepreneurs, they may be discovered as possessors of prohibited goods. The sub-rosa economy is especially mirrored by the women's rule violations listed in table 3.9, suggesting women's strong interest in making the life of penal confinement more comfortable. Those violations associated with transactions in prohibited articles were very numerous among women, comprising 29.1 percent of all their infractions, compared to 9.7 percent of all male violations. Deviant conduct may raise difficulties for the prison management but essentially is opposed by moral values. Self-injury includes damage to one's body in a genuine suicide attempt or as a suicidal gesture and also the males' tattooing denoting yakuza membership. Gambling is largely male conduct in Japanese prisons. Tobacco smoking (exclusively a male infraction) has been prohibited traditionally because early prisons were constructed of wood. Sexual indecency involved twenty males and only one female.

Length of Sentence and Prison Admissions

Do rule violations—or at least the *detection* of rule violations—become more frequent as the length of incarceration is extended? Perhaps the frustrations of being locked up involuntarily multiply over time. Perhaps the early success in concealing violations evaporates as they are repeated. Perhaps compliance with official expectations becomes routine and habitual once completing the learning and adjustments of the first months of imprisonment.

Among the annual statistics on rule violations of prisoners published by the Ministry of Justice, one of the tables relates the kind of rules being violated to number of months served before release. In table 3.10 I record the complicated patterning of these relationships according to gender.

On average, women violators in 1993 had served a longer time in prison than had men before incurring punishment—24.18 versus 23 months. But, as table 3.10 shows, the difference stems from a greater concentration of women in the twelfth to thirtieth months of penal confinement, rather than from women resembling men throughout the span of imprisonment. Inmates with the longest period of incarceration drew the fewest punishments; both sexes had less than 2 percent of all violations assigned to individuals completing at least seven years of incarceration.

The mean numbers of months are only a crude indicator of variance among the categories of infractions, but they suggest that for women rulebreaking usually comes earlier in the prison career than for men. Participation in the sub-rosa economy (a major female endeavor) especially persists through the range of penal confinement. Violence against staff—rather uncertainly surfacing as a female infraction—is more short-lived. Deviant conduct by women is rather rare, but the few incidents tend to occur with longer exposure to penal confinement. The women without infractions are well distributed throughout the span of the prison experience, but compared with men, they are more represented in the category of confinement from one to seven years. The great variety of miscellaneous infractions helps explain their rather even distribution throughout the length of incarceration.

To compare the sexes by crimes, the absolute number in each length of imprisonment (say, the 453 women discharged on completing a prison stay of twelve to twenty-four months) was traced through the categories of rule violations in table 3.10. In 1993 19 women, or 4.19 percent of 453, had been punished for violence against inmates. Of the 8,437 men discharged in 1993 after being confined from twelve to twenty-four months, 751, or 8.9 percent, had been punished for violence against inmates.

Of course, the comparison according to those percentage distributions for each length of confinement would result in women having a concentration over the men in some of the infraction categories. The most noteworthy category is participation in the sub-rosa economy, in which women's advantage over men was definite and persisted through the range of stays within prison. Women also drew greater punishment for violence against staff, but the absolute number of incidents undermined the significance of that

Table 3.10
Rule Violations by Length of Penal Confinement, 1993

Rule Violations	Mean Length of Confinement (in months)	Under 12	12–24	24–36	36–84	Over 84
Violence Against Staff						
Women	23.00	2.67	1.54	2.64	1.16	0.00
Men	28.49	1.02	0.98	1.05	1.56	2.78
Violence Against Inmates						
Women	22.41	2.67	4.19	3.53	3.49	0.00
Men	31.19	4.16	8.90	12.71	16.05	23.46
Reactions Against Prison Control						
Women	28.18	0.67	3.31	3.53	3.49	6.67
Men	27.99	4.53	7.24	9.61	10.44	14.81
Improper Inmate Relations						
Women	22.93	0.67	1.77	1.76	1.16	0.00
Men	27.95	2.66	4.97	6.52	7.25	7.41
Participation in Sub-Rosa Economy						
Women	33.18	4.00	7.95	13.65	16.28	40.00
Men	29.07	2.47	4.93	7.31	8.44	8.33
Deviant Conduct						
Women	34.19	0.67	0.88	1.76	1.16	6.67
Men	27.65	0.62	1.26	1.77	2.13	0.93
Miscellaneous						
Women	27.12	7.33	8.17	10.13	12.79	13.33
Men	25.51	8.39	12.42	13.64	14.78	14.20

Table 3.10 cont. on next page

Table 3.10 continued

Rule Violations	Mean Length of Confinement (in months)	% Distribution by Length of Confinement (in months) Under 12	12-24	24-36	36-84	Over 84
None						
Women	22.25	81.32	72.19	63.00	60.47	33.33
Men	19.38	76.15	59.30	47.38	39.35	28.08
All						
Women	24.18	16.11	48.66	24.28	9.24	1.61
Men	23.00	26.93	40.06	19.87	11.60	1.54

Source: Research and Statistics Section 1994a

pattern, and that form of misconduct withered in the longer periods of confinement.

For men violence against inmates and reaction against prison control are spread throughout the prison confinement and gain precedence as the experience is prolonged. For women violence against inmates is less prevalent but comes earlier in imprisonment. Women have the slightly higher mean number of months for reaction against prison controls, because of few incidents for women released before a year of imprisonment. Otherwise, both sexes are more prone to resist the custodial measures as penal confinement is lengthened.

Difficulties in inmate relationships are mostly a male phenomenon and gain importance for men as the exposure to incarceration is extended. Deviant conduct comes later for women than for men, largely because of particular concentration in female confinement for seven years and more.

In 1993 both sexes had substantial portions of their infractions in the miscellaneous category, which includes infractions that the officials had difficulty classifying at the moment or that did not seem to fit into the usual plan for regulating behavior. Examples of incidents falling into the miscellaneous category are unauthorized talking without permission, spreading false rumor, and unattended walking without permission.

For both sexes the number of persons without rule violations was greater than the number punished while imprisoned, but women exceeded men in that regard. They held to their advantage throughout the range of confinement lengths, but the advantage tapered off when imprisonment exceeded seven years.

Recidivism and Women Inmates

In an early study of the effects of compulsory penal confinement, Clemmer (1958, 299) defined *prisonization* as the taking on by the inmate "in a greater or less degree of the folkways, mores, customs, and general culture of the penitentiary." The term refers generally to the newcomers' adaptation to prison life, accepting the humble role of prisoners, internalizing new habits and sleeping, and learning new behavioral standards and specialized language.

American criminologists usually identify the process with taking on mores of prisoners in opposition to the prison system. I discussed with Japanese prison officials whether or not that perception also holds for Japanese inmates. Most of them denied vigorously that a prisoner subculture exists; a few argued that penal confinement inevitably stimulates resistance among inmates in any institution receiving unwilling inmates.

In my opinion the social psychology of the Japanese generally weakens any tendency toward strong cohesion among the inmates—the yakuza excepted—but repeated commitments to prison favor an adaptation to the incarceration as though it were a setting for regularized and conventional conduct. For some experienced prisoners, an environment intended to punish the deviant becomes a shelter against the tribulations of the outside world. Official leniency is extended to offenders who public prosecutors and judges believe are capable of, and willing to undertake, self-correction. But, as summarized by Wagatsuma and Rosett (1986, 477), "Japanese not only believe that human character is mutable but view an excessively bad person as 'nonhuman.' " Previous imprisonment is one of the criteria for deciding that the defendant is "nonhuman" and thereby an apt candidate for another prison sentence. When deciding whether or not to suspend a prison sentence, the judges will consider several qualities of the case and the defendant: deliberateness in planning of the crime, coldheartedness in execution of the criminal plan, whether or not excessive pain was imposed on the victim, repetition of offenses, and other evidence of moral depravity (Suzuki 1979).

The risk of repetitive imprisonment for female defendants is enhanced by the "evil woman" perspective that, in light of their previous imprisonment, they are unqualified for official leniency either because their repeated crimes demonstrate an evil nature, because their "evil nature" violates standards applied to "good women," or because stern measures must be taken to protect these defendants from negative influences to which they are susceptible.

From either point of view, the decisions of public prosecutors and judges result in a high proportion of convicted women, compared with the men, entering prisons and later joining the prisoners released on completion of incarceration. Judicial decisions mirror in some degree the convergence of changes in patterns of crimes of women and the public interpretations of gender issues raised by socioeconomic changes affecting the status of women.

Probably, some female offenders without previous imprisonment will go to prisons for the first time because their previous offenses, though discounted by judges, were serious. The rise of new public issues stimulates reassessments. Japanese women's prisons have received a greater number of women convicted of drug offenses; half of them in 1993 were in prison for the first time (see table 3.11). Few women were imprisoned for traffic offenses; those few signal the greater number of women who drive motor vehicles, and the few in prison probably have been selected as the most flagrant violators of traffic laws.

Crimes commonly identified with the imprisonment of Japanese women are homicide (especially infanticide), shoplifting and other forms of petty theft, and arson. Those crimes are associated with the high proportion of first prison admissions among women; the proportion among men is also high, although short of the female proportion. Male recidivism is more likely to involve multiple kinds of crime in the past; the chances of first admissions to prison among males are thus reduced.

Other female crimes are symptomatic of changes in the misconduct of women, although the incidents remain infrequent quantitatively when compared with male offenses. First imprisonments of women appear in conjunction with their relatively few admissions for robbery, forgery, and embezzlement. Illicit commerce involves gambling, prostitution, and pornography by both sexes. Only ten women came to prison for those law violations, and the high proportion of first imprisonments suggests the possibility of a slight increase in the number of female managers.

Rule violations of women prisoners discharged in 1993 is on our analytic plate, however, and the discussion of prison admissions is intended to reveal the relationships between crimes and the presence of women in prison. The published statistics on rule violations do not touch that relationship. On the whole, serial imprisonment was more of a male than female experience. In table 3.12 the total violations are distributed by percentages according to the number of prison admissions. Women had a lower average number of admissions (2.39) than men (3.51). Almost 70 percent of the women had been imprisoned once or twice, but not quite 53 percent of the men had been. At the other end of the continuum, 25.98 percent of the men and only 12.23 percent of the women had been imprisoned five or more times.

To compare the relationships between kinds of rule violations and previous prison experience, table 3.12 traces by percentages the distribution of kinds of violations for each number of admissions to prison. Special attention should be directed to the very high shares held by persons who left prison without being punished for an infraction. The enforcement of official rules was uniform and stern, prison officials insisted; nevertheless, a major proportion of the persons leaving prisons had avoided punishment. In that regard women had the advantage over men for every category of numbers of prison admissions. The advantage increased from one through three admissions before stabilizing. The percentages of inmates committing no violations declined with the increase of prison admissions for both sexes but was always substantial.

For all kinds of infractions, men had a greater average number of incidents than women during the stay in prison, but the comparison becomes more complicated when the number of imprisonments is considered. For individuals experiencing confinement for the first time, women were more represented than men for violence against staff, participation in the sub-rosa economy, and deviant conduct. Those incidents suggest a combination of unsophistication in adjustment to conditions of penal confinement and the urge to make the experience as comfortable as possible. Confrontation of prison officers is likely to involve physical aggression as an effect of emotions. The women, unlike the men, abstained from conflicts with prison officers resulting in serious physical injury. Women punished for participating in the sub-rosa economy were predominately engaged in prohibited trade of articles. Their deviant conduct was infrequent and usually self-injury in the form of either self-mutilation or tattooing, interpreted in connection with the yakuza.

For certain violations the trend was toward more inci-

Table 3.11.
Number of Prison Admissions by Crime, 1993

Crimes	Admissions of Women No. of Inmates	% First Admissions	Times per Inmate	Admissions of Men No. of Inmates	% First Admissions	Times per Inmate
Violence	81	95.1	1.18	3,714	41.4	3.12
Homicide	(12)	(100.0)	(1.00)	(386)	(63.5)	(2.18)
Bodily Injury	(47)	(91.7)	(1.17)	(1,245)	(34.3)	(3.31)
Robbery	(17)	(88.2)	(1.42)	(538)	(71.2)	(2.10)
Extortion	(3)	(100.0)	(1.00)	(764)	(36.5)	(3.09)
Other[a]	(2)	(50.0)	(3.00)	(781)	(79.2)	(4.00)
Property	271	46.7	3.08	7,715	31.5	4.28
Larceny	(172)	(34.9)	(3.86)	(5,688)	(27.5)	(4.37)
Fraud	(71)	(62.0)	(1.82)	(1,337)	(36.9)	(4.46)
Arson	(18)	(77.8)	(1.28)	(188)	(65.4)	(2.80)
Forgery	(6)	(83.3)	(1.33)	(117)	(59.8)	(2.16)

Table 3.11 cont. on next page

Table 3.11. continued

	Admissions of Women			Admissions of Men		
Crimes	No. of Inmates	% First Admissions	Times per Inmate	No. of Inmates	% First Admissions	Times per Inmate
Property						
Embezzlement	(3)	(100.0)	(1.00)	(186)	(78.0)	(1.78)
Other[b]	(1)	(0.0)	(7.50)	(199)	(19.1)	(5.65)
Sex[c]	0	0.0	0.00	557	68.0	1.99
Illicit Commerce[d]	10	50.0	2.10	172	33.7	3.00
Drug	501	51.5	2.08	5,393	27.6	3.48
Traffic	38	100.0	1.00	1,935	63.1	2.01
Other[e]	18	83.3	1.05	837	41.3	3.00
All	919	56.5	2.23	20,323	36.7	3.51

Source: Research and Statistics Section 1994a.

[a] Assault, kidnapping, intimidation, gross negligence, illegal possession of firearms or explosives, and violations of the violence law.
[b] Intrusion, counterfeiting, and possession of stolen property.
[c] Rape and indecent assault.
[d] Gambling, prostitution, and pornography.
[e] Violations of public order, other penal laws, and other special laws.

Table 3.12
Rule Violations by Number of Prison Admissions, 1993

Rule Violations	Mean No. of Admissions	1	2	3	4	5+
Violence Against Staff						
Women	3.53	1.49	1.15	1.01	4.06	4.38
Men	4.48	0.72	0.93	1.11	1.42	1.60
Violence Against Inmates						
Women	3.04	1.49	6.32	7.07	5.40	4.38
Men	3.67	9.10	8.61	9.88	9.13	10.31
Reactions Against Prison Control						
Women	2.96	3.18	1.72	0.00	4.06	6.14
Men	4.12	5.30	7.33	8.50	9.24	9.34
Improper Inmate Relations						
Women	2.21	1.27	1.15	4.04	1.35	0.88
Men	3.72	4.57	4.47	5.49	5.51	5.33
Participation in Sub-Rosa Economy						
Women	2.45	8.91	10.35	13.13	12.16	9.65
Men	4.04	3.80	5.09	5.49	6.56	6.51
Deviant Conduct						
Women	1.54	1.70	1.15	0.00	0.00	0.88
Men	3.32	1.16	1.49	1.72	1.15	1.13
Miscellaneous						
Women	2.77	7.86	9.77	8.08	9.46	13.16
Men	4.10	8.20	11.86	13.42	15.07	14.96

% Distribution by No. of Prison Admissions

Table 3.12 cont. on next page

Table 3.12 continued

Rule Violations	Mean No. of Admissions	% Distribution by No. of Prison Admissions				
		1	2	3	4	5+
None						
Women	4.51	74.10	68.39	66.67	63.51	60.53
Men	3.21	67.15	60.22	54.39	51.92	50.82
All						
Women	2.39	50.54	18.67	10.62	7.94	12.23
Men	3.51	34.79	17.78	12.42	9.03	25.98

Source: Research and Statistics Section 1994a.

dents as the confinement was prolonged. For both sexes the pattern held for violence against staff and reactions against prison control. For men there was also a marked increase in incidents of violence against inmates. Resistance of some inmates to the compulsory and unusual features of prison life was the common thread for this trend.

Another trend was toward fewer incidents as the prison experience lengthened. Both sexes followed that trend for deviant conduct. Women seemed to become more proficient with time in managing relationships with other inmates and avoiding violent confrontations with them.

Other rule violations fluctuated but, on the whole, remained rather stable throughout the time behind bars. Participation in the sub-rosa economy was an important part of prison life for both sexes but was definitely more prominent among women. Men were more involved in violence with other inmates throughout the prison experience.

A wide variety of infractions falls in the category of miscellaneous. Compared with women, men had greater and increasing shares of their infractions so classified throughout the span of time in prison. The pattern for women was a gradual and irregular increase over time. Men were more likely to be punished for comparatively minor infractions.

Women and Probationary Supervision

Community programs draw a larger share of women than the prisons: 4.39 percent of all prison admissions in 1990, 8.4 percent of 1990 admissions to probation, and 5.8 percent of 1990 admissions to parole (Research and Statistics Section 1991a, 1991c). But women are a minority in community programs as well as in prisons. During my conference with a group of volunteer probation officers (VPOs) in Sendai, participants commented on particular aspects of supervising women probationers and parolees. "For female cases, it is easier than for men to find a place for them to stay," said an official of the Rehabilitation Bureau, who explained: "They are received by parents or the spouse; on the contrary, male offenders are single more usually and some tend to be violent and alcoholic. It is easier to find part-time work for women even when they have been convicted of a crime; wages are lower than for men, and Japanese women are gentle and quiet. Single mothers with children have difficulties in seeking work, but the social welfare service will support them for a while."

A male VPO outlined a problem for supervising single females: "If you visit her home, the neighbors will become suspicious of a man coming so often. I say that I am an uncle or other relative." A woman commented: "Even an uncle can start gossip. Why don't you have her meet you in a nearby coffee shop?"

Some fifty thousand unsalaried volunteer probation officers are responsible for supervision of most probationers and parolees.[7] Women have increased their share of the

VPOs: 7 percent in 1953 and 21 percent in 1990. Many of the VPOs are housewives and retired persons; the percentage of all VPOs over sixty years of age has risen from twenty-six in 1953 to sixty-five in 1990.

Probationary supervision is a possible effect of the authorization of judges (by Article 25 of the Penal Code) to suspend prison sentences less than three years in length when there are extenuating circumstances. "Simple suspensions" return the convicted offender without supervision, and these do not qualify as probation when strictly defined. Established legally as "protective supervision," probation holds less than one-fifth of all the suspended sentences to prison. The women on probation are supposed to be more worthy than those sent to prison but less worthy than those granted simple suspensions.

In 1993 over half of the women beginning probation had been convicted of drug offenses (see column A in table 3.13). Property offenses are of secondary importance. Crimes of violence except homicide are few in the caseload. Japanese women are unlikely to be traffic offenders.

According to an administrative summary of the Rehabilitation Bureau, the women placed on probation in 1993 (476) are few when compared with the males (4,492) and the women entering prison (919). For every 100 male probationers, there were 10.6 female probationers. Drug convictions were especially prominent among female probationers; the ratio of 26.5 is more than two times larger than the general 10.6 ratio. Prostitution cases (largely "entrepreneurs") were numerically few, but the representation of women was high. Homicide is heavily represented among female probationers. Other violent offenses were not remarkable. For property offenses, the ratios suggest that arson, fraud, and forgery won women reasonable access to probation; that advantage did not hold for larceny, a crime of varied nature. The representation of women among traffic cases on probation was low and less than for prison admissions.

Table 3.13
Offense Trends of Women Admitted to Probation and Parole, 1993

Offenses	A	B	C[a]	D	E	F[a]
Drug	52.5	26.5	49.9	55.2	12.3	85.0
Property	32.8	8.5	57.6	31.1	5.1	88.6
Larceny	(23.7)	(7.4)	(65.7)	(20.0)	(4.2)	(89.6)
Fraud	(6.1)	(17.2)	(40.8)	(7.4)	(9.1)	(80.3)
Arson	(1.3)	(23.1)	(33.3)	(2.5)	(19.4)	(105.5)
Forgery	(1.1)	(13.2)	(83.3)	(0.5)	(3.6)	(66.7)
Embezzlement	(0.4)	(6.7)	(66.7)	(0.8)	(4.4)	(200.0)
Violent	6.1	4.5	35.8	9.2	4.0	87.6
Homicide	(2.9)	(140.0)	(29.8)	(6.2)	(15.4)	(102.1)
Bodily Injury	(1.5)	(2.4)	(58.3)	(1.4)	(2.1)	(91.7)
Extortion	(0.8)	(2.0)	(133.3)	(0.6)	(1.4)	(166.7)
Robbery	(0.2)	(2.6)	(5.9)	(0.5)	(1.1)	(23.5)
Traffic	5.2	3.3	65.8	1.9	1.3	39.5
Prostitution	1.9	30.0	112.5	1.3	23.8	125.0
Other	1.5	2.6	47.8	1.2	4.3	211.1
All	100.0	10.6	51.8	100.0	6.6	83.9

Source: Data from administrative summary of the Rehabilitation Bureau.

Note: Column headings are as follows:
A. % Distribution of Offenses for Female Probationers
B. Rate of Female Probationers per 100 Male Probationers
C. Rate of Female Probationers per 100 Female Prisoners
D. % Distribution of Offenses for Female Parolees
E. Rate of Female Parolees per 100 Male Parolees
F. Rate of Female Parolees per 100 Female Prisoners

[a]Based on the total number of female admissions in 1993: 919 to prisons, 476 to probation, and 771 to parole.

The number of women entering probation (476) was about half the number of the women entering prisons (see column C in table 3.13). Judges in Japan consider probation an unnecessary burden for the genuinely worthy offenders but less of a penalty than imprisonment. Doubts about female drug-law violators increased their imprisonment rate, but the probation admissions of those violators approximated the use of probation for all women offenders.

The numbers of convicted women are few for prostitution and traffic offenses; their few cases weaken the reliability of their remarkably high rates per one hundred women prisoners (see column C in table 3.13). Larceny is second only to drugs in the number of female probationers and wins a high degree of the courts' preference for probation over imprisonment. Fraud and arson dampen the rate for all property offenses. Forgery and embezzlement put few women on probation but reflect high preference for probation. As would be expected, crimes of violence have low chances for probation, but considering the few cases, probation for bodily injury and homicide occurs often.

Parole and Rehabilitation Aid Hostels

Release from prison may be through either completion of the prison sentence (expiration) or parole. In 1993 departures from women's prisons were 83.5 percent on parole and 16.5 percent at expiration. Men were less likely to benefit from parole: 55 percent of their 1993 departures were on parole, and 44.3 percent were at expiration (Research and Statistics Section 1994a).

All women released at expiration average fewer months in prison before release than parolees, because inmates serving less than a year are less likely to be recommended for parole. If recommended they usually avoid parole, because after a relatively short time in prison, expiration returns them to the community without the inconvenience of parole supervision. Women averaged shorter incarceration than men—19 versus 21.5 months for expiration and 21.9 versus 23.5 months for parole (Research and Statistics Section 1994a).

Parolees, of course, had been imprisoned; earlier, sentencing judges had found them ineligible for probation. In table 3.13 we find the women parolees exceeding women probationers in the proportions of offenses usually denied probation: drugs, homicide, robbery, fraud, and arson. Compared with male parolees, women parolees were especially drawn from drugs, arson, homicide, and fraud cases. Larceny was a "popular" offense for both men and women. Arson and homicide are among the "female" offenses.

Former prisoners are supposed to depend primarily on families for easing the transition from imprisonment to community life. Operated by private organizations and partially subsidized by the Rehabilitation Bureau, hostels are buffeting facilities for those former prisoners not served by families. Of the persons referred in 1993, more women than men had been refused help by their families (28.1 versus 13.9 percent). Men were more likely to have no family ties (70.2 percent versus 62.5 percent of women) or to refuse to rejoin their families (15.9 percent versus 9.4 percent of women) (Research and Statistics Section 1994b).

Of the ninety-seven rehabilitation aid hostels, seven are devoted to women only, and three receive both sexes. Typically, accommodations are for from ten to twenty women. Concerned individuals and organizations established the hostels. Ryozenkai Hostel in Tokyo originated in a private home in 1908. A Buddhist monk began to assist released female inmates in Tochigi City; in 1910 postrelease quarters were established on the grounds of Tochigi Women's Prison. The Baiko Volunteer Probation Officers Association, established in Fukuoka City by women VPOs in 1952, opened Baikoryo Hostel in 1956. Nishihonganji Byakkoso Hostel was opened in 1950 on the grounds of a temple in Kyoto.

A Parolee Who Killed Her Yakuza Husband

On 12 August 1989, at 4 A.M., a parolee, Mrs. A., had killed her husband, a member of the yakuza, with a cooking knife during a violent quarrel.[8] Her case is an appropriate conclusion to this chapter on women offenders. It illustrates some features of the feminine role in Japan that are latent in the offenses of women and are considered in parole administration.

Candidate's background. One of Mrs. A.'s two elderly brothers suffered a serious disease requiring the mother's intensive care. The girl felt abandoned by her parents. Her father was violent when drunk. After completing junior high school, Mrs. A. failed to complete a course in a school for beauticians. She lived for a year with a male friend and returned to her parents' home. At age twenty-one she was married to a member of the yakuza.

Victimization in marriage. In the first five years of marriage, Mrs. A became a mother and suffered the violence of her husband, including broken ribs in one incident. When she complained about the violence to her husband's mother and grandmother, they said he was so confirmed in misconduct that they could do nothing. His sister urged her to accept the responsibilities of the Japanese wife to care for her husband. Learning that he had a lover, Mrs. A. asked the family court in June 1989 for arbitration preliminary to divorce. In July 1989 she accepted the husband's appeal that she return to him. A month later she knifed her husband. She was twenty-seven years old.

Three-year prison sentence. Mrs. A. received the minimum sentence to prison for homicide, because sentencing investigation established the following factors. She had acted in self-defense when the victim suddenly attacked her. The incident was one in a series of violent incidents against her. After the killing she talked to the wife of the victim's yakuza boss, who urged her to call her parents. The parents took her to the hospital and then to the police to report the offense. (Acknowledgment of a crime is crucial to receiving leniency from the court.)

Qualifying for parole. Mrs. A. was granted parole after serving 72 percent of her sentence. The Regional Parole Board (RPB) interviewed her at the prison and authorized further investigation. A volunteer probation officer (VPO) investigated the place where she would reside (her parent's home) and the attitudes of neighbors about her return from prison. Her situation was approved. The RPB usually places priority on whether or not the offender had expressed regrets and offered financial compensation to the victim's family. The latter expectation was deemed inappropriate because of the husband's violence, but the board wondered if a "comfort letter" had been sent to the victim's family. A full-time probation officer accompanied the VPO to the victim's family and brought Mrs. A.'s comfort letter and a bouquet of flowers.

When interviewed by a probation officer at the prison, Mrs. A. expressed attitudes favorable for her parole case. She said that though she was admittedly angry in the crime incident, overall she did not hate her husband. She said she did not want to restore her premarital name; her mother and sister-in-law had done so without her knowledge. She acknowledged ignoring her mother's advice before the incident. She told the RPB that her parents had sought the divorce without her knowledge and that she resented acts of her own family as well as the violence of her husband. Mrs. A. had no criminal record, despite her husband's affiliation.

Conduct on parole. Mrs. A. lived with her parents, a brother's family, and her child. Her search for employment was interrupted by hospitalization and medical care for angina, low blood pressure, and a stomach ulcer. The VPO reported good conduct without special problems; supervision was terminated.

4

Traffic Offenders: The Impulse for Penal Innovation

The Japanese government has adopted a wide variety of measures in striving to cope with an escalating traffic crisis. Among the measures, increased criminalization has placed more traffic offenders under probationary supervision or sent more of them to prisons or juvenile training schools.

In resorting to extended criminalization, the policymakers broadened police responsibilities, strengthened the sentencing authority of the courts, and modified the characteristics that it sent to the Rehabilitation Bureau and the Correction Bureau. The unprecedented conviction of traffic offenders—usually considered reputable, if excessively rash—illustrates the introduction of new kinds of offenders into the field of corrections. Targeting traffic offenders required special care because of the public attitude that they are "regular" persons rather than "real criminals." The policymakers framed a multifaceted national program that gave priority to preventive approaches, traffic engineering, and mobilization of public rejection of flagrant traffic offenders. The singular circumstances created the opportunity for innovation by correctional agencies. Probation became relevant as a community-oriented approach. Ichihara Prison for Traffic Offenders appeared as a remarkable combination of features that may occur singly elsewhere: it receives only imprisoned traffic offenders, it qualifies as an open institution, and it constitutes a full-fledged prison in its staffing and breadth of programs.

The Multifaceted Reaction to Traffic Crisis

As an instrument of rapid and personal mobility through space, the automobile has become a major element in the ecology of the city, its economic activities, fundamental functions of the contemporary families, and the pursuit of pleasure by individuals. Since World War II, car ownership in Japan has expanded greatly to produce a traffic crisis that has magnified fatalities and injuries. Registration of passenger cars, trucks, and two-wheeled vehicles grew from 109,586 in 1946 to 82,204,643 in 1993; for each vehicle on the roads in 1946, there were 750 in 1993. In coping with that accumulation, Japan has been handicapped by urban congestion, narrow streets and roads, and the heavy expense of modern traffic engineering. The traffic fatalities soared from 3,848 in 1948 to 16,765 in 1970, declined to 8,466 in 1979, and then resumed an increase to 10,942 by 1993. The gain in injuries was much greater, increasing from 17,609 in 1948 to 981,096 in 1970, falling to 598,719 in 1980, and then rising to 878,633 in 1993 (Traffic Bureau 1986, 1994).

The accident toll per 10,000 vehicles is a better measurement than the absolute figures. Injuries per 10,000 vehicles have declined from 415.3 in 1958 to 345.6 in 1970 and 99.8 in 1984, and they have bottomed between 101 and 107 from 1985 through 1993. Fatalities per 10,000 vehicles have declined from 23.6 in 1958 to 1.3 in 1993 (Traffic Bureau 1986, 1994).

As early as May 1955, the national government endeavored to reduce traffic accidents. At that time the Head Office for Traffic Accident Prevention Measures was afforded cabinet rank; it was replaced in 1960 by the Head Office for Traffic Policy. The Traffic Safety Policies Law was enacted in 1970, and in 1971 the first of several five-year programs with massive budgets was initiated. As only one phase of the multifaceted reaction since 1955, new laws were enacted to further criminalize traffic offenses, to increase the level of penalization, and to strengthen the rigor of law enforcement (Traffic Safety Policy Office 1991).

Traffic engineering brought new construction and improvement of roads. Traffic signals, signs, and control centers were installed in cities; police tightened regulations. Emergency rescue services were expanded. Traffic safety education received priority at day-care centers and schools, within families, and in national campaigns. Vehicular traffic has been prohibited in some areas, and additional children's and neighborhood parks and bicycle road networks have been constructed. In 1971 seat belts were made obligatory. Enforcement of standards for obtaining driver's licenses placed a premium on the quality of designated driver's schools, especially for operation of mini-sized vehicles and mopeds.

Traffic Offenses and Criminalization

Motor vehicles are symbols of the effects of technological developments on human relationships. Moving rapidly through distance, the operators have little contact with the drivers with whom they share streets and highways. Anonymity favors the impression that persons outside the motorized capsule are "things" deserving little consideration. When personally controlling the vehicle, the individual can select among sites that satisfy personal wishes. The casual contacts among motorists are insufficient for the usual face-to-face controls and blur the distinctions between responsibility and irresponsibility. Some drivers exploit the maneuverability and speed of their vehicles in competing for space and priority on crowded streets.

Low income groups are especially vulnerable to apprehension for theft and assault, but the higher status persons share with them the possibility of traffic misconduct that is particularly visible for police apprehension. The "reputable" and influential citizens see law enforcement protecting them from "criminals" but may appear in court for traffic offenses. Resentment of the law enforcement radiates throughout the population. Cressey (1974, 218) illustrates the point: "The distinguished Automobile Association began in 1905 as an organized group of motorists who employed bicycle patrols to warn drivers of policemen operating speed traps."

Members of the general public are inclined to regard traffic misconduct as only "minor" rulebreaking, sometimes find the "daring heroics" admirable, and otherwise identify themselves with the transgressors. Such attitudes complicate enforcement of laws, especially raising resistance to more rigorous enforcement. The traffic offenders benefit from the Japanese expectation that "worthy" rulebreakers are capable of self-correction. The traffic offenders also agree that they are not "genuine criminals."

The ultimate goal of extended criminalization is to broaden general observance of driving standards so that serious accidents are prevented, rather than simply punishing flagrant drivers. The behavioral standards enunciated (or implied) by the written law are to become binding on all drivers as "good" and "proper." Without that moral support, law enforcement raises several difficulties: it adds to the demands on the public purse, obscures the difference between lawbreakers and "normal" persons, generates technical violators without necessarily targeting the serious transgressors, encourages tolerance of the transgressors as victims of "dictatorial" policing, and raises negative reactions of political constituencies the extended criminalization is supposed to serve.

Traffic law enforcement in Japan raises delicate issues, notes Bayley (1976, 40): "The police are forced to calculate the value of preventing accidents against losses in public respect for law and the police." The "delicate issues" are especially salient for the Japanese, who give priority to duty and to the group over individual interests. To avoid undermining internalized controls, the legislators had to be careful in resorting to criminal sanctions. The national government decided that criminalization would be limited to the most flagrant offenders. Priority would be given to the mobilization of moral indignation and interest groups in favor of new countermeasures, as suggested by the following statement.

> In thinking about future traffic safety countermeasures, and based upon the principle of placing value on human life, our purpose or goal should be to create a traffic society of safety and optimum pleasures and comfort. In particular, our purpose is to establish a road-traffic environment where pedestrians, bicycle riders, small children, old people, and the handicapped can move about with a maximum degree of safety and lack of anxiety. (Traffic Safety Policy Office 1985, 8)

Trends in Enforcement of Traffic Laws

The police and courts became more involved in traffic control through the revision of laws and greater penalization of traffic offenders. The Road Use Control Ordinance and Automobile Traffic Control Ordinance, enforced in 1919, were replaced by the Road Traffic Control Law in 1948. That law was replaced, in turn, by the current Road Traffic Law in 1960, in light of new traffic conditions after World War II. Revision of the Penal Code in 1968 increased the penalty for grave traffic offenses. Imprisonment with forced labor was added as a more stern option, and the maximum prison term for imprisonment without forced labor was lengthened to five years. The Road Traffic Law revised after 1960 is one of the "special laws" that are not part of the Penal Code. From 1932 through 1939, traffic violations were about 40 percent of all offenses against the special laws. After World War II, that share increased rapidly to reach 93 percent in 1960 and 97 percent in 1965 (Shikita and Tsuchiya 1990, 12, 56, 63; Research and Training Institute 1993, 26).

In criminalization of traffic misconduct, two bodies of law are employed: the Road Traffic Control Law and Article 211 of the Penal Code, which defines professional negligence resulting in death or bodily injury: "A person who fails to use such care as is required in the conduct of his profession or occupation and thereby kills or injures another shall be punished with imprisonment at or without forced labor for not more than five years or a fine of not more than 1,000 yen.[1] The same shall apply to a person who by gross negligence kills or injures another" (UNAFEI n.d., 72). The application of the Penal Code prohibition of "professional negligence" to gross traffic incidents is unique in Japan and a legal expedient accepted into practice. Yokoyama (1990, 24) explains that in the earlier history of motor vehicles in Japan most drivers were professional chauffeurs. The public prosecutors and judges, when encountering traffic fatalities and injuries, adopted the fiction that all drivers are professional chauffeurs. That fiction opened the way to increasing the severity of punishment in traffic cases causing fatalities or serious injuries.

In 1946 the police cleared only 2,905 suspects charged with professional negligence in traffic incidents, but regulating traffic took up more and more law enforcement resources. The number of professional negligence cases mark that trend. There were 692,620 by 1970. The number declined in the following years and then resumed the increase, with 606,386 cases in 1990 and 660,750 in 1993 (Research and Training Institute 1994, 40).

The two legal authorizations of criminal justice actions have differed over the years in the delivery of convicted traffic offenders to correction agencies. Table 4.1 traces the two trends and also demonstrates that only a small propor-

TRAFFIC OFFENDERS

Table 4.1
Sentencing and Imprisonment of
Convicted Traffic Offenders, 1979–92

Year	A	B	C	D	E	F	G	H
1979	298	3.12	0.62	1,835	1,673	0.52	0.13	2,154
1980	304	3.18	0.59	1,799	1,655	0.54	0.14	2,253
1981	316	2.90	0.54	1,710	1,692	0.47	0.14	2,315
1982	324	2.75	0.51	1,654	1,729	0.45	0.13	2,196
1983	337	2.77	0.46	1,577	1,878	0.39	0.11	2,085
1984	339	2.82	0.50	1,716	1,972	0.38	0.11	2,135
1985	352	2.83	0.46	1,609	1,976	0.40	0.10	2,054
1986	374	2.67	0.40	1,508	1,841	0.43	0.11	2,068
1987	291	3.31	0.50	1,464	1,265	0.59	0.15	1,962
1988	237	3.75	0.55	1,316	1,023	0.68	0.17	1,771
1989	222	3.61	0.56	1,238	943	0.70	0.18	1,703
1990	171	4.62	0.67	1,149	1,000	0.69	0.16	1,622
1991	117	5.43	0.81	956	1,001	0.63	0.14	1,377
1992	109	5.33	0.80	868	1,038	0.61	0.13	1,310

Sources: Research and Training Institute 1985, 97; 1987, 99; 1992a, 102; 1994, 90.

Note: Column headings are as follows:
A. No. Convicted, Professional Negligence (in thousands)
B. % Sentenced to Prison, Professional Negligence
C. % Imprisoned, Professional Negligence
D. No. Imprisoned, Professional Negligence
E. No. Convicted, Road Traffic Law Violations (in thousands)
F. % Sentenced to Prison, Road Traffic Law Violations
G. % Imprisoned, Road Traffic Law Violations
H. No. Imprisoned, Road Traffic Law Violations

tion of the convictions in courts results in prison admissions. In 1979 the Road Traffic Law led to 1,673,000 convictions in courts, of which 0.13 percent (2,154) resulted in imprisonment. In 1992 the convictions had dropped to 1,038,000, and 0.13 percent (or 1,410) of these convicts were put behind bars. Arrests for professional negligence involved the incidents in which persons were killed or injured. Fewer violators were convicted for professional negligence than for Road Traffic Law offenses (298,000 in 1979 and 109,000 in 1992), but a higher proportion of those convicted were sent to prison (0.62 in 1979 and 0.80 in 1992, or 1,835 and 868, respectively, in absolute numbers).

In determining who were tried, public prosecutors shut off much of the flow of traffic offenders to prison. They also sent a considerable number to lower courts for summary proceedings that do not culminate in imprisonment. Of persons accused of professional negligence, only 9.2 percent were referred for formal trial in 1946, 6.1 percent in 1951, and between 2 and 4 percent from 1956 to 1988. Also, few were tried for violations of the Road Traffic Law: 1.6 percent in 1946 and less than 1 percent thereafter (Shikita and Tsuchiya 1990, 124–27).

In 1968 the traffic infraction notification system was introduced to reduce the heavy volume of traffic cases. It simplified the collection of fines and exempted most traffic offenders from the criminal stigma. Nonserious offenders were given blue tickets and could pay a fine when notified by the prefectural police. If motorists refused to pay and requested trial in a summary court, they would receive a red ticket and join motorists not considered eligible for an administrative fine (Yokoyama 1990; Shikita and Tsuchiya 1990, 63, 124–27; Araki 1985).

After ordering a prison sentence, the judge may suspend its execution (under conditions set by Articles 25 and 25-2 of the Penal Code) and decides whether or not probationary supervision is necessary. The sentence may not be more than three years in length. The offender must not have been previously sentenced to prison; if previously sentenced, the prohibition is lifted after five years since the execution of the previous imprisonment, but the judge must order probationary supervision.

Traffic Offenses and Imprisonment

It is in keeping with the central concern of this book to question whether or not the imprisonment of traffic offenders increased while the imprisonment of all offenders declined over the years. Has the traffic crisis motivated the Japanese people—or at least their policymakers—to suspend their usual reluctance to employ imprisonment as an instrument for maintaining the public order?

Broadly speaking, prison admissions of all traffic offenders increased from 1968 to at least 1973 but, according to two yardsticks, subsequently dropped consistently and sharply (see table 4.2). The first yardstick is male traffic admissions, which were 12 percent of all male prison admissions in 1968, up to 19.2 percent in 1973, and down to 9.6 percent by 1994. In other words, the number of new traffic prisoners initially increased their share of all prison admissions but later joined the trend away from imprisonment.

The imprisonment rates per one hundred thousand male adults in Japanese society—the second yardstick—also support the conclusion that, except for a few initial years, the imprisonment of traffic offenders fails to oppose the general decline in the use of incarceration. The rates in table 4.2 show that for offenses other than traffic offenses, the rate of male prison admissions per one hundred thousand Japanese male adults declined over the years, and that except for the years 1968–72, the rates for traffic offenses joined the trend. The ratios in table 4.2 also confirm a declining trend, after 1971.

The imprisonment rate is a severe test of our hypothesis but also has the advantage of linking imprisonment and

Table 4.2
Male Traffic Admissions to Prison for All Traffic Offenses, 1968–94

Year	No.	% of All Admissions[a]	Rate per 100,000 Population[b] Traffic	Other	Ratio[c]
1968	3,450	12.0	10.8	78.6	13.7
1969	3,833	14.6	11.6	68.0	17.1
1970	4,215	16.6	12.5	62.7	19.9
1971	5,418	20.3	15.8	62.1	25.4
1972	5,547	19.9	15.8	63.6	24.8
1973	4,931	19.2	13.8	58.3	23.7
1974	4,700	18.6	13.0	56.9	22.8
1975	4,011	15.4	10.8	58.4	18.5
1976	3,807	14.2	10.1	61.3	16.5
1977	3,721	13.7	9.8	61.5	15.9
1978	3,916	13.8	10.2	63.7	16.0
1979	3,747	13.3	9.6	63.0	15.2
1980	3,817	13.9	9.7	60.5	16.0
1981	3,896	13.3	9.8	64.1	15.3
1982	3,635	12.0	9.1	66.4	13.7
1983	3,486	11.8	8.6	65.7	13.1
1984	3,675	11.9	9.0	66.0	13.6
1985	3,524	11.6	8.5	64.5	13.2
1986	3,414	11.6	8.1	61.9	13.1
1987	3,235	11.4	7.6	59.4	12.8
1988	3,018	11.2	7.0	55.9	12.5

Table 4.2 cont. on next page

TRAFFIC OFFENDERS

Table 4.2 continued

Year	No.	% of All Admissions[a]	Rate per 100,000 Population[b] Traffic	Other	Ratio[c]
1989	2,716	11.5	6.2	47.9	12.9
1990	2,589	11.9	5.9	43.7	13.5
1991	2,261	11.2	5.1	40.1	12.7
1992	2,084	10.4	4.6	39.5	11.6
1993	1,940	9.5	4.2	40.1	10.5
1994	1,957	9.6	4.2	39.5	10.6

Sources: Research and Statistics Section 1971a, 1976a, 1981a, 1986a, 1991a, 1994a.

[a] Equals percent of total prison admissions of males aged 20 years and over.

[b] Equals prison admission rates per 100,000 male Japanese aged 20 years and over in Japan's total population.

[c] Equals rate for traffic offenses divided by rate for other offenses and multiplied by 100.

developments in general society in the analysis of public issues. The linkage implies that if unchanged over the years, (a) the degree of traffic misconduct and (b) the policy of imprisoning flagrant traffic offenders will generate the same imprisonment rate despite gains in the number of persons vulnerable to imprisonment for traffic crimes. Then, the more recent decline in the traffic admissions to prison signals either (a) a reduction in the degree of traffic misconduct or (b) an easing of the stern policy toward flagrant traffic offenders.

The total prison admissions of traffic offenders, however, does not conclude the discussion. As I already explained, the criminalization of traffic offenders is two-pronged (involving both professional negligence and Road Traffic Law violation), and revision of the Road Traffic Law has been more directly related to the rather recent recourse to greater criminalization of traffic offenders.

In Japan imprisonment for traffic offenses is almost entirely a male experience (see table 4.2). Thus, my analysis of prison statistics is largely limited to adult males, though published statistics on probation do not differentiate by gender.

In the early years, the decline of the general imprisonment rate was opposed by admissions authorized by both professional negligence and the Road Traffic Law. The two legal justifications for imprisonment of traffic offenders follow opposing trends over the years. Professional negligence is an increasing factor through 1971, when the drive against traffic crimes was enthusiastic. The upsurge in absolute number of prison admissions was prolonged until 1981 by the Road Traffic Law.

The absolute number of convictions increased until the mid-1980s (see table 4.1). The percentage of convictions resulting in prison sentences increased in the long run, especially until the mid-1980s, but the percentages of prison sentences were very modest compared with the great number of convictions. The sentences imposed by the courts, as I have already explained, were markedly reduced by actions of the public prosecutors and the traffic infraction notification system. Convictions under the Road Traffic Law were especially numerous, but the relatively more tolerant handling of those violations is indicated by the heavy use of fines and the lower percentage of cases receiving prison sentences. The courts suspend a substantial proportion of the prison sentences, especially in professional negligence cases. However, because of their much greater volume, the Road Traffic Law cases deliver more violators to prison gates in absolute numbers, despite the smaller proportion of cases sentenced to prison before the judges decide whether or not to suspend the sentence.

In that way, the Road Traffic Law has generated greater recourse to imprisonment of traffic offenders than of male offenders in general (see table 4.3). In trends opposing those of professional negligence cases, the Road Traffic Law recorded (a) higher imprisonment rates and (b) growing shares of all male prison admissions until 1982. Thereafter, the general trends were downward.

Assuming consistency in the courts' decision making, the quality and quantity of traffic cases resulted in a greater volume of convictions into the mid-1980s, but the flow into the prisons was sustained because of the sheer volume of the Road Traffic Law cases. After the mid-1980s, the Road Traffic Law cases joined the professional negligence cases in the general decline in the use of imprisonment.

Whether professional negligence or Road Traffic Law cases, the convictions were more numerous until the mid-1980s, but the percentages of prison sentences among convicts and the percentage of prison sentences actually executed dropped off (see table 4.1). Despite the referrals to summary courts by public prosecutors and the introduction of the traffic infraction notification system, the number of convictions did not drop until the mid-1980s. Meanwhile, executed prison sentences lost percentage shares of court dispositions. Whether they reflect a change in the quality of traffic cases or in the sentencing policy of judges, the courts' decisions on suspending prison execution of prison sentences contributed to the reduction of traffic offenders in prison admissions.

Traffic Offenders and Probation

The access of convicted traffic offenders to probation depends in part on the prevalence of the program for offenders in general. (Parole of traffic offenders is not considered here; parole rates depend more on the number of inmates than on the choice of imprisonment among alterna-

TRAFFIC OFFENDERS

Table 4.3
Male Traffic Admissions to Prison, by Offense, 1968–94

		Professional Negligence			Violation of Road Traffic Law	
Year	No.	% of All Admissions[a]	Rate per 100,000 Population[b]	No.	% of All Admissions[a]	Rate per 100,000 Population[b]
1968	2,633	9.2	8.2	817	2.8	2.5
1969	3,475	13.2	9.9	363	1.4	1.0
1970	3,809	15.0	11.3	406	1.6	1.2
1971	4,750	17.8	13.1	668	2.5	1.8
1972	4,515	16.2	12.9	1,032	3.7	2.9
1973	3,880	15.1	10.4	1,051	4.1	2.8
1974	3,210	12.7	8.9	1,490	5.9	4.1
1975	2,585	10.1	6.7	1,426	5.6	3.7
1976	2,289	8.5	6.1	1,518	5.7	4.0
1977	2,037	7.5	5.1	1,684	6.2	4.2
1978	1,940	6.8	5.0	1,976	7.0	5.1
1979	1,680	5.9	4.1	2,067	7.3	5.1
1980	1,586	5.8	4.0	2,231	8.1	8.2
1981	1,481	5.0	3.6	2,415	8.2	5.8
1982	1,390	4.6	3.5	2,245	7.4	5.6
1983	1,347	4.6	3.2	2,139	7.2	5.0
1984	1,532	4.9	3.7	2,152	7.0	5.2
1985	1,439	4.7	3.3	2,085	6.9	4.8
1986	1,348	4.6	3.2	2,066	7.0	4.9
1987	1,329	4.7	3.0	1,906	6.7	4.3
1988	1,231	4.5	2.9	1,787	6.6	4.2
1989	1,039	4.4	2.3	1,677	7.1	3.7

Table 4.3 cont. on next page

Table 4.3 continued

	Professional Negligence			Violation of Road Traffic Law		
Year	No.	% of All Admissions[a]	Rate per 100,000 Population[b]	No.	% of All Admissions[a]	Rate per 100,000 Population[b]
1990	1,044	4.8	2.4	1,545	7.1	3.5
1991	882	4.4	1.9	1,379	6.8	2.9
1992	785	3.9	1.7	1,299	6.5	2.9
1993	723	3.6	1.6	1,217	6.0	2.6
1994	697	3.4	1.5	1,260	6.2	2.7

Sources: Research and Statistics Section 1971a, 1976a, 1981a, 1986a, 1991a, and 1994a.
[a] Equals percent of total prison admissions of males aged 20 years and over.
[b] Equals prison admission rates per 100,000 male Japanese aged 20 years and over in Japan's total population.

tive dispositions of courts.) Judges are reluctant to attach probationary supervision to the suspension of a prison sentence when there are extenuating circumstances. They see supervision as an additional burden and prefer to return the more worthy recipients of suspension to the streets without supervision. Furthermore, another suspension would be denied if the individual commits a new crime. The net effect is that probationary supervision signals the judge's belief that the probationers are the least favorable of the successful candidates for suspended prison sentences (Kouhashi 1985; Nishikawa 1990). The proportion of suspensions requiring probationary supervision has dropped from 18.5 percent in 1981 to 14.3 percent in 1992 (Research and Training Institute 1985, 106; 1987, 98; 1990a, 121; 1993, 73).

Adult traffic offenders have held impressive but recently declining proportions of all probations. Nevertheless, granting of probation in lieu of execution of the prison sentence gives traffic offenders the benefit of leniency and indicates the judge's more favorable evaluation of the convicted defendant.

Comparison of the data of tables 4.2 and 4.3 reveals that adult traffic offenders were more likely to receive probation as the years unfolded. Statistics drawn from the tables show that 611 men (517 convicted for professional negligence and 144 under the Road Traffic Law) became probationers in 1968 and that 3,450 men were admitted to prison in 1968. In that year 5.2 adult traffic offenders entered prison for every one beginning probation. The ratios fluctuated over the ensuing years, but the general trend was downward, reaching 2.5 probationers per admitted prisoner in 1993. Although prison admissions always exceeded probation admissions, the increasing willingness of judges to authorize probation contributed to the decline of prison admissions of traffic offenders.

Convictions for professional negligence usually involved more serious traffic misconduct than convictions under the Road Traffic Law. Altogether, Road Traffic Law violations were much more numerous, but most of those offenders were diverted into administrative fines and summary proceedings. In the early years, professional negligence cases were more directed toward imprisonment than those Road Traffic Law cases convicted in district courts, from a ratio of 5.1 in 1968 down to 3.1 in 1977. After 1981, both kinds of cases tended to have about the same number of prison admissions per probation admission for traffic offenders—about 2.5 prison admissions per probation admission. In 1968 professional negligence sent 2,633 men to prison (see table 4.3), but only 517 were granted probation (see table 4.4): a ratio of 5.1. The equivalent comparisons produce ratios of 3.1 in 1977, 2.2 in 1982, and 2.6 in 1993.

Over the years, traffic offenders gained greater shares of all probations, from 8.8 percent in 1968 to 22.6 percent in 1980 (see table 4.4). They then hovered around 20 percent until 1992 and dropped off in 1993. At first professional negligence was the chief basis for the convictions resulting in suspension of prison sentences with probationary supervision. In 1968 that was the basis for 6.8 percent of all probation authorized that year, compared with only 1.9 percent for Road Traffic Law cases. Tracing those percentages in table 4.4 reveals, first, the continued preeminence of professional negligence until 1975, when Road Traffic Law cases assumed the dominant position; and, second, that the Road Traffic Law cases made significant contributions thereafter, to maintain the relative stability of all the traffic cases at about 20 percent of all probationers.

Adult probation has failed to keep pace with the growth of the Japanese population. It has held very low rates per one hundred thousand Japanese of both sexes. Again, for adults, professional negligence initially had the highest rates when compared with Road Traffic Law cases, but it gave up that position after 1974.

Open Facilities: An Innovative Approach

In establishing Ichihara Prison, Ryozo Katsuo, then director general of the Correction Bureau, and Haruo Sato, a psychologist who was its first warden, seized the opportunity for innovation. The opportunity emerged as a combination of the policymakers' wish to minimize public resistance to the extended criminalization of traffic offenses, the public tolerance of a "folk crime," and the assumption that traffic offenders are especially likely to undertake self-correction. The combination made possible the establishment of Ichihara as the Correction Bureau's premier example of an open institution. The following official statement captures the philosophy of an open facility for inmates convicted of traffic offenses.

> The traffic offenders imprisoned there are allowed to enjoy a freedom of atmosphere. In order to facilitate them

Table 4.4
Admissions to Probation of Adult Traffic Offenders, 1968–93

Year	All Admissions No.	All Admissions % of All Admissions	Professional Negligence No.	Professional Negligence % of All Admissions	Professional Negligence Rate[a]	Road Traffic Law Violations No.	Road Traffic Law Violations % of All Admissions	Road Traffic Law Violations Rate[a]
1968	7,542	8.8	517	6.8	0.78	144	1.9	0.22
1969	7,161	9.7	556	7.8	0.81	141	2.0	0.21
1970	6,908	12.0	693	10.0	0.99	135	1.9	0.19
1971	6,771	13.2	694	10.2	0.97	200	2.9	0.28
1972	7,228	14.4	782	10.8	1.07	262	3.6	0.36
1973	7,187	17.4	740	10.3	1.00	514	7.1	0.69
1974	7,014	21.0	754	10.7	1.00	717	10.2	0.95
1975	7,048	17.9	552	7.8	0.72	711	10.1	0.93
1976	8,068	18.8	694	8.6	0.89	825	10.2	1.06
1977	7,897	21.2	657	8.3	0.84	1,016	12.9	1.29
1978	8,501	21.2	648	7.6	0.82	1,155	13.6	1.45
1979	8,128	21.7	622	7.7	0.77	1,144	14.1	1.42
1980	8,058	22.6	667	8.3	0.82	1,157	14.4	1.42

Table 4.4 cont. on next page

Table 4.4 continued

Year	All Admissions No.	All Admissions % of All Admissions	Professional Negligence No.	Professional Negligence % of All Admissions	Professional Negligence Rate[a]	Road Traffic Law Violations No.	Road Traffic Law Violations % of All Admissions	Road Traffic Law Violations Rate[a]
1981	8,336	20.7	655	7.9	0.80	1,069	12.8	1.30
1982	8,223	20.4	633	7.7	0.76	1,045	12.7	1.26
1983	7,798	20.4	659	8.4	0.78	932	11.9	1.11
1984	7,692	20.1	634	8.2	0.75	909	11.8	1.07
1985	7,180	20.0	614	8.5	0.71	825	11.5	0.96
1986	6,456	19.1	501	7.8	0.58	735	11.4	0.85
1987	6,477	19.9	638	9.8	0.73	652	10.1	0.74
1988	6,076	21.6	590	9.7	0.66	720	11.8	0.81
1989	5,205	19.4	439	8.4	0.49	571	11.0	0.63
1990	4,793	20.7	398	8.3	0.44	596	12.4	0.66
1991	4,645	17.7	304	6.5	0.33	519	11.2	0.56
1992	4,732	18.3	290	6.1	0.31	577	12.2	0.62
1993	4,968	15.8	280	5.6	0.30	506	10.2	0.53

Sources: Research and Statistics Section 1971a, 1976a, 1981a, 1986a, 1991a, 1994a.
[a]Equals rate per 100,000 adult Japanese of both sexes in Japan's total population.

to return to normal society without trouble and to prevent them from committing any other traffic crime, they are given special corrective education for the purpose of cultivating the spirit of law observation, sense of responsibility, respect for human life and other moral characteristics through daily activities, etc. (Traffic Safety Policy Office 1985, 128)

In that spirit, Ichihara Prison for Traffic Offenders was established in November 1969. Some traffic prisoners had been assembled in Toyohashi Prison on an experimental basis in 1961, as well as in Kakogawa Prison and a branch of Chiba Prison in 1963. Special prisons for traffic offenders were authorized in 1964; their criteria only allowed acceptance of inmates having their first exposure to imprisonment, serving sentences no longer than three years, having no serious mental or physical disabilities, and otherwise qualified for minimum security. Of the approximately 1,500 traffic prisoners received annually in the Kanto area around Tokyo, 10 to 14 percent are selected to go to Ichihara. Seven other facilities are designated to receive adult males sentenced for traffic offenses: Hakodate Juvenile Prison, Kakogawa Prison, Ohita Prison, Onomichi Branch Prison, Saijo Branch Prison, Toyohashi Branch Prison, and Yamagata Prison.

As the prototype open prison in Japan, Ichihara opposes the principle of containment exemplified by the custodial prison. "Containment here means not only that prisoners must be kept out of circulation," explain Jones, Corres, and Stockford (1977, 1–2), "but that their deviations, even within the prison, must not be on such a scale as to disturb the peace of mind of the man-in-the-streets." In architecture and other features of its physical environment, the ideal open institution is supposed to convey the willingness of officials to engage in free and easy social intercourse with inmates. Authorities strive to make the environment as similar as feasible to life in the free community. Movement within the buildings and on the grounds is free. The residents are selected for their self-responsibility in a social-psychological environment that substitutes inner controls for the surveillance and regimentation of the custodial prison.

Ichihara is the most exact and prominent example of open facilities in Japan, but other correctional facilities present some features of open institutions. In addition to Ichihara, four small and independent institutions, affiliated with private enterprises, qualify essentially: the Ohi Shipbuilding Dockyard Camp, a branch of Matsuyama Prison on Shikoku Island; Arii Dockyard Camp in Onomichi, on the Inland Sea of Seto; the Kagamihara Metal Industrial Camp near Gifu City; and Kitsuregawa School for Agriculture and Civil Engineering in Tochigi Prefecture. In addition to the five institutions, fourteen "live-out" programs are satellites of regular prisons, but selected inmates commute on workdays from a regular prison to private workshops contracting for prison labor. Three "live-out" programs are on farms, and one is a forestry camp.

Akira Masaki was the earliest pioneer introducing open facilities in Japan. As director general of the Correction Bureau, he put prisoners in the Ishikawajima Dockyard, Tokyo, for construction of ships during World War II. Masaki recalled that he intended to combine the concept of the open prison with the industrialization of inmate labor. In 1942 fifty men in the final level of the progressive grade system employed in Japanese prisons were dressed in civilian worker garb, granted three days off their sentence for each day of diligent labor, and placed in the dormitories of free workers (Masaki 1964).

An abortive and small experiment was introduced at Fuchu Prison by Warden Nobuo Gotoh on 2 September 1968 but was canceled on 15 March 1969. Inmates approved for parole (fifty-seven during the experiment) rode a bus and train and then walked ten minutes to the Nikko Pen factory in Chofu City, a suburb of Tokyo. They were housed in a warehouse and part of a cell block.

Three persons were prominent in introducing the Ohi Shipbuilding Dockyard Camp in 1961. A former prison officer (Mr. Arita) was on the staff of the rehabilitation aid hostel for prisoners released from Matsuyama Prison. To suggest that prisoners be employed at the dockyard, he approached Hisao Tsubouchi, president of the Kurushima Dockyard Company and vice-president of the Volunteer Council for Rehabilitation Aid Hostels of Ehime Prefecture. Tsubouchi had been a prisoner of war during World War II and doubted that prisoners need strict supervision. Nubuo Gotoh was warden of Matsuyama Prison, where the Ohi inmates were selected to work alongside free workers in welding, drilling, and grinding the steel components of a ship.[2]

The Arii Dockyard Camp was initiated later, while Gotoh was warden of Hiroshima Prison. It is sponsored by Kosin-Sangyo, Inc., for dismantling obsolete vessels for steel scrap. As at Ohi, traffic offenders are heavily represented there.

The Kagamihara Metal Industrial Camp was the brainchild in 1970 of Yoshio Takahashi, then head of the Nagoya Correction Region, and Yukio Nishi, then warden of Gifu Prison, of which the camp is a branch. They persuaded ten private contractors, who operated small industrial shops, to sponsor the nearby camp in a residential suburb and to employ carefully selected traffic offenders.

Established in 1970, the Kitsuregawa School for Agriculture and Civil Engineering was then a branch of Utsunomiya Prison; the prison was replaced in 1971 by Kurobane Prison. The school was chiefly the creation of Takeji Yagishita, warden of Kurobane, and a project team of the Correction Bureau. Kiyoshi Arai, director of the school, implemented the training center for construction machinery, agriculture, and animal husbandry.

Ichihara's Staff and Programs

Located on forty-nine acres outside Ichihara City in Chiba Prefecture, the prison for traffic offenders is still as described by Watson (1971) in nature and operations. It has a wire perimeter fence surrounding the receiving cell block, a semiopen dormitory, a staff office building, a dining hall, a congregate bath building, an auditorium with classrooms, and five workshops. The grounds are attractively landscaped, with a Japanese-style park in the rear for visits. Outside the perimeter are a sports field, facilities for safe-driving instruction, three open dormitories for impending releases, and a Japanese-type cottage for inmate meditation and prayer.

After a reception period of two to three weeks, inmates are moved to the semiopen dormitory adjacent to the receiving cell block. They are free to move about the dormitory building. Instead of the usual cells, the dormitory has four-person sleeping units resembling sections of European railroad cars but without a door to the corridor. Instead of the sleeping mats of ordinary Japanese cells, there is a two-level bunk of dark wood on each side of the unit. Sliding curtains enclose each bunk at night. Study tables face ordinary windows.

Consistent with the premises of the open institution, Ichihara orients its staff and its battery of programs toward changing the behavior of imprisoned traffic offenders. Ichihara residents have provided evidence of self-discipline in an open setting. Rule violators appear before the prison's disciplinary committee, which determines guilt and, when appropriate, the kind of punishment. Because infractions are few, the committee meets seldom.

Ichihara's commitment to treatment over security purposes is demonstrated by its staffing and its organizational structure. Of a staff of one hundred, only forty-one members are assigned security duties, whereas conventional prisons devote the bulk of their personnel to security functions. Forty-two members of the staff have earned at least a bachelor's degree. The staff is well rounded and includes psychologists for testing, as well as counselors, teachers, and medical personnel. Usually, Japanese prisons have five divisions: general affairs, security and industry, education, medical, and classification. Ichihara has only three divisions: general affairs, medical, and treatment (with classification, education, and security and industry as subdivisions).

Ichihara benefits from being a component of a single national correction system incorporating all prisons and pretrial detention centers. The distribution of inmates is effected through an integrated classification system that supplies a sufficient number of selected inmates for Ichihara and that implies that less worthy individuals can be sent to other facilities. Ichihara also benefits from well-established staff recruitment and training programs. Candidates for correctional officer positions must pass a written examination administered annually by the National Personnel Board. The Training Institute for Correctional Personnel, located in a suburb of Tokyo, is the hub of in-service training, offering the most advanced courses for senior executives and administrators and for selected specialists, including teachers, counselors, and classification specialists.

Ichihara adds an unconventional element to the industrial activity of Japanese prisons. Instead of the forty-hour workweek of most Japanese prisons, Ichihara inmates have a thirty-hour workweek; ten hours are added to the treatment activities. The Ichihara industrial program pays for safe-driving instruction as a kind of vocational training.

The programmed activities focus on attitudes and behavior believed to be among the basic causes of traffic deaths and injuries. The approach relies on the Japanese psychology that presses individuals to be dutiful. As an Ichihara psychologist explained to me, traffic offenders are believed to lack concern about the effect of their misconduct on others, and they should be encouraged to develop responsibility. The emphasis on moral reeducation is symbolized by the Monument of Atonement, a large rectangular stone on a pyramid platform. Constructed in 1978, it was dedicated in 1986 in a semireligious ceremony to which twenty retired Ichihara officers and volunteer chaplains were invited. On the polished floors in the traditional Japanese cottage are mats for Buddhist and Zen expressions of regret for killing or injuring others.

Naikan therapy, freely translated as "inner self-observation," is employed to move inmates toward more positive social behavior. Two members of the education section at Ichihara have earned a license in the method at a Naikan Training Institute in Nara Prefecture. For two weeks some half-dozen residents, who have volunteered for the therapy, go to a solitary cell in the receiving cell block on weekdays from 5:30 to 9:30 P.M., on Saturday afternoons, and all day on Sundays. Staff members go from cell to cell, asking what the individuals are thinking and advising them on how to think about themselves, but offering no specific advice. It is expected that the traffic incident will dominate the inmate's inner self-observation.

Naikan therapy proceeds through three stages, as Ishii and Bindzus (1987) explain, to counter negative childhood memories that, by being interpreted by the individual as lack of devotion and love, have produced strong feelings of rejection and hate. The feelings, transferred against society, are believed to cause criminal behavior. Naikan therapy is supposed to break that cycle by mobilizing the individual's inner energies through recollection. In the first stage, by considering what the counselor has done positively for him, the inmate relives the concern and love he once experienced. The ability to confront negative experiences of the past is reinforced in the second stage, when the inmate considers what he has done positively for the persons involved in those experiences. In the third stage, the inmate is ready to accept the negative aspects of the past and to liberate himself from them. New and more positive behavioral patterns are supposed to favor social responsibility after release from prison.

Newly arrived inmates are encouraged to set personal goals in prison and to develop safe-driving aptitudes and attitudes. In addition to psychological tests, machines test the inmates' responses to typical driving situations. Individuals are selected for a four-week safe-driving course involving study of road traffic laws, instruction on first-echelon automobile maintenance, experience in driving simulators, and demonstrated competence in an arena of mock city streets.

Each group, under the leadership of a staff member, engages in free discussion of causes and solutions for traffic accidents. The groups are formed according to the inmates' traffic offenses: drunken driving, driving without a license, repeated minor violations, and offenses for which the offenders were given short sentences. Lectures on Saturday mornings emphasize morality, driving safety, industrial safety, and avoidance of drug abuse.

In exploiting extended criminalization as a part of far-ranging reactions to the traffic crisis, Japanese policymakers recognized the need for careful targeting because of the unusual public tolerance of traffic violators. The necessity opened a window of opportunity for correctional innovation but also shaped the programming for adult and juvenile traffic offenders.

As a primary example of the possibilities of open institutions, Ichihara draws on the Japanese faith in the capacity of most deviants for self-correction without intervention of external controls. The emphasis on duty and moral responsibility also underlies the special programs for juvenile traffic offenders and the treatment orientation for juveniles. Those bases for the criminalization of traffic offenders have inhibited their admissions to prisons and training schools and have given impetus to adult, and especially to juvenile, probation.

The Monument of Atonement at the Ichihara Prison for Traffic Offenders was built in 1978 with donations from many volunteers, so that inmates who realize the serious nature of their offense and have a sense of repentance and atonement would be provided with opportunities to pray for the repose of their victims' souls.

According to their wishes, the inmates at Ichihara Prison for Traffic Offenders are given opportunities to pray for the repose of victims' souls.

At Ichihara Prison for Traffic Offenders, a course in safe driving concludes with demonstrated competence on an arena of mock city streets.

Male foreign civilians have been concentrated in Fuchu Prison in metropolitan Tokyo. The increasing number of foreign prisoners has necessitated the recent referral of some of them to Osaka Prison.

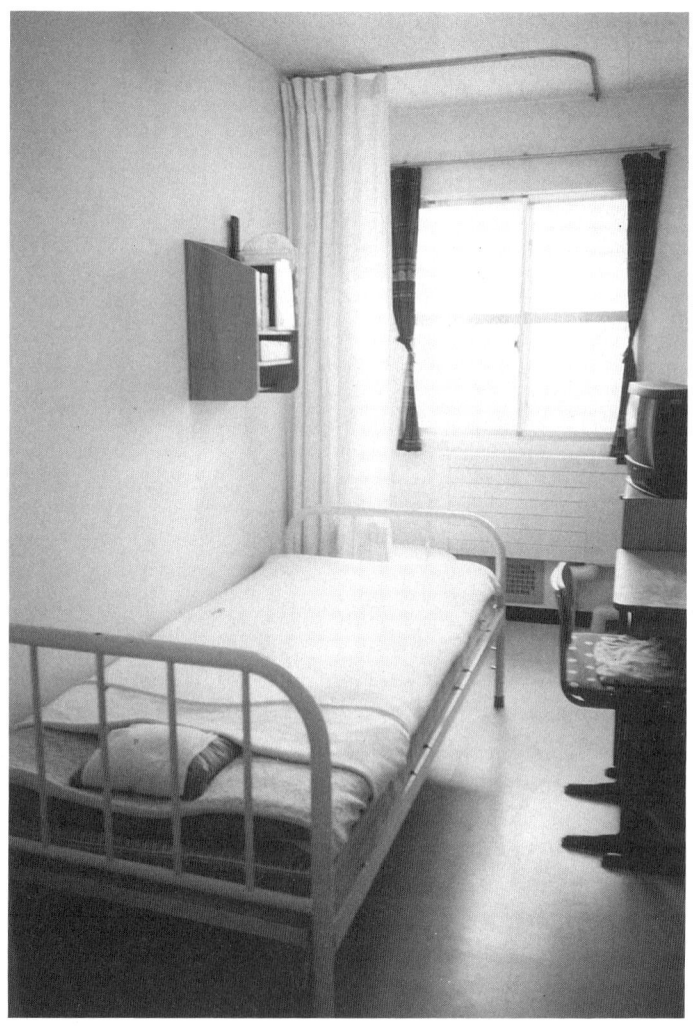

The room at Tochigi Women's Prison is typical of one-person "cells" for foreign inmates in class F.

Renovated in 1991, Kasamatsu Women's Prison is an example of the design of many of the Japanese correctional institutions.

In response to the upsurge in the number of women inmates, the former juvenile prison at Iwakuni was completely reconstructed in 1989 in a modern design to become the fifth women's prison.

The Osaka Juvenile Classification Home administers group psychological tests to adolescents referred by the juvenile court for diagnosis. The findings will assist the court in deciding whether or not the juveniles should be sent to training schools.

This Kendo tournament (traditional Japanese fencing) was conducted at the public gymnasium near Tama Juvenile Training School for boys in the Tokyo Correction Region.

As a phase of physical education, the girls at Haruna Juvenile Training School engage in the Naginata, an exercise featuring the use of feudal-era halberds.

At a Juvenile Training School, the graduates of the junior high school program receive certificates.

The Onomichi Branch Prison, Hiroshima Correction Region, specializes in the care of inmates beyond 60 years of age.

5

Juvenile Offenders: Reactions to Drug and Traffic Offenses

In the last quarter century, increased numbers of juveniles involved with either drug or traffic offenses have arrived at juvenile training schools or were received by probation offices as probationers. The two sets of juveniles qualify as another cohort that is a segment of a subpopulation of persons subject to the authority of a correction agency.

The juvenile cohort is a concern here for two general reasons. First, we are interested in whether the cohort becomes more numerous as the years proceed, while the general inmate population loses numbers. For juveniles, are the total admissions to correction facilities declining but the number of admissions for certain law violations increasing? This is the basic question raised for each cohort addressed in this book.

Second, the escalating admissions of drug and traffic offenders among juveniles qualify as extended criminalization, in which the scope of the law and official policy has been broadened. In a major public crisis, laws were revised to authorize greater efforts of the police and juvenile courts to cope with young drug and traffic offenders. As I already stated, training schools and probation offices have encountered unprecedented numbers in the juvenile cohort.

JUVENILE OFFENDERS

Table 5.1
Admissions to Juvenile Training Schools, 1969–94

Year	Total Juvenile Population[a]	JTS Admissions Total	Traffic	Drug	Adjusted[b]	Rate per 100,000 Population[c] Actual	Adjusted
1969	11,401	4,409	41	1	4,367	38.7	38.3
1970	10,668	3,965	69	3	3,893	37.2	36.2
1971	10,187	3,290	114	1	3,175	32.3	31.2
1972	9,984	2,940	94	8	2,838	29.4	28.4
1973	9,787	2,276	65	8	2,203	23.2	22.5
1974	9,668	1,969	89	9	1,871	20.4	19.3
1975	9,522	2,549	136	27	2,386	26.8	25.1
1976	9,501	2,662	128	39	2,495	28.0	26.3
1977	9,602	3,277	234	78	2,965	34.1	30.9
1978	9,697	3,779	236	329	3,214	39.0	33.1
1979	9,863	4,074	257	461	3,356	41.3	34.0
1980	9,717	4,720	410	574	3,736	48.6	38.4
1981	10,008	5,004	469	693	3,842	50.0	38.4
1982	10,263	5,253	512	747	3,994	51.2	38.9
1983	10,514	5,787	536	789	4,462	55.0	42.4
1984	10,752	6,062	545	855	4,662	56.4	43.4
1985	10,962	6,029	578	778	4,673	55.0	42.6
1986	11,541	5,747	517	744	4,486	49.8	38.9
1987	11,745	5,222	487	656	4,079	44.5	34.7
1988	11,924	4,831	427	576	3,828	40.5	32.1
1989	11,953	4,811	499	553	3,759	40.2	31.4

Table 5.1 cont. on next page

JUVENILE OFFENDERS

Table 5.1 continued

Year	Total Juvenile Population[a]	JTS Admissions Total	Traffic	Drug	Adjusted[b]	Rate per 100,000 Population[c] Actual	Adjusted
1990	11,847	4,234	527	462	3,245	35.7	27.4
1991	11,653	4,329	572	610	3,147	37.1	27.0
1992	11,335	4,356	546	625	3,185	38.4	28.1
1993	11,028	4,229	532	588	3,109	38.3	28.2
1994	10,804	4,000	487	464	3,049	37.0	28.2

Sources: Research and Statistics Section 1971b, 1976b, 1981b, 1986b, 1995b.
[a] In thousands, ages 14–19.
[b] Equals total admissions minus traffic and drug admissions.
[c] Equals rate per 100,000 juveniles aged 14–19 in Japan's total population.

The Drug and Traffic Cohort and Juvenile Corrections

This book's basic question about cohorts rests on the existence of two opposing trends: a drop in the number of admissions to correctional institutions versus an increase in a cohort's members over the years. In conformity with the first trend, the total number of juvenile training schools is declining. But in opposition to the second trend, the members of the juvenile cohort who are involved in drug and traffic cases are also becoming fewer in time. The answer to the basic question of this book is thus complicated for the admissions of young persons involved with drug or traffic violations.

Table 5.1 lists the actual rates of total juvenile training school admissions per one hundred thousand Japanese aged fourteen to nineteen years. The declining trend in the total number of admissions is related to the number of people in that age group in Japanese society. From 1969 to 1975, both the rates and the absolute number of juvenile training school admissions decline in conformity to this book's basic expectation. Then, until 1984 both statistics show an increase in value, in opposition to the basic expectation. From 1984 to 1991, the actual rates rejoin the downward trend. Thereafter, the trend has been erratic.

What about the trend of the drug and traffic admissions and its affect on the trend for total juvenile training school admissions? Through 1985 the trend was upward, in keeping with the expectation that cohorts add numbers as the years proceed. From 1985 through 1994, a reversal sent the numbers downward. Thus, overall, the cohort did gather numbers over the years in conformity with the expectation, but recently the drug and traffic admissions dropped in absolute numbers.

If the effect of drug and traffic admissions is removed, has the adjusted total admissions to training schools come closer to conformity with the expectation of declining rates per one hundred thousand young Japanese? Table 5.1 presents the admissions with the drug and traffic admissions subtracted. Conformity with the expected increase of the admission rate per one hundred thousand youths continues to be imperfect. The absolute number of adjusted admissions and the adjusted rates generally declined for the 1969–74 period and the 1985–94 period, but the intervening years recorded increases. Again, the hypothesis has been only partially confirmed.

Three sources of distortion contribute to the exceptions to the downward trend of the general juvenile training school admission rate and the upward trend of the drug and traffic admissions. First, as table 5.1 shows, the total population aged fourteen to nineteen years has not followed a consistently upward trend. Earlier birthrates affect the size of the later youthful population. The youthful population from which juvenile training school inmates are drawn declined until 1976, increased for 1977-79 and 1981-89, and declined thereafter. The declines cut the value of the denominator of the admission rate; the admission rate would be inflated. Thus, the fluctuations in the number of Japanese youth would have modest distorting effect.

Second, the policy of the family courts also is a major influence; their administrative "faucets" regulate the flow of juveniles to training schools as one of the dispositions of cases. As early as the 1960s, the Correction Bureau had experimented with short-term treatment, but official introduction of the program came in 1977. The family courts reduced juvenile training school intake, contending that stays in the schools were excessively long and had negative effect on some juveniles. The Correction Bureau adjusted to meet the criticism and in response to the unprecedented appearance of some kinds of gang members. For greater flexibility, short-term and long-term programs were introduced. The family courts increased juvenile training school referrals in subsequent years.

Third, an upsurge occurred in the juvenile training school admissions of drug and traffic offenders. The upsurge was an exercise of extended criminalization in that the scope of the law and policy was broadened in the spirit of a major crisis. Later in this chapter, table 5.5 records the enlarged shares of juvenile training school admissions taken by the drug and traffic offenders into the 1980s.

The trend is significant. First, the juvenile drug and traffic inmates in combination qualify as another cohort that is becoming more numerous despite the more general decline in the inmate population. Table 5.5 documents the long-term trend, although not fully consistent.

Second, the upsurge in the drug and traffic admissions is an example of the weakened Japan's reluctance to employ institutionalized corrections. In this sense, we speak of the "distorting influence" of the growing presence of drug and traffic offenders in training schools.

Juveniles and Reactions to Crises

Traffic and drug offenses had been subject to criminalization, but the social-psychology of a public crisis produced a demand for further criminalization. Intense recourse to criminalization has been unprecedented because traffic misconduct usually is not evaluated as a form of crime, but young drivers have been identified with particularly high offense rates. As for similar adults, the traffic and drug delinquents are singled out for special attention. In addition to new willingness to incarcerate them, concern about juvenile drug offenders' vulnerability to drug abuse has stimulated new interest in protecting them from evil.

After a decline from the high of 16,765 in 1970, traffic fatalities reached 10,942 in 1993 (Traffic Bureau 1986, 1994). The Traffic Safety Policy Office (1994, 15–25) offers evidence that young drivers are responsible for the upturn. From 1979 to 1992, the percentage of people aged twenty to twenty-four years with driver's licenses rose from 65 to 84, while the percentage for all ages rose from 47 to 63. Single persons less than thirty years of age scored the greatest gain in ownership of motor vehicles. Although 16 percent of all licensed drivers in 1992, persons aged sixteen to twenty-four years were held to be the most negligent party in 38 percent of traffic fatalities.

Perceiving a major crisis, representatives of related ministries and agencies framed a six-point agreement in September 1980 on how to manage the young reckless drivers: (1) promotion of "comprehensive and organizational measures," (2) cultivating public opinion antagonistic to reckless acts, (3) "guidance" of youths at home and in their communities, (4) "creation of a social environment which disallows their reckless acts," (5) strengthening the control and prevention of repeated recklessness, and (6) preventing illegal modification of vehicles. The Road Traffic Law was amended in 1978 to make punishable by law incidents when side-by-side driving puts the public in danger and to revoke driver's licenses for that misconduct (Traffic Safety Policy Office 1985, 160–63).

Criminal justice agencies balanced law enforcement, prevention, and public education. The police intensified their control strategies; probationary supervision focused on factors motivating young traffic law violators to form their own groups and on the perceptions of those group members. Publicity, special campaigns, and mobilization of organizations were to create local opposition to reckless drivers. High schools were to deal with any educational maladjustment.

Abuse of opium and narcotics has been very limited. The first wave of stimulant drug abuse (methamphetamines) came immediately after World War II. The Stimulant Drug Control Law was enacted in 1951 and amended in 1954 and 1955. The Mental Health Law was amended in 1954 to compel hospitalization. By 1958 the crisis appeared to have been overcome, but a second wave of drug abuse appeared, including narcotics use. The Narcotics Control Law was amended in 1963, and the number of drug abuse cases dropped thereafter. Stimulant drugs again became more prevalent in the 1980s. The prevalence was, in part, due to the drug traffic of the yakuza (Ministry of Health and Welfare 1979; Yoshimura 1991).

Around 1962 some juveniles began putting solvents, such as toluene and acetone, in a plastic bag and sniffing the fumes, recalls Yokoyama (1992, 16). "At that time juveniles were free to buy solvents at stationery or paint stores," he says. In 1968 the police reported 20,812 juvenile abusers, mostly in Tokyo, and by 1971 the numbers had more than doubled and were distributed about the country. In 1972 revision of the Poisonous and Hazardous Substances Control Law also penalized those dealers who sold solvents to juveniles knowing their abusive purpose (Shikita and Tsuchiya 1990, 244).

The Family Court as Gatekeeper

The contemporary Juvenile Law took effect in 1949 and established the present juvenile justice system, including the contemporary training schools, family courts, and juvenile classification homes. Juvenile institutions existed previously, but the Juvenile Training School Law of 1949 is the basis for the training schools operated by the Correction Bureau. The Juvenile Law introduced modern probation; the Rehabilitation Bureau is responsible for community-based corrections throughout Japan.

According to the Juvenile Law, any person under twenty years of age is a juvenile. Article 3 grants the family court jurisdiction over (a) "any juvenile who is alleged to have violated any criminal law or ordinance," (b) "any juvenile under 14 years of age who is alleged to have violated any criminal law or ordinance," and (c) "any juvenile who is prone to commit any offense or violate a criminal law or ordinance in view of his character or environments" (UNAFEI n.d., 165).

Established in 1949, the family court deals with family affairs and juvenile delinquency cases. Article 1 states that the Juvenile Law is dedicated to "the wholesome rearing of juveniles, to carry out protective measures relating to the character correction and environmental adjustment of delinquent juveniles and also to take special measures with respect to the criminal cases of juveniles and adults who are harmful to the welfare of juveniles" (UNAFEI n.d., 165). The family court uses casework in a merger of "the principles of law, the conscience of the community, and the social sciences" (General Secretariat 1989, 4).

The court's special investigators inquire into the juvenile's total situation and relationships with others. The judge may send juveniles to a Correction Bureau's juvenile classification home. The fifty-three such homes are located adjacent to the family courts for assessment of intelligence, attitudes, and other elements of personality; for determining personal history and antecedents; and, when deemed necessary by the family court, for temporary "protective detention" for seven days during case investigation. Processing of detainees is limited to a medical checkup, a preliminary interview, and access to family members, concerned employers or teachers, an attorney, and the police investigator.

Because the ideal of the Juvenile Law is to provide guidance, care, protection, and education, declares Assistant Judge Hiroshi Kouhashi (1985, 7–9), the family court "can choose community-based treatment concerning a juvenile no matter how serious the type of committed offense may be." The judges refrain from committing juveniles to training schools, he continues, "considering its injurious effect such as labeling or stigmatization." When the individuals are "more advanced in delinquent tendencies," probation is likely.

To supervise some one hundred thousand probationers and parolees, the fifty probation offices of the Rehabilitation Bureau depend on some 48,000 unsalaried volunteer probation officers (VPOs) and on one thousand professional probation officers. The VPOs are in advanced ages in contrast to the youth of juvenile probationers and parolees. The proportion of VPOs over sixty years of age has gone from 29 percent in 1953 to 65 percent in 1990. The probation offices are responsible for supervising probationers and parolees, whether juveniles or adults; assessing and preparing families for paroling of inmates; aftercare of offenders discharged from prisons and detention houses without parole; investigation for pardons; and promoting crime prevention in the community.

As the gatekeeper to the juvenile justice system, the family court diverts to the public prosecutor (a) those defendants older than twenty years of age and thus not under the family court's jurisdiction and (b) any case that should be processed as that of an adult criminal. In the latter instance, the family court deems the referral to the public prosecutor justified by the nature of the offense, the circumstances within which it happened, and the personal characteristics of the offender.

The Family Court's Dispositions of the Cohort

The campaigns against traffic and drug offenses of juveniles, especially traffic offenses, have inflated the cases brought to the family courts. How have the family courts' dispositions of these cases affected the admissions to juvenile probation and juvenile training schools? How have the major types of those offenses been affected differentially by the dispositions?

Family courts are very reluctant to send juveniles to training schools except for stimulant drug offenses, and even then probation is favored over the training schools. The courts place heavy emphasis on returning the juveniles to the community without further official intervention. Traffic cases are more likely to be dismissed, increasingly over time, without formal hearing. Juveniles involved with stimulant drugs trail those violating the Poisonous and Injurious Substances Control Law in being sent home without further actions. Ordering probation is the most frequent disposition for stimulant drug offenders and the second favorite for offenses involving poisonous substances.

Tracing the dispositions of most family court cases, table 5.2 reports that about 90 percent were dismissed, mostly without a formal hearing. Less than a half-percent were sent to the public prosecutors to be processed as adult cases because of the serious nature of the offense, its situation, and the offender. (Referrals of defendants older than twenty years of age were removed from table 5.2.) Probation was ordered three times as often as referrals to juvenile training schools, but both dispositions fall far short of dismissals.

Compared with all offenses, the traffic and drug of-

JUVENILE OFFENDERS

fenders were less likely to be dismissed without a hearing, but except for stimulant drug cases, they were more likely to be dismissed after a hearing. The comparison suggests that, though they favored dismissals (except in stimulant drug cases), the family courts took unusual care in considering traffic and drug cases.

Compared to both total offenses and drug offenses, traffic offenders had the much larger share of dispositions taken up by referrals to public prosecutors. Yet traffic cases were less likely than drug cases to go to the training schools. Professional negligence drew probation more often than did violations of the Road Traffic Law. Probably, the professional negligence offenders were more split between the more aggravated and least serious cases.

Of the two kinds of drug violations, those involving organic solvents received the more tolerant dispositions. Dismissals were frequent, whether with or without a hearing; referrals to the public prosecutors were exceptional; few cases remained for probation, but the preference over training schools applied. Use of stimulant drugs drew greater penalization. Dismissals without a hearing were few, but when dismissal did occur, it was apt to occur after a hearing. Compared with organic solvents, the slack left by the fewer dismissals was taken up by more referrals to public prosecutors, training schools, and probation.

Paradoxically, offenses involving stimulant drugs exceeded those involving organic solvents and both kinds of traffic offenses in shares of dispositions taken up by both training schools and probation. The high share for training school referrals may reflect the higher ages and companionate nature of the stimulant drug offenses. Although dismissals were relatively infrequent and referrals to the public prosecutors were less than for the traffic cases, the family courts expressed low regard for stimulant drug users. When training schools were avoided as excessively stern, probation was utilized as a stronger action than dismissals. The total number of cases for stimulant drugs was

168
JUVENILE OFFENDERS

Table 5.2
Family Court Dispositions of Juvenile Traffic and Drug Cases, for Selected Years

% Distribution of Family Court Dispositions

Year	Total Cases	Public Prosecutor	Training Schools	Probation	Dismissals With Hearing	Dismissals Without Hearing
Total Offenses[a]					
1982	197,543	0.44	2.22	7.77	19.35	70.22
1985	190,478	0.45	2.71	7.89	18.68	70.27
1988	190,022	0.38	2.21	7.33	16.13	73.95
1990	168,902	0.29	2.10	7.35	17.54	72.72
Professional Negligence Offenses					
1982	48,190	11.23	0.39	24.98	54.69	8.71
1985	53,243	11.34	0.29	26.83	51.59	9.95
1988	59,749	6.74	0.20	28.46	54.45	10.15
1990	60,005	4.88	0.16	28.93	54.10	11.93
Road Traffic Law Violations					
1982	256,255	13.78	0.08	11.70	55.84	18.60
1985	330,810	17.14	0.10	12.65	51.08	19.03
1988	208,910	11.90	0.12	17.67	50.03	20.28
1990	192,748	12.26	0.19	22.81	46.50	18.24
Stimulant Drug Offenses					
1982	2,071	8.16	26.51	40.90	17.87	6.56
1985	1,513	6.68	34.37	41.04	12.56	5.35
1988	872	7.68	32.91	43.58	11.81	4.02
1990	578	4.33	34.26	44.81	14.01	2.59

Table 5.2 cont. on next page

Table 5.2 continued

		% Distribution of Family Court Dispositions				
					\multicolumn{2}{c}{Dismissals}
Year	Total Cases	Public Prosecutor	Training Schools	Probation	With Hearing	Without Hearing
		Organic Solvent Offenses				
1982	18,276	0.05	1.54	11.20	35.10	52.11
1985	15,057	0.92	2.31	13.13	36.96	46.68
1988	14,735	0.69	2.24	13.19	36.01	47.87
1990	16,914	0.48	1.96	12.03	34.84	50.69

Sources: Research and Training Institute 1984, 144–45; 1987, 142–43; 1990a, 166–67; 1992a, 148–49.

Note: Published data also include referrals of a small number of the youngest offenders to child guidance centers, child education or training homes, or homes for dependent children.

[a]Exclude some traffic professional negligence and predelinquent offenses.

less among the four kinds of juveniles; comparatively low numbers would inflate the percentages.

The Bosozoku and the Traffic Crisis

The universal appeal of the motor vehicle has drawn many Japanese adolescents and young adults into groups that the mass media began to speak of as the *bosozoku* (*boso* means "running wild," and *zoku* means "tribe"). Suttles (1991, xii) captures the enchantment: "It can be truly fun to go roaring down the main street of Kyoto in unison, toying with the police, swapping drivers in midcourse, alarming pedestrians, drawing the willing and unwilling attention of girls." By modifying their vehicles to create noise, adds Ikuya Sato (1991, 41–44), they draw public attention and rancor. Automobiles receive a "low-rider" suspension system, wide tires, special horns and lights, "designer wheels," and greater horsepower.

From one point of view, as Sato (1991, 158-62) declares, "It is assumed that youths' participation in gang activity is a sort of youthful fever which can be healed by self-healing, as in the case of measles, if one matures enough." Those who had been involved in traffic delinquencies told Sato that they perceived the misconduct as mere "mischief." After becoming adults, they recognized the risk of penal sanctions on their later job careers.

In field research of the Ukyo Rengo, a motorcycle gang confederation in Kyoto, Sato (1991, 2) found the bosozoku to be engaged in "extreme expressiveness and playfulness," rather than being the extreme deviants portrayed in the mass media. "The majority of those who participate in gang activities are from middle-class families," he says, "and gangs are rarely involved in illicit underworld activities as groups." The bosozoku borrow the shaved eyebrows, haircut style, and other outer symbols of the yakuza, but Sato (1991, 169) relays statements of his informants that bosozoku boys rejected yakuza overture because of the risks and poor economic returns of yakuza operations.

The police have expressed less understanding of the bosozoku values. In 1972 a riot occurred in Toyama City when bosozoku groups protested police actions against them. The mass media gave them fuller attention; after the Road Traffic Law was amended in 1978, arrests of members increased for lack of a driver's license, improperly equipped vehicles, excessive passengers, and various other traffic violations (Yokoyama 1983, 2-4).

The police report stronger measures to control "hot rodders" in 1989, after "citizens were assaulted and killed by groups of hot rodders." The police note an increased number of "hot rodders" not affiliated with any group, more small groups annoying residents with violent exhaust noise

JUVENILE OFFENDERS

after midnight, and twenty-two intergang fights in 1989 (National Police Agency 1991, 104-5). The control measures were ambushes in which the police waited in areas where bosozoku rallies occurred; cultivating opposition in local communities; persuading gasoline stations, automobile parts dealers, and late-night food shops to reject hot-rodders; organizing taxi drivers to report incidents; and improving traffic control. In June 1992 the police "intensified crackdowns on illegally remodeled vehicles" during the "Month for Stepping Up Control on Hot Rodders and Poorly Maintained Vehicles, Etc." Vehicles were seized, and car mechanics were held responsible for illegal modifications. The public was urged not to allow hot-rodding and not to go out "to watch hot-rodding" (National Police Agency 1994, 135).

Programs for Juvenile Traffic Offenders

A short-term probation program was introduced in 1977 for selected juveniles who had been convicted in family court for traffic incidents causing death and injury. The probation offices assign the juveniles to either general probation or a traffic program. Admissions to the traffic program were 33,083 in 1981, 44,361 in 1985, 50,298 in 1990, and 48,021 in 1991 (Research and Training Institute 1984, 160; 1987, 159; 1992a, 166). Only 30 percent of the juveniles in the special traffic program had been identified with delinquent groups. Among them 89 percent were bosozoku (Research and Statistics Section 1994c, 92).

The probation offices require juveniles in the special program to attend two group sessions conducted by professional probation officers and to report to the probation office for four months. The verbal report is supplemented by written answers to such questions as: What did you do this month? Did you drive this month? Do you have a problem to discuss with the probation officer? At the intake session, the nature of the program is explained, and the conditions are specified. After three or four months, the second session deals with the responsibilities of drivers, traffic safety, and how to avoid traffic accidents. Usually, discussion groups separate certain kinds of traffic offenders: those without a driver's license versus those possessing the license, the bosozoku versus the nonbosozoku, or offenders convicted of professional negligence causing death or injury versus those convicted of professional negligence not resulting in death or injury. After the second session, the probation officer can terminate supervision if the monthly reports have been satisfactory. A few juveniles are kept under supervision for a maximum of six months when authorized by the family court.

In admissions to juvenile training schools, the bosozoku increased their representation from 9 percent in 1985 to 26 percent in 1993. The Correction Bureau identifies four delinquent gangs: delinquent students, neighborhood (or local) gangs, organized (or yakuza-type) gangs, and the bosozoku. The bosozoku added to their share of all gang admissions from 18 percent in 1985 to 44 percent in 1993 (Research and Statistics Section 1994c).

The training schools offer "treatment courses" varying from "basic social training for disciplined social life" through vocational training and academic education to medical care for the physically or mentally handicapped. The scheme also differentiates between short-term courses (two to four months) for juveniles believed to be more amenable to behavioral change and long-term courses (no longer than two years) for those deemed more difficult to resocialize (Correction Bureau 1990, 56–59).

In June 1977 the Minister of Justice announced a long-term program and two short-term programs for training schools. Lasting up to two years, the long-term program was for juveniles difficult to resocialize in shorter time. One short-term program was oriented toward juveniles amenable to intervention for four to six months. The second specialized in juveniles who had caused death or bodily injury in traffic incidents (Correction Bureau 1982, 44).

Nine juvenile training schools conducted the short-term program: Harima, Ichihara, Matsuyama, Miho, Oitama, Okinawa, Sasebo, Toyogaoka, and Tsukigata. I observed the program at the Ichihara Juvenile Training School. Lectures were on the psychology of drivers and pedestrians, the Road Traffic Law, and defensive driving. The inmates analyzed traffic accidents from newspapers, participated in role-playing, read essays of victims and offenders, wrote to traffic victims, prepared safety posters, and so on. Discussions were on a given topic, such as the bosozoku, bodily injuries and deaths in accidents, or driving without a license.

In September 1991 the general short-term program took over the program for the traffic offenders and a special short-term program was introduced for open treatment. In the open scheme, individuals commute from the institution and a school in the community on weekdays and stay with their families on weekends. If the juveniles have regular jobs, they usually commute between the training school and the workplace and stay at the training school on weekends. More rarely, the juveniles may spend weekday nights with their families if the work is near their home, in which case they stay at the training school on weekends.

In 1993 the bosozoku differed from other delinquent groups represented in the juvenile training schools in the greater proportion of their members assigned to short-term academic education, short-term vocational training, and preparation for senior high schools. Of the 341 inmates on the open program, 164 were bosozoku and 112 had not been affiliated with any gang. Inmates without a history of drugs held a 72 percent share of the open program and a 55 percent share of all inmates (Research and Statistics Section 1994b).

Distributions of Juvenile Offenders among Programs

Correctional agencies rely on either probation in the community or confinement in juvenile training schools or prisons. Table 5.3 portrays the distribution among two of the programs for juvenile traffic and drug offenders and, for comparison, the distribution for adult traffic and drug offenders. The family courts choose between probation and training schools when they decide that other dispositions—referral to the public prosecutor or dismissal—are not appropriate. (Parole is not relevant to the family court dispositions.) How have the choices differed for traffic and drug offenders?

The case of a young defendant going to a juvenile classification home has presumably been selected by the family courts as requiring careful study before disposition. In juvenile classification home cases for 1993, traffic offenders accused of violating the Road Traffic Law had more favorable backgrounds than those arrested for professional negligence. Only 7 percent had previously experienced training schools (12 percent of the professional negligence group). A larger proportion of the Road Traffic Law violators were living with their families (89 versus 75 percent).[1]

The Road Traffic Law group was younger (17.5 versus 18 years), and its crimes were heavily companionate. Only 19 percent were aged nineteen or twenty years, compared with 46 percent of those accused of professional negligence. Almost all the professional negligence incidents (92 percent) involved only a single juvenile, but for Road Traffic Law cases, 78 percent had more than four participants, and 73 percent of those juveniles were officially identified as members of a "delinquent group." The bosozoku were prominent among groups the police linked to traffic offenses.

Whether involved with stimulants or chemical solvents, only 11 percent of the juvenile drug abusers at the juvenile

JUVENILE OFFENDERS

Table 5.3
Correctional Approaches to Juvenile and Adult Traffic and Drug Offenders, 1970–90

Correctional Approach	1970	1975	1980	1985	1990
Juvenile Traffic Offenders					
No. of Admissions					
Probation	14,326	12,269	11,286	11,682	11,309
Training School	69	136	410	578	527
Ratio[a]	207.62	90.21	27.53	20.21	21.46
Adult Traffic Offenders					
No. of Admissions					
Probation	846	1,275	1,831	1,442	994
Prison	4,223	3.965	3,805	3,537	2,615
Ratio[a]	0.20	0.32	0.48	0.41	0.38
Juvenile Drug Offenders					
No. of Admissions					
Probation	13	69	2,629	2,505	2,290
Training School	3	27	574	778	462
Ratio[a]	4.33	2.55	4.58	3.22	4.96
Adult Drug Offenders					
No. of Admissions					
Probation	47	533	1,744	1,663	897
Prison	136	1,717	6,270	8,600	5,884
Ratio[a]	0.35	0.31	0.28	0.19	0.15

Sources: Research and Statistics Section 1971a, b, c; 1976a, b, c; 1981a, b, c; 1986a, b, c; 1991a, b, c.

[a] Equals admissions to probation divided by admissions to correctional institutions.

classification homes had been in juvenile training schools previously, but the stimulant group was less likely to have experienced probation (36 versus 45 percent). The juveniles who committed offenses involving organic solvents tended to be living with their families (81 versus 61 percent), probably because they were younger (17.3 versus 18.1 years). Users of stimulants were more companionate (65 versus 55 percent). Recreational contacts were predominant for both types of drugs. In keeping with their more advanced age, stimulant users mentioned coworkers and casual acquaintances as coparticipants in use of drugs, more often than did the group abusing organic solvents.

Juvenile traffic offenders have been definitely more numerous than drug offenders. Drug offenders were few in 1970 and added great numbers, although always short of traffic offenders, in the following years. As the very high ratios in table 5.3 demonstrate, probation was preferred over training schools, especially for traffic offenders. Few traffic offenders went to training schools in 1970; thereafter, the training schools gained higher numbers and shares of the family court decisions. Probation clung to very high ratios, but their decline attested to the greater absolute number of training school referrals.

In comparison to juvenile traffic cases, the adult traffic offenders were much more prone to be imprisoned than to be granted probation on the basis of a suspended prison sentence. Although probation for adult traffic offenders always held the inferior numbers, it gained favor over imprisonment, from a ratio of 0.20 in 1970 to 0.38 in 1990. In granting probation the courts were less lenient for adult drug offenders than for adult traffic offenders. Furthermore, the ratios increased irregularly over the years for traffic offenders but dropped for drug offenders.

Juvenile drug offenders also had many more individuals on probation than in training schools, but they failed to accumulate absolute numbers on probation that were as high as those accumulated by traffic offenders. The short-term probation program for young traffic offenders was responsible for the difference. The number of juvenile drug cases were very few in the 1970s, but their increase in later years wiped out the difference between them and juvenile traffic cases. Since the absolute numbers of juvenile drug cases were less than those for juvenile traffic cases, their percentage superiority trailed that of juvenile traffic cases. Yet probation continued to be favored over training schools. Adult drug offenders faced greater prospects of being imprisoned than the juveniles, and their prospects increased with the years.

Traffic Offenders and Juvenile Corrections

Family courts have made greater use of juvenile probation than of the training schools. As table 5.4 shows, the probation offices received 25,999 juvenile probationers in 1969; table 5.1 reports that 4,409 entered training schools that year. Thus, there were 5.9 probationers for every training school. In the following years, the number of probation admissions wandered up to 28,613 in 1983 (dropping to 4.7 probationers per training school admission) and thereafter declined to 19,796 in 1993 (again 4.9 probationers per training school admission). The probation offices have received a rather steady number of juvenile probationers over the years, always much greater than training school admissions, but gradually reducing the advantage.

Although family courts and adult criminal courts have doubts about probation, they prefer probation to sending the offenders to correctional institutions. The doubts help explain the relatively modest use of training schools. Juvenile probationers were more likely to have been convicted under the Road Traffic Law than for professional negligence, but the two groups differed less in absolute numbers for training school admissions. Although professional negligence cases average greater seriousness, family courts,

Table 5.4
Admissions to Juvenile Probation for Traffic and Drug Offenses, 1969–93

Year	A	B	C	D	E	F[a]	G	H[b]	I
1969	25,999	4,107	7,909	15.8	30.4	5(3)	—	0.02	—
1970	27,383	4,820	9,430	17.6	34.4	13(7)	—	0.05	—
1971	25,403	4,410	9,058	17.4	35.7	18(9)	—	0.07	—
1972	23,900	4,375	9,279	18.3	38.8	21(7)	—	0.09	—
1973	20,686	3,737	8,425	18.1	40.7	36(9)	—	0.19	—
1974	19,992	3,630	7,862	18.2	39.4	36(5)	—	0.33	—
1975	21,384	3,579	8,663	16.7	40.5	69(7)	—	0.14	—
1976	23,981	3,881	10,121	16.2	42.2	197(6)	—	0.82	—
1977	21,264	3,186	8,704	15.0	40.9	173(5)	—	0.81	—
1978	20,971	3,182	6,649	15.2	31.7	187(8)	—	3.69	—
1979	21,559	3,362	6,255	15.6	29.0	488(4)	1,781	2.26	8.26
1980	25,684	3,626	7,626	14.1	29.7	608(1)	2,021	2.37	7.87
1981	26,131	3,683	7,919	14.1	30.3	850(1)	1,874	3.25	7.17
1982	27,877	3,848	8,288	13.8	29.7	876(4)	1,999	3.14	7.17
1983	28,613	3,860	9,017	13.5	31.5	841(2)	1,993	2.94	6.96
1984	27,834	3,498	8,012	12.6	28.8	835(8)	2,005	3.00	7.20
1985	27,050	3,509	8,148	13.0	30.1	663(2)	1,842	2.45	6.81
1986	26,769	3,710	8,135	13.9	30.4	544(2)	1,695	2.03	6.33
1987	25,182	3,727	7,216	14.8	28.6	466(4)	1,773	1.85	7.04
1988	24,268	3,868	6,630	15.9	26.9	400(7)	1,955	1.65	8.06
1989	23,736	4,168	6,492	17.6	27.3	346(5)	1,893	1.46	7.97
1990	23,481	4,037	7,247	17.2	30.9	287(6)	2,003	1.22	8.53
1991	22,663	3,827	6,938	16.9	30.6	332(1)	2,093	1.46	9.23

Table 5.4 cont. on next page

Table 5.4 continued

Year	A	B	C	D	E	F[a]	G	H[b]	I
1992	22,693	3,688	7,364	16.2	32.5	350(5)	1,840	1.54	8.11
1993	19,796	3,154	6,266	15.9	31.6	363(5)	1,243	1.83	6.28

Sources: Research and Statistics Section 1971c, 1976c, 1981c, 1986c, 1991c, 1994c.

Note: Column headings are as follows:
A. Total Probation Admissions
B. Traffic Admissions, Professional Negligence
C. Traffic Admissions, Road Traffic Law Violations
D. % of All Admissions, Professional Negligence
E. % of All Admissions, Road Traffic Law Violations
F. Drug Admissions, Stimulant Drugs
G. Drug Admissions, Organic Solvents
H. % of All Admissions, Stimulant Drugs
I. % of All Admissions, Organic Solvents

[a] Figures in parentheses denote narcotic admissions.

[b] Includes narcotic admissions.

Kouhashi (1985) has told us, are prone to order probation even for offenders who are assessed officially as being more advanced in delinquent tendencies—an assessment implying that they are unlikely to abandon criminal tendencies. For adults, judges are inclined to prefer outright release into the community to probation. The judges typically regard probationary supervision as a form of punishment less severe than imprisonment.

The responsibilities of the two correctional bureaus for young traffic offenders fell into major patterns. First, in the earlier years professional negligence was the chief basis for admissions to juvenile training schools and to juvenile probation. As the years passed, the Road Traffic Law assumed the greater role. Second, probation drew the larger number of cases.[2]

The number of juvenile training school admissions for

Table 5.5
Admissions to Juvenile Training Schools for Traffic and Drug Offenses, 1969–94

Year	No. of Traffic Admissions Pro. Negli.	Road Law	% of All Admissions[a] Pro. Negli.	Road Law	No. of Drug Admissions Stim. Drugs[b]	Org. Solv.	% of All Admissions[a] Stim. Drugs[c]	Org. Solv.
1969	15	26	0.34	0.59	1	—	0.22	—
1970	33	36	0.83	0.91	3(1)	—	0.08	—
1971	42	72	1.28	2.19	1	—	0.03	—
1972	52	42	1.77	1.43	8(3)	—	0.27	—
1973	39	26	1.71	1.14	8	—	0.35	—
1974	49	40	2.49	2.03	9	—	0.46	—
1975	73	63	2.86	2.47	27(4)	—	1.06	—
1976	60	68	2.25	2.55	39	—	1.46	—
1977	109	125	3.33	3.81	78	—	2.38	—
1978	120	116	3.17	3.07	174(1)	155	4.60	4.10
1979	116	141	2.85	3.46	258(1)	203	6.33	4.98
1980	202	208	4.28	4.41	336(1)	238	7.12	5.04
1981	152	317	3.04	6.33	469	224	9.37	4.48
1982	135	377	2.57	7.18	531(4)	216	10.11	4.11
1983	171	365	2.95	6.31	566(5)	223	9.78	3.85
1984	146	399	2.41	6.58	583	272	9.62	4.49
1985	173	405	2.87	6.72	528(2)	250	8.76	4.15
1986	153	364	2.66	6.33	469(1)	275	8.16	4.78
1987	103	384	1.97	7.35	405(2)	251	7.76	3.14
1988	111	316	2.30	6.54	299(1)	277	6.19	5.73
1989	92	407	1.91	8.46	253	300	5.26	6.24
1990	105	422	2.48	9.97	195(2)	267	4.61	6.31

Table 5.5 cont. on next page

JUVENILE OFFENDERS

Table 5.5 continued

Year	No. of Traffic Admissions Pro. Negli.	Road Law	% of All Admissions[a] Pro. Negli.	Road Law	No. of Drug Admissions Stim. Drugs[b]	Org. Solv.	% of All Admissions[a] Stim. Drugs[c]	Org. Solv.
1991	99	473	2.29	10.93	330(3)	280	7.62	6.47
1992	87	459	2.00	10.54	325(2)	300	7.46	6.89
1993	74	458	1.75	10.83	356(3)	232	8.42	5.49
1994	76	411	1.90	10.27	281(1)	183	7.02	4.57

Sources: Research and Statistics Section 1971b, 1976b, 1981b, 1986b, 1995b.
[a]Equals % of total JTS admissions.
[b]Figures in parentheses denote narcotic admissions.
[c]Includes narcotic admissions.

traffic misconduct were only a few score until 1977, after which the chief source of the gain was the convictions under the Road Traffic Law. Table 5.5 uses percentages of total training school admissions for tracing the trends. For most years the Road Traffic Law delivered the greater number of traffic offenders to training schools. After 1981 Road Traffic Law increased its share of all admissions to a rapid pace that professional negligence could not match. Professional negligence usually scored gains through 1980, then it dropped off. The percentage shares for Road Traffic Law admissions followed a similar general increase through 1982, but the rates were higher. After 1982 the share expanded rather greatly, to become about 10 percent in the 1990s.

Traffic offenders were predominately a probation responsibility. The Road Traffic Law contributed more youngsters to probation than did professional negligence over the years (see table 5.4). Both classes of offenders were more heavily and consistently represented among probation admissions than among training school admissions. The share of probation admissions for professional negligence floated between 12.6 and 18.3 percent but ended up at almost exactly the same level in 1993 as in 1969 (15.9 and 15.8 percent, respectively). The share of probation admissions for the Road Traffic Law fluctuated similarly, but its share topped at 42.2 in 1976 and terminated at 31.6 in 1993.

Drug Offenders and Juvenile Corrections

The juvenile convictions for drug violations have increased the caseloads of training schools and probation offices in Japan. The combined numbers of juvenile drug offenders admitted to the two correctional programs have been fewer than the equivalent number of juvenile traffic offenders, but the drug offenders began with only six admissions in 1969 and subsequently followed an impressive rate of increase until 1983 (see tables 5.4 and 5.5). The combined admissions for drugs topped at 3,695 in 1984 and thereafter slacked off to 2,194 in 1993. The equivalent figures for juvenile traffic admissions were comparatively steady over the years, but always at a much higher absolute number of admissions. Narcotic offenses (combined for probation and training schools) were few, ranging from one in 1981 to eleven in 1975. Stimulant drugs had the longest effect on the combined admissions to probation and training schools; "poisonous substances" first appeared in caseloads in 1978 and 1979, but in great numbers.

Stimulant drugs brought 308 juveniles to the attention of public prosecutors in 1956, but their numbers dropped to only 11 in 1969 before beginning an increase. From 152 in 1973, the referrals to public prosecutors rose to 2,750 in 1982 before beginning to decline again. The Poisonous and Injurious Substances Control Law was amended in 1972 and produced an abrupt and persistent increase in referrals to the public prosecutors, from 1,243 in 1972 to a peak of

JUVENILE OFFENDERS

29,254 in 1982 (Shikita and Tsuchiya 1990, 243-44). The law was amended again in 1982 to raise the maximum penalty to one year for solvent abuse. As a consequence, the training school admissions for that offense rose from 223 in 1983 to 300 in 1989 (see table 5.5).[3]

The family courts had a slightly more favorable estimate of juvenile poisonous substance offenders over juvenile stimulant drug offenders. That conclusion rests on the greater proportion of admissions to training schools for stimulant drugs: 34.6 percent of the combined admissions in 1979, with a rise to 41.4 percent in 1993. The equivalent percentages for poisonous substances were 10.2 in 1979 and 15.7 in 1993.

Stimulant drugs had a trivial effect on training school and probation admissions until 1978. The data suggest a comparatively negative perception of stimulant drug use over organic solvent use among juveniles. The percentage shares of total admissions for stimulant drug use consistently favor training schools over probation. Youthful users of organic solvents draw a less stern reaction; juvenile probation exceeds the training schools in percentage shares held by organic solvents.

6

Foreigners in Japanese Prisons: Adaptation and Accommodation

Since World War II, sweeping socioeconomic changes have strengthened the interdependence of nations and have stimulated the growth of alien populations in economically developed societies. Many purposes motivate the arrival of foreigners in a prosperous country. They come as tourists, foreign students, employees of foreign enterprises, asylum seekers, undocumented workers, and persons hoping to raise their standard of living through job opportunities. Among them are persons who violate the criminal laws of the host society.

Japan is an apt setting for examining two interrelated challenges presented by foreign prisoners. First, as cultural strangers, they have their particular perspectives and difficulties in adapting to penal confinement in Japan. Second, the administrators must fit the strangers into ongoing management of Japanese prisoners. The Rehabilitation Bureau receives even fewer foreigners as probationers and parolees but must also adapt to their particular characteristics.

Foreigners' Greater Presence in Prisons

The Correction Bureau has differentiated those foreigners who adapt rather well from those who have serious difficulties (class-F foreigners). Class-F inmates have primarily been concentrated in three prisons: male civilians in Fuchu Prison in a suburb of Tokyo, female civilians in Tochigi Women's Prison, and American military personnel in Yokosuka Prison. Fuchu has experienced overcrowding of the class-F section, and a number of other male prisons have been assigned some class-F inmates. On 1 January 1995, some foreigners were transferred to Osaka Prison; they have lived in Japan for a considerable time, speak Japanese to some extent, and are habituated to the Japanese style of life.

The Correction Bureau has few foreign inmates in absolute numbers; table 6.1 shows that there were only 1,504 foreigners in 1983, or 3.35 percent of all prisoners present on the last day of the year. The absolute numbers rose from 1,504 to 1,584 in 1985 (or 3.44 percent), dropped in irregular fashion to reach 1,424 (or 3.83 percent) in 1993, but revived to 1,568 (4.19 percent) in 1994.

Foreigners have assumed greater shares of the entire prisoner population and thereby opposed the decline in the total number of prisoners. Again we find a cohort of prisoners who are increasing their representation among all prisoners, despite the decline in the general imprisonment rate. Along with the elderly, the foreigners are becoming more numerous among prison inmates, not through the process of criminalization, but because of the increased number of foreigners in Japan. We call that development responsive incarceration because the increased number of foreign prisoners is the product of the growth of foreigners in Japan.

The class-F inmates present an even better case for the hypothesis. Among the classification categories, class F is allocated to "foreigners who need different treatment from that of the Japanese" (Correction Bureau 1990, 30). Class F is reserved for the subgroup of foreign inmates who cannot understand the Japanese language, who require a diet other than that preferred by the Japanese, and who prefer Western beds and showers to the Japanese-style futons and communal baths.

Table 6.1
Foreigners' Share of All Inmates in
Year-End Prison Population, 1983–94

Year	Total Foreign Inmates No.	% of All Inmates	Male Foreign Inmates No.	% of Male Inmates	Female Foreign Inmates No.	% of Female Inmates
1983	1,504	3.35	1,419	3.29	85	5.04
1984	1,539	3.39	1,457	3.34	82	4.67
1985	1,584	3.44	1,491	3.37	93	4.89
1986	1,526	3.31	1,433	3.25	93	4.84
1987	1,565	3.40	1,483	3.37	82	4.26
1988	1,555	3.40	1,462	3.33	93	4.92
1989	1,505	3.53	1,428	3.49	77	4.43
1990	1,380	3.46	1,291	3.38	89	5.37
1991	1,342	3.55	1,255	3.47	87	5.53
1992	1,369	3.68	1,277	3.57	92	6.08
1993	1,424	3.83	1,329	3.72	95	6.24
1994	1,568	4.19	1,447	4.04	121	7.57

Sources: Research and Statistics Section 1987a, 1990, 1995a.

The number of class-F prisoners at year-end has risen consistently; the civilians exceeded the American military inmates in numbers and consistency of numerical increases from 1983 to 1994 (see table 6.2). Primarily because of the civilian trend, the class-F males have taken over a greater share of the total male prisoners held by the Correction Bureau, from 0.18 percent in 1983 to 1.35 percent in 1994. The

Table 6.2
Class-F Inmates' Share of Year-End Prison Population, 1983–94

	No. at Year-End				% of All Inmates by Gender			
Year	A	B	C	D	A	B	C	D
1983	79	44	35	7	0.18	0.10	0.08	0.41
1984	109	79	30	9	0.25	0.18	0.07	0.51
1985	127	102	25	12	0.29	0.23	0.06	0.63
1986	164	141	23	20	0.37	0.32	0.05	1.04
1987	188	166	22	12	0.43	0.38	0.05	0.62
1988	196	177	19	13	0.45	0.40	0.04	0.69
1989	212	192	20	17	0.52	0.47	0.05	0.98
1990	230	202	28	17	0.60	0.53	0.07	1.02
1991	245	221	24	22	0.68	0.61	0.07	1.40
1992	303	276	27	30	0.85	0.77	0.08	1.98
1993	362	344	18	39	1.02	0.96	0.05	2.56
1994	485	417	23	47	1.35	1.16	0.06	2.94

Source: Data from the Correction Bureau.

Note: Column headings are as follows:
A. Class-F Male Inmates
B. Class-F Civilian Male Inmates
C. Class-F American Military Male Inmates
D. Class-F Female Inmates

percentages were smaller than those for all foreigners, of course, but the rate of increase transcended that of all foreigners. Class-F women were less numerous than class-F men, but their gain in percentage share of all women prisoners (from 0.41 to 2.94) was even more impressive than the increased share of class-F men.

Migrant Control and Criminal Justice

Since World War II, its strong economy has earned Japan a place among the prosperous nations of the world and has attracted a growing number of visitors from other countries. Aliens are coming to Japan in progressively greater numbers, 1,296,000 in 1980 and 3,040,719 in 1993—a 135 percent gain in thirteen years (National Police Agency 1991; Research and Training Institute 1994). From 1980 through 1985, only a minute fraction of the foreigners were arrested for crimes, but the fraction rose from 0.06 percent in 1985 to 1 percent in 1989. Violators of immigration regulations represented 0.23 percent of the foreigners in 1984 and 0.56 percent in 1989. Although they too were exceptional among all foreign visitors, the immigration law violators were 3.7 times more numerous than the Penal Code arrestees in 1984 and 5.6 times more numerous in 1989 (National Police Agency 1991).

Foreigners were accused of 7,276 violations of the Penal Code in 1993, traffic offenses excluded, for a gain of 5.6 times in ten years. Larceny and dealing in stolen property held almost 90 percent of their crimes in 1993. Foreigners also had a greater proportion of homicides and robberies than Japanese suspects. Violations of special laws increased 2.1 times in ten years by 1993, especially for immigration infractions (69.7 percent of the foreigners' special-law violations) and drug offenses (10.2 percent) (Research and Training Institute 1994).

Japan is not alone in experiencing a flood of foreigners; the Council of Europe reports increased foreigners in the prisons of its member states. The increases between 1983 and 1992 often exceeded that of Japan; for example, the numbers of foreign inmates increased from 22 to 34 percent in Belgium, from 27 to 40 percent of the small population of Luxembourg's prison, from 25 to 30 percent in France, and from 9 to 15 percent in Germany (Tournier and Barre

1990; Council of Europe 1992). The flow of migrants has reflected the changing geopolitical map of Europe as well as more persistent socioeconomic developments, and as Tomasevski (1994) points out, it has obscured the distinction between migrant control and the administration of criminal justice.

Japan also has recognized greater pressure on the migrant controls. Between 1 May and 1 November 1993, 297,000 foreign visitors had exceeded their legal stay. Refusals to admit foreigners have increased fourteen times in the last ten years; there were 18,960 in 1993. Expulsion orders on charges of violating the Immigration Control and Refugee Recognition Act were instigated ten more times in 1993 than ten years before, with 70,404 actions in 1993. Most of those cases were for overstays and for being illegally employed (National Police Agency 1991; Research and Training Institute 1994).

As revised, the Immigration Control and Refugee Recognition Law (1989) specified three classifications of foreigners who could work legally in Japan: (1) diplomats, artists, religious personnel, and journalists; (2) professional and technical personnel; and (3) a variety of specific experts. Temporary visitors, students, and family visitors are prohibited from working. Among the purposes of the revisions has been to restrict and control the inflow of unskilled and semiskilled workers, declares Sassen (1994).

The emergence of a service economy in Japan has added to the labor shortage already existing in manufacturing (Sassen 1994). The shortages are aggravated by the retirement of Japanese employees from low-skill service jobs, the rejection of such jobs by the young and highly educated Japanese, and the low growth of the population. To cope with the labor shortage and to avoid having to close their factory, some employers risk the law's maximum penalty of the fine of two million yen for knowingly hiring an illegal migrant, but Sassen (1994) predicts that the labor shortage probably will persist in a society with a "fairly homogeneous" population and without a belief in the positive contributions of immigration.

Criminal Justice and the Strangers

Criminal laws applied by Japan to the alien suspects have been in force for many decades. The actions taken against the foreign suspects qualify as responsive incarceration because imposing the criminal status on selected foreigners is not a new policy. Rather, the volume of its impositions has grown in absolute numbers because of developments in the society at large.

Conferring the criminal status is a political act that nations may take properly and legally to defend their borders. The presence of foreigners has become a political issue in Europe. Tomasevski (1994) mentions general statements offered in defense of the management of some foreigners by means of the criminal justice system, such as "most crimes are committed by foreigners" or "drug trafficking is in the hands of foreigners." Those arguments suggest the tendency of all people to stand aloof from "strangers."

"Foreigners" are of great variety, but they share the status of "stranger." Early in the twentieth century, Simmel (1908) pointed out that the mobility of strangers makes them physically near but socially remote in relations within a community. When serving legitimate economic, social, or political functions, the strangers may gain a recognized place in the community's social structure. That outcome may stem from the key characteristic Simmel noted for strangers. Their spatial mobility exempts them from the personality conditioning experienced by the orthodox members of the community. They stand out because of the objectivity with which they regard values esteemed by natives.

Movement through physical space is not enough to exempt the strangers from the personality conditioning of the society they enter, says Park (1967, 199–200), but nomads (for example, the gypsies) cling to their "ancient tribal organization and customs" despite their symbiotic presence in various communities. The stranger tends to stand aloof from the natives' value commitment. Park applies the term *marginal man* to "the emancipated individual" or the "cosmopolitan" who "learns to look upon the world in which he was born and bred with something of the detachment of a stranger" (201).

When a "marginal man" qualified as a "cultural hybrid," the foreigner may be "living and sharing intimately in the cultural life and traditions of two distinct peoples" (Park 1967, 205), but when the status of the stranger is combined with the status of the criminal, discriminatory treatment is especially possible. Adverse discrimination is difficult to prove, because, as Albrecht (1987, 274) notes, the marginal status of foreign minorities has "objective and perceptual dimensions." Objectively, the minority actually differs from the majority in race, color, religion, and language, and the minority has inferior access to employment, formal education, and equal treatment by the criminal justice system. In the perceptual dimensions, the majority is subjective in evaluating the minority according to preconceived judgments; foreigners are branded as dangerous or crime prone whether or not they are objectively different.

Foreign Suspects and Management of Cases

When referred to public prosecutors and possibly later to courts for trial, the foreign suspect in Japan usually suffers special disadvantages: ignorance of the details of case processing in Japan and lack of understanding of the Japanese language, including the technical terms used in case processing. Whether innocent or guilty of the crime being charged and whether or not experienced with the workings of criminal justice elsewhere, the foreign suspect is unlikely to be aware of the assumptions and procedures whereby only a small proportion of convicted Japanese are sent to prison.

The public prosecutors are authorized and inclined to avoid referrals for trial, and the sentencing judges are similarly authorized and inclined to suspend prison sentences after conviction when the defendant admits fault, expresses repentance, and makes restitution to the victim, and when the nature of the offense justifies leniency. The Ministry of Justice reports that foreign suspects enjoyed a lower rate of referrals for trial in 1993: 54.4 percent versus 60.3 percent for Japanese suspects (Research and Training Institute 1994). The high proportion of foreigners in migrant control cases handled administratively partially accounts for the difference.

To increase the availability of interpreters, reports the Ministry of Justice (Research and Training Institute 1994), a national directory of interpreters has been distributed, fees for interpretation have been increased, a legal glossary and manual on Japanese criminal procedures has been prepared for interpreters, a special administrative section for recruiting interpreters has been established in six major cities, and language training programs have begun for personnel of public prosecutors offices. The ministry says that an interpreter or translator aided only 320 of 2,650 tried foreigners in 1984 and 3,521 of 4,760 in 1993.

To test whether or not foreigners suffer discrimination in the courts' suspensions of sentences to prison, the Research and Training Institute (1992a) compared outcomes for sixty-eight Japanese and fifty-six foreigners convicted of larceny but not granted suspension of sentence, in one district court and twelve summary courts in twenty-three wards of Tokyo in 1989 and 1990. Japanese judges are more apt to refuse suspension when the individual denies guilt despite evidence that seems to be conclusive. Among the foreigners 35.7 percent (versus 1.5 percent of the Japanese) denied guilt in court or attributed the offense to certain circumstances. Although the foreigners especially had partners in the offense (64.3 percent versus 20.6 percent of Japanese offenders), they were more apt (25 versus 1.5 percent) to refuse to disclose the codefendant's name. Foreigners also were less likely (7.1 versus 29.4 percent) to have witnesses testify in their favor.

The larcenies of foreigners were more likely to be picking pockets (mostly) or stealing metal balls from *pachinko* machines (similar to pinball machines). The larcenies of the Japanese were more likely to be burglaries and thefts from sleeping persons on subways and trains. Foreigners also showed signs of original intent. More foreign offenders used special tools or sold stolen goods in illegal transactions (30.4 percent versus 14.7 percent of Japanese offenders). More foreign offenders possessed unexplained large sums of cash when arrested or had sent such amounts outside of Japan (28.6 versus 1.5 percent). A significant proportion (57.1 percent) had either come to Japan for a criminal purpose or had committed a crime within thirty days after arrival. Of course, only foreigners had also violated immigration laws (32.1 percent) or obtained employment in violation of their status as foreign visitors (16.1 percent).

Those Japanese convicted of larceny and also denied a suspended sentence differed from counterpart foreigners in certain ways. More Japanese offenders usually had a known record of property crimes (91.2 percent versus 25 percent of foreign offenders), had a known history of previous imprisonment (32.4 versus 16.1 percent), and were already under a suspended sentence when they committed another offense (55.9 versus 10.7 percent). The researchers of the Research and Training Institute concluded that no discriminatory practice was found.

Foreigners admitted to prison in 1993 were a small minority when compared with nonforeigners. There were 669 foreign and 19,654 nonforeign males admitted, 65 foreign and 854 nonforeign females. Only 220 males and 25 females were classified as class-F inmates. In the distribution of offenses for persons entering prisons in 1993, the foreigners differed fundamentally from the other inmates, and the class-F inmates differed from the total foreigners (see table 6.3).[1] The general trend mirrored official leniency; a selective process removed the less serious offenses of foreigners and culminated in the heavy representation among class-F inmates of those crimes the public prosecutors and sentencing judges regard as most reprehensible.

For men, the total foreigners had proportionately more violent offenses than the other new inmates, and class-F offenders (a subgroup among the foreigners) had an even greater percentage share. Robbery was most instrumental in shaping that trend, and homicide had similar, but minor, influence. Larceny and stimulant drug offenses held sizable percentages but definitely declined when compared with the Japanese admissions. Narcotics—a relatively rare but very serious offense—was noteworthy among reasons for imprisonment of class-F offenders. Class-F women were too few (25) for reliable conclusions, but women's shares of robbery, homicide, and narcotics offenses exhibited trends similar to those for the men.

Community Corrections and Foreigners

When convicted for a crime against Japanese laws, foreigners are unlikely to be placed under probationary supervision. Many are deported to their native country. The relatively few foreigners sent to prison makes parole even less likely. The Rehabilitation Bureau issues monthly internal administrative reports on the number of probationers and parolees under supervision. The reports offer statistics on the number of foreigners on probation and parole in recent years: 950 for 1991, 911 in 1992, 936 in 1993, and 983 in 1994.

The figures on foreigners in these reports include per-

Table 6.3
Distribution of Prison Admissions for Nonforeign, Foreign, and Class-F Offenders, 1993

	% Distribution					
	Nonforeign Admissions		Total Foreign Admissions		Total Class-F Admissions	
Offenses	Male	Female	Male	Female	Male	Female
Violent	18.0	8.6	26.5	12.3	32.3	24.0
Bodily Injury	(6.1)	(1.3)	(6.6)	(1.6)	(4.5)	(—)
Robbery	(2.5)	(1.8)	(8.4)	(3.1)	(20.0)	(8.0)
Homicide	(1.8)	(5.0)	(3.4)	(6.1)	(5.9)	(12.0)
Extortion	(3.8)	(0.4)	(3.4)	(—)	(0.5)	(—)
Firearms	(1.6)	(—)	(1.9)	(1.6)	(0.5)	(4.0)
Violence Law	(1.5)	(0.1)	(1.3)	(—)	(—)	(—)
Other	(0.7)	(—)	(1.5)	(—)	(1.0)	(—)
Property	38.4	29.5	25.3	29.2	19.1	8.0
Larceny	(28.3)	(18.7)	(18.7)	(18.5)	(11.4)	(4.0)
Fraud	(6.7)	(7.9)	(3.9)	(6.1)	(4.5)	(—)
Arson	(0.9)	(1.9)	(0.9)	(3.1)	(—)	(4.0)
Other	(2.5)	(1.0)	(1.7)	(1.6)	(3.2)	(—)
Sex	2.9	0.1	2.8	—	3.6	—
Drug	26.4	55.3	29.5	44.6	22.3	48.0
Stimulants	(26.3)	(55.3)	(23.2)	(33.8)	(4.5)	(28.0)
Narcotics	(0.2)	(—)	(6.3)	(10.8)	(17.7)	(20.0)
Prostitution	0.3	0.5	0.3	6.1	—	4.0
Gambling	0.4	0.1	0.6	—	—	—
Traffic	9.6	4.3	5.7	1.6	1.3	—
Other	4.0	1.6	9.3	6.2	21.4	16.0
Total %	100.0	100.0	100.0	100.0	100.0	100.0

Source: Research and Statistics Section 1994a.

sons officially defined as Koreans although long-term residents of Japan, including persons of Korean descent born in Japan. Of the total number of "foreigners" on probation or parole in the four years (3,780), 76.9 percent were classified as coming originally from the Republic of Korea or North Korea. They have been granted permanent residence in Japan. Another 95 probationers and parolees (2.5 percent of the total 3,780) have been granted permanent residence but are from countries other than Korea. We are left with 778 persons (20.6 percent of the 3,780) who have special permission to be permanent residents; often they have a Japanese wife.

The Rehabilitation Bureau's monthly reports also show that the number of probationers and parolees not granted permanent residence is increasing, from 115 of the 950 on probation or parole in 1991 to 121 of the 911 cases in 1992, 234 of the 936 cases in 1993, and 308 of the 983 cases in 1994. Adults outnumber juveniles, and their predominance increased from 1991 to 1994. Parole has tended to gain a longer proportion of the cases; probation cases especially lagged behind the paroles for adults.

The distribution of cases is listed in table 6.4. Whether adults or juveniles, parolees exceeded probationers in number. Adult parolees were heavily involved with drugs and crimes of violence. Adult probationers have been convicted primarily for crimes against property and involvement in the trade of prostitution. Juvenile probationers tended toward traffic and property offenses. A few juveniles were predelinquents who had not been convicted of law violations and who were placed on parole or probation as a protective measure.

The foreigners placed in either of the two community-based programs came primarily from Asiatic countries, especially probationers. Adult parolees were distributed most widely about the world. The United States and South American countries were well represented in 1994 (see table 6.5).

Probation officers are encouraged to study foreign

FOREIGNERS IN JAPANESE PRISONS

Table 6.4
Offenses of Probationers and Parolees Not
Permanent Residents of Japan, 1994

Offenses	Juvenile Parole	Juvenile Probation	Adult Parole	Adult Probation	Total Cases
Robbery	4	2	48	3	57
Bodily Injury	5	1	4	4	14
Homicide	—	1	8	1	10
Firearms	—	—	6	—	6
Larceny	18	3	18	17	56
Other Property	1	—	3	4	8
Drug	9	1	79	7	96
Stimulants	(3)	(—)	(30)	(6)	(39)
Cannibus	(1)	(—)	(21)	(1)	(23)
Poison Substances	(5)	(1)	(—)	(—)	(6)
Narcotics, Opium	(—)	(—)	(28)	(—)	(28)
Traffic	12	—	1	4	17
Prostitution	—	—	1	15	16
Immigration	—	—	8	3	11
Sex	—	—	4	1	5
Predelinquency	1	3	—	—	4
Other	4	—	2	2	8
Total	54	11	182	61	308

Source: Data from an internal monthly report of the Rehabiliation Bureau.

tongues. Voluntary probation officers (VPOs) speaking foreign languages and professional interpreters have been listed. As expected, foreigners are less responsive to supervisory relationships based on Japanese customary respect for older persons, which VPOs tend to be.

Table 6.5
Nationality of Probationers and Parolees Not
Permanent Residents of Japan, 1994

Nationality	Juvenile Parole	Juvenile Probation	Adult Parole	Adult Probation	Total Cases
Northeast Asian	17	4	41	25	87
Southeast Asian	21	2	64	30	117
Southwest Asian	—	—	9	2	11
Oceanian	—	—	5	—	5
Middle Eastern	—	—	15	—	15
European	—	—	9	1	10
African	—	—	5	—	5
North American (U.S.)	7	2	28	2	39
South American	9	3	6	1	19
Total	54	11	182	61	308

Source: Data from an internal monthly report of the Rehabilitation Bureau.

Adaptations by Foreign Inmates

The imprisoned foreigner has been relegated as a convicted criminal to the outcast status suffered by all prisoners. But foreigners must adjust their behavior as prisoners to legal standards, behavioral norms, and cultural values other than those of their own society. Imprisoned intellectuals usually emphasize the prison's lack of concern for their personal dignity and individuality. Admission procedures impose a series of petty humiliations: fingerprinting, assignment of an impersonal number, deprivation of personal possessions, standardized haircuts, and issuance of prison garb. The new prisoner is tested and queried on matters usually regarded as private. Information disappears into files, to be ready for future decisions that have serious effects—good or disadvantageous—beyond the control of the prisoner. Inmates are subject to a code of conduct framed to counter any intransigence.

Even if they had been confined in a prison in their own country, the foreigners now confined in Japan must adapt to unfamiliar roles and rules. As Suzuki (1979, 143) has commented, "The history of Japan provides many instances in which a sincere attempt to copy a foreign institution resulted in the development of a system not dissimilar in form but quite different in substance from the original."

For foreigners, the impact of imprisonment in another society is aggravated by their own concerns about whether their individualities, dietary preferences, medical needs, religious beliefs, and living habits will be respected by the authorities of the other culture. Will representatives of their governments provide the services orthodox travelers expect when emergencies occur? Subjected to policies and practices that are oriented to managing native prisoners, foreigners especially need advice on regulations, administrative routes for appeals, and customs.[2] In that sense, the class-F inmate is not, contrary to the assumption of Park (1967, 201), "emancipated" from the "world in which he was born and bred." He or she is less able to melt into the regular prison population and thus to attract less attention from officials and Japanese inmates.

As a subcultural minority, foreigners must make a quick study of two sets of role norms: those of the keepers, on the one hand, and, on the other, those of the kept, among whom the more intimate associations occur. Unfamiliarity breeds misunderstanding of the behavioral cues to which Japanese inmates would respond intelligently.[3] Officers need fewer words when addressing Japanese inmates. Westerners of both sexes, I was told, require fuller explanations of instructions.

A few foreign women vigorously voice medical complaints; an American loudly charged mistreatment while on remand. Another foreign woman attempted suicide by drinking shampoo because an acquaintance had stolen all her possessions from her residence. Women from other Asian societies are particularly obedient, I was told, because their status at home is lower than the status of women in Japan.

Prison officials disagreed on the work attitudes of foreigners. Some report that the prison officers find them "lazy" by the workaholic standards of Japan and that those who see themselves as professionals in legitimate occupations disdain prison labor as beneath their station in life. Other officials contend that the foreigners are diligent after they have learned the tasks.

Americans were reported to be especially prone to deny any guilt for crimes and to seek release through technical aspects of the criminal law. Their attitudes oppose the Japanese expectation that the accused persons will admit their guilt, when the evidence indicates it, and will earn official leniency by making restitution to the victims.

Allocation of Foreign Inmates

A key advantage of the Japanese correctional system for development of consistent policies and procedures is the operation of all detention centers, prisons, and juvenile training schools by a national agency (the Correction Bureau). Relatively few, the sentenced foreigners can be concentrated in Fuchu Prison or Osaka Prison, in Yokosuka Prison, or in Tochigi Women's Prison. After being convicted and sentenced to prison, all inmates are classified at the detention houses and allocated to prisons according to these classes: those with "advanced criminal tendencies" (class B), those without "advanced criminal tendencies" (class A), those sentenced to more than eight years (class L), those adults under twenty-six years of age (class Y), juveniles sentenced to adult prisons (class J), and foreigners who need different treatment than Japanese (class F).

Fuchu Prison received only twenty foreigners in 1972; admissions rose in 1977 to sixty-five, plus one foreigner at Nakano Prison in a suburb of Tokyo.[4] After 1977 admissions of foreign offenders to Fuchu decreased until 1982, when they began a progressive climb from 32 to 344 in 1993 and 417 in 1994.

American military offenders admitted to Yokosuka numbered twenty-one in 1972, plus one held in Okinawa Prison. Until opened in a new site in 1978, Yokosuka lacked space for all military offenders. From 1973 to 1977, Sasebo Prison also received them, as did Okinawa Prison from 1972 through 1978. Admission of the American military to all the prisons skyrocketed to 147 in 1974 and then declined in irregular fashion to 24 in 1994 (Research and Statistics Section 1991a, 1995a).

Prison law and regulations require censorship of all correspondence and reading materials. Administration of such regulations is complicated when interpreters are needed. Since foreign inmates often cannot afford to pay for the service, the prisons seek the assistance of volunteers, including embassy personnel. Most embassies are responsive; for example, the American Embassy in Tokyo and consulates elsewhere maintain direct contact with citizens in detention centers or prisons. However, some embassies ignore their imprisoned nationals as outcasts. Some foreigners ask that their embassies not be contacted for fear of retaliation when they return home.

The menu of meals is crucial to the morale of prisoners in all countries. Steamed white rice is the basis of the three typical meals each day for the Japanese. Breakfast may add seaweed, a pickled vegetable, and a slice of grilled fish or a fried egg. The lunch box may add curry, vegetables, or fish. Dinner may have one or two pickled or quick-cooked vegetables, seaweed, a slice of grilled fish, and a soup (Seward 1972). Western-style meals have been provided class-F inmates from America and Europe who could not tolerate Japanese menus, but now there are few inmates from those countries.

On 1 April 1995, the revision of the Food Supply Ordinance authorized the prison wardens to permit special diets because of religious belief, vegetarianism, illness, and other major dietary customs. The new food policy reduces the proportion of staples, such as rice and wheat; increases side dishes; and raises the number of proteins and vitamins. Designed for inmates who stand at work for at least fifteen hours a week, dietary menu A calls for 2,000 kilocalories, 399 grams of rice, and 171 grams of wheat. Menu B is for those standing for less than fifteen hours a week; it requires 1,700 kilocalories, 339 grams of rice, and 147 grams of wheat. For inmates remaining in cells during the day, menu C provides 1,600 kilocalories, 318 grams of rice, and 147 grams of wheat. Side dishes are delivered in equal quantities for all three menus. The nutritive value of all meals must conform to health standards. The warden and other relevant senior officials taste-test the sample delivered to their respective offices. Sample meals for each three-day period are displayed in a glass case in the prison kitchen.

As is customary in their country, Japanese inmates sleep in comforters (futons) on tatami mats. The futons are rolled up in the daytime. Class-F inmates are provided with raised beds, mattresses, blankets, pillows, and chairs in their cells. Western-style toilets and showers are available. For all prisoners, chapels serve persons of Shinto, Buddhist, or Christian beliefs. Volunteer visitors offer counseling and religious services.

The exceptions granted class-F inmates exist within the general requirement that they be accorded the same benefits as Japanese inmates and be subject to the same conduct norms. All inmates receive benefits when promoted along the four levels of the progressive grade system introduced in 1934. Article 17 of Ministry of Justice Ordinance No. 56 rewards exceptional merit: "The grade of treatment of a prisoner who is strong in the sense of responsibility and promises to be fit for collective living may be advanced to a proper grade" (UNAFEI n.d., 243). The amount of monetary remuneration for prison labor made available for the inmate's own use increases from one-fifth of their remuneration at grade four to one-half at grade one. Second grade permits play in sports or attending athletic events. First grade offers freedom from search of body and cell.

Foreign Women at Tochigi

Tochigi Penitentiary opened in 1868 within the town of Tochigi and became a women's institution in 1906. Reconstructed after a fire in 1907, it was renamed Tochigi Prison in 1948. Kocher (1961) describes the facility as it stood within the boundary of the town. Four main wooden buildings housed an industrial shop, cells and a library, the hospital and center for admission of new prisoners, and the administrative offices. The buildings were joined by outside corridors. A ten-foot stone wall circled the prison.

In 1979 the prison was relocated outside the city in its present site, which had been a large farm. It has capacity for 398 prisoners, including 248 in congregate cells, 142 in one-person cells, and 8 in a small cottage-type building for prerelease. The prerelease building has three rooms for sleeping, a recreation room, a kitchen, and a laundry area. A twenty-five-foot concrete wall surrounds the prison, with a two-story administration building outside the wall. All buildings are of modern construction.

Tochigi receives all foreign women sentenced to Japanese prisons. Deportation is an alternative that especially reduces prison admissions of foreign women. Although the absolute numbers of female foreigners in Japanese prisons are few, the trend in recent years has been toward an increasing proportion of foreigners to all women inmates in Japan (see table 6.1), even more so for class-F women (see table 6.2). For Tochigi's population, the foreigners increased their proportional share from 2.6 percent in 1987 to 7.2 percent in 1992. I was told at Tochigi that the foreigners there in 1987–92 were drawn predominately from eastern Asia, especially Taiwan, Thailand, and the Philippines. Of the total Tochigi inmates for those years, the United States held 13 percent, the greatest share of any country other than the three eastern Asian nations.[5]

The majority of foreigners present at Tochigi in October 1992 had been imprisoned for narcotic offenses (42.3 percent) or for stimulant drug or marijuana offenses (23.1 percent). Robbery and prostitution (at 11.5 percent each) were the causes of imprisonment for most of the rest. Foreign prostitutes usually are deported; those women imprisoned under the Antiprostitution Law are likely to be managers or to have forced other women into prostitution. Single cases of homicide, arson, and violation of the social security law made up the remainder. All women admitted to prison in 1992 were heavily involved with drugs (56 percent, mostly with stimulant drugs), but to an extent short of the involvement of Tochigi's foreigners. Property offenses took up 31 percent of the total admissions, and homicide and arson (at 7 percent) comprised most of the remainder.

The foreigners at Tochigi in October 1992 averaged sixty-two months in length of sentence. All women entering prisons in 1992 received considerably shorter sentences (twenty-three months), but the mix of offenses differed. The foreign women at Tochigi were younger on average than the Japanese women admitted to prisons in 1992 (32.15 versus 39.82 years).

As do all women's prisons in Japan, Tochigi receives a wide variety of inmates, rather than particular classifications of inmates as do the prisons for males. Immediately after being sentenced to prison, the women are transferred from the detention houses to Tochigi for classification. Those with serious mental or medical problems are transferred to Hachioji Medical Prison. Otherwise, assignments to various cell blocks differentiate the general classes of inmates. When designed as a facility, Tochigi did not receive foreign women, and it is not prepared to concentrate their relatively small number in a particular area. When they earn placement in second grade in the progressive grade system, they are eligible for one-person cells at night. Of the thirty-one women foreigners present in November 1992, six requested and were obtaining Western meals. Volunteers offer the inmates counseling and religious services.

Most women work in industrial shops, and inmates are assigned selectively; three shops are for recidivists, and three are for women in prison for the first time. One is a laundry for institutional wash; the inmates do their own personal laundry. Other workshops assemble parts for automobiles or make men's suits, children's caps, or lunch boxes. One workshop is in an independent area, outside the wall and surrounded by a high wire fence. Trusted inmates sleep in that area. In a small kitchen, they prepare their own meals on weekends.

Near that area is a large meeting room; among its functions, it serves as the place where annual national examinations are administered for female applicants for prison officer positions. Within the prison is a large gymnasium for entertainment, physical exercise, volleyball, softball, and folk dancing. The hospital building includes a nursery for the infants of staff members. The two visiting rooms present no barriers between the inmate and the visitor; the inmate and prison officer sit on one side of a table. The second room is furnished with a low table and pillows for sitting in the Japanese fashion. The two-floor cell blocks have spotless, light-colored wooden floors. A large kitchen, security offices, and the classification section have their own buildings.

Academic education includes a course in the Japanese language for foreigners; other courses offer training in bookkeeping, abacus instruction, and guidance for a certificate in cooking. A two-year course in beautician services offers practical experience in a shop serving the female staff. A course in sewing lasts three months. Group activities are in flower arranging, the tea ceremony, calligraphy, recitation of poems, traditional dance, drawing, music, penmanship, and English.

Fuchu Prison and Male Civilian Foreigners

Fuchu Prison is the culmination of a history extending back to the Ishikawajima Workhouse for Criminal and Homeless Paupers established in 1790 by the Tokugawa shogunate. In 1885 a new plant was built in the village of Nishi-Sugamo and called Sugamo Penitentiary. The Ministry of Justice assumed control of that plant in 1903 and renamed it Sugamo Prison in 1922. It was relocated as Fuchu Prison to its present site in 1935 and reconstructed in 1992.

In its 1935 design, the two-floor cell blocks radiated like spokes in a wheel. The inadequate cells, dimly lighted corridors, and physical deterioration necessitated extensive renovation. The old cells were small with narrow, barred windows. Later introduction of toilets in the cells was improvised by a wooden unit that also served as a table, a chair, and shelves. For bathing, the inmates had to go through a tunnel to another cell block. The industrial shops were inadequately lighted and suffered deterioration.

Along with other large prisons, Fuchu is undergoing major reconstruction, which is expected to be completed in 1997. The new buildings are white, are well designed, and have three floors to permit greater spaciousness. The congregate and one-person cells are larger and have larger windows. Each cell block has a large bathing pool of bright color, with forty showers along the wall for washing before entering the pool. The new industrial shops are well lighted and more spacious. The new cell block for class-F inmates is similar to those for the Japanese, with certain exceptions:

the cells are more spacious, showers are available, and the furniture is Western.

The distribution of offenses, as compiled at Fuchu Prison, suggests that both class-F and Japanese males felt the impact of the criminal justice campaign against drugs. Drug trafficking, other than drug abuse, drew a large proportion of the imprisonments for illegal drugs. In 1992 thirty-seven class-F men were at Fuchu for violating the Stimulant Drug Control Law, but only four had used the drug. Twenty-six foreigners abused other drugs, but eighty-five were imprisoned for violating laws concerned with those drugs. The class-F group at Fuchu was heavily involved in drug offenses but was more inclined toward narcotics and marijuana (32 percent of their number were so inclined in 1992) than were the Japanese males in the nation's prisons (only 0.4 percent of their number were so inclined). Another 14 percent of the foreigners and 26 percent of the Japanese had been imprisoned for violations of the Stimulant Drug Control Law. Drug smuggling was more common among foreigners. The lower-level members of trafficking groups are likely to be deported, and the criminal elite are usually imprisoned.

The foreign inmates had the greater share of the incidents of robbery (24 percent versus 3 percent of Japanese inmates), whereas the Japanese inmates were more inclined toward theft (28 percent versus 9 percent of foreign inmates), traffic offenses (9.5 versus 1.5 percent), fraud (6.6 versus 1.1 percent), bodily injury (6.1 versus 2.6 percent), and sex offenses (2.7 versus 1.9 percent).

The class-F male civilians in 1992 drew longer sentences (five years and seven months) on average than either other Fuchu inmates (thirty months) or all male prisoners in Japan (twenty-two months). The difference was partially due to the respective menus of crimes.

Over the years, male civilians among foreign inmates at Fuchu have been drawn from an extending range of nationalities. Information supplied to me at Fuchu lists seventeen nationalities in 1976, twenty-five in 1988, and thirty-two in 1992. The largest share of the men came from Asia: 48 percent in 1976, 88 percent in 1988, and 77 percent in 1992. Despite the appearance of foreign inmates from the People's Republic of China in 1992, those from eastern Asia failed to keep pace with the upsurge from Malaysia and the nations of southwest Asia (primarily Pakistan and Iran). The inmates from North and South America held a 37 percent share in 1976, 5.1 percent in 1988, and 13.5 percent in 1992. Europe took up the slack.

Average ages in 1992 also differentiate the class-F civilian males (average age 32.2 years at Fuchu) from other Fuchu inmates (average age 44.2 years, with one inmate aged 81 years) and from all male prisoners (average age 39.5 years). Migrants tend to be drawn from the younger members of the originating society. A violent crime is more characteristic of young adult males but relatively infrequent in Japan; robbery sends to prison an appreciable number of foreigners. In 1992 foreigners exceeded the other Fuchu inmates in average schooling (10.9 years versus 9.8 years), but the class-F distribution was bimodal. Inmates from south Asia had a lower average level of education than the Japanese; other foreigners (especially Westerners) had attended colleges.

The International Affairs Division of Fuchu Prison deals exclusively with foreign inmates. Its staff includes interpreters in English, Chinese, Spanish, and Persian, but the prison administration hopes that instruction in Japanese will provide a common language. The staff orients the newly arrived foreigners on the rules of conduct, the programs at Fuchu, opportunities for counseling, and means of communicating with officials and individuals on the outside. The International Affairs Division translates letters, and sometimes the interpreters counsel inmates not familiar with the Japanese language.

Language barriers, of course, block communication with staff and among inmates. In 1992 more class-F inmates than before could not speak Japanese, English, or Chinese; only three of the class-F inmates could speak Japanese when entering prison. Among those from Thailand, Pakistan, Indonesia, and some other parts of Asia, some individuals could read English but could not speak it adequately. Instructions on prison regulations and procedures have been translated into eight languages by the Fuchu staff and embassy personnel. Language tapes, broadcast from the Education Section office, offer Japanese language instruction for foreigners who speak English or Chinese.

Fuchu's location in Tokyo has advantages for access to embassies and contacts with a range of specialized services in the community. The class-F inmates are housed separately, but they are assigned with the Japanese to workshops producing shoes, metal boxes, heavy iron grills, electronic harnesses, and parts for automobiles, printing equipment, and toy animals.

The Education Section coordinates the participation of volunteer counselors and religious workers. The number of applications make recruitment unnecessary. The section investigates the background of applicants, and, when appropriate, the warden refers the application to the Tokyo Correction Region, which is authorized to issue warrants. The volunteers come to the prison once or twice a month, especially on weekends, at times adjusted to their other activities.

The Education Section issues newspapers and books from the library, including six thousand in foreign languages. Class-F inmates who read English receive the *Japan Times*; Chinese inmates are given a newspaper in the Chinese language. The embassies are asked to contribute additional books. Prisoners are permitted to purchase approved books. A prisoner-edited magazine in Japanese, *Fujimi*, is issued monthly; its title, meaning "By Mt. Fuji," is a symbol of special meaning to the Japanese.

In 1992 only 9 percent of the class-F inmates were rated medically as invalids or physically handicapped; 29 percent of the other prisoners at Fuchu were so diagnosed, partly because of their higher average age. The prison hospital has a pharmacy, a dental clinic, an operating theater, a minor surgery theater, offices for physicians, and two wards for patients (one for contagious diseases). The staff is made up of four general practitioners, three surgeons, one dentist, two pharmacists, one X-ray technician, and eleven nurses (three female). Most surgery occurs at the prison hospital; some referrals are made to a hospital in Tokyo. Most serious cases go to the Hachioji Medical Prison.

Visitors to the prison register at a booth resembling the ticket office of a theater and wait in a nearby room. Inmates await their visitors in a unit resembling a tall telephone booth. The visits take place in rooms where tables are separated by a perforated screen.

American Military at Yokosuka

Yokosuka Prison is located on the shore of Tokyo Bay, where Commodore Matthew C. Perry landed in 1853. It was a naval prison constructed in 1883, mostly of wood in the fashion of that time. It had deteriorated by 1945, when it was transferred to the Ministry of Justice to become a branch of Yokohama Prison.[6] In 1951 Yokosuka became an independent prison; in 1955 it became the place of confinement for the American military and their dependents imprisoned for offenses against Japanese law. The original site was sold to permit construction of a public school and an apartment complex operated by the local government. On a new site on the fringe of Tokyo Bay, the present modern plant was opened in 1978 as a pretrial detention facility and as a class-A prison receiving inmates classified as not having "advanced criminal tendencies."

The administrative offices are in a two-story building outside the concrete perimeter wall. A steep, forested hill is outside the wall on one side, and Tokyo Bay is directly outside. Next to the locked entrance through the wall, the security office manages fifty-four prison officers, seven chief guards, seven assistant chief guards, and fourteen sergeants. The rest of the staff is made up of the warden, two deputy wardens, one instructor, two technicians, a physician, and seven clerks. The prison's capacity is 227, including the Americans, Japanese prisoners, and Japanese in pretrial detention.

On the last day of 1994, the Americans in Yokosuka were from the following elements of the U.S. armed forces, in the following numbers: fourteen from the navy, eight from the marines, and one from the air force. The total number was small, but the presence of American military personnel in Japanese prisons is remarkable in itself. That result of negotiations demonstrated American respect for Japan's sovereignty and Japanese patience with the presence on its territory of the military of a foreign power.

Yokosuka receives Americans under conditions of the Status of Forces Agreement between Japan and the United States. A U.S. Armed Forces Prison Liaison team represents the American military in contacts with Japanese authorities about military personnel or their dependents who are in either pretrial detention or prisons. Excerpts of Article 17 of the agreement follow.

> 1. Subject to the provisions of this Article,
> (a) the military authorities of the United States shall have the right to exercise within Japan all criminal and disciplinary jurisdiction conferred on them by the law of the United States over all persons subject to the military law of the United States;
> (b) the authorities of Japan shall have jurisdiction over the members of the United States armed forces, the civilian component, and their dependents with respect to offenses committed within the territory of Japan. . . .
> 3. In cases where the right to exercise jurisdiction is concurrent the following rules shall apply:

(a) the military authorities of the United States shall have the primary right to exercise jurisdiction over members of the United States armed forces or the civilian component in relation to
    (i) offenses solely against the property or security of the United States, or offenses solely against the person or property of another member of the United States armed forces or the civilian componentor of a dependent;
    (ii) offenses arising out of any act or omission done in the performance of official duty.
(b) In the case of any other offense the authorities of Japan shall have the primary right to exercise jurisdiction. . . .

5. (a) The authorities of Japan and the military authorities of the United States shall assist each other in the arrest of members of the United States armed forces, the civilian component, or their dependents in the territory of Japan and in handing them over to the authority which is to exercise jurisdiction in accordance with the above provisions.
(b) The authorities of Japan shall notify promptly the military authorities of the United States of the arrest of any member of the United States armed forces, the civilian component, or a dependent.
(c) The custody of an accused member of the United States armed forces or the civilian component over whom Japan is to exercise jurisdiction shall, if he is in the hands of the United States, remain with the United States until he is charged by Japan. . . .

9. Whenever a member of the United States armed forces, the civilian component or a dependent is prosecuted under the jurisdiction of Japan he shall be entitled:
    (a) to a prompt and speedy trial;
    (b) to be informed, in advance of trial, of the specific charge or charges made against him;
    (c) to be confronted with the witnesses against him;
    (d) to have compulsory process for obtaining witnesses in his favor; if they are within the jurisdiction of Japan;

(e) to have legal representation of his own choice for his defense or to have free or assisted legal representation under the conditions prevailing for the time being in Japan;
(f) if he considers it necessary, to have the services of a competent interpreter; and
(g) to communicate with a representative of the Government of the United States and to have such a representative present at his trial....

The absolute number of Americans at Yokosuka has been too few to influence the class-F share of all prisoners. Warden Toichi Ohtsuka of Yokosuka Prison has offered a three-fold explanation for this decline. First, when the military draft in the United States ended, voluntary enlistments resulted in more stable individuals serving in Japan. Second, major military combat had been absent between the end of World War II and the time of his statement (1988); the more aggressive personalities are not as socially rewarded in peace as in wartime. Third, the American armed forces have been increasingly effective in persuading military personnel to avoid drug abuse and to respect Japanese customs and people. The U.S. Naval Base at Yokosuka does not allow individuals under the influence of alcohol or drugs to go out the main gate.

The American inmates at Yokosuka in 1994 were younger and had more schooling than the Japanese inmates at the prison. Average ages for the Americans and the Japanese were 25 and 37 years, respectively; respective average education levels were 12 and 10.8 years.[7] The average lengths of sentences also were greater for the Americans (sixty-one months versus twenty-seven for Japanese), because of different distributions of crimes. The twenty-three military prisoners present at the end of 1994 were serving terms for more violent offenses: four for murder, two for rape, fourteen for robbery, one for bodily injury, one for a fatal traffic accident, and one for embezzlement. The fifty-seven Japanese prisoners were inclined more toward drug and property crimes: fourteen were serving for stimulant drug offenses, one for a heroin offense, one for a poisonous substance offense, thirteen for larceny, eight for fraud, five for embezzlement, one for injury in a traffic accident, one for murder, two for rape, two for bodily injury, two for robbery, three for illegal firearms, and four for other crimes.

The prison's pamphlet in English, *Regulations for Prisoners*, announces: "This book for prisoners indicates how you will lead prison life here. The contents are taken into consideration for foreigners who have different customs and habits. If anything contained herein is not clear to you, do not hesitate to ask for an explanation from us. . . . Try to rehabilitate yourself as soon as possible observing this regulation book and obtaining regular live behavior."

The American military receive certain benefits not offered the Japanese inmates at Yokosuka. Steam heat is provided in the morning and evening only on the northern island of Hokkaido. This policy is consistent with the Japanese tradition that, in lieu of heating the entire residence in the winter, individuals warm themselves with heavy undergarments, bulky sleeping comforters (futons), and the *kotatsu* (a low table covered by a heat-holding quilt and sitting over a well in the floor with a hibachi at the bottom). Yokosuka provides American inmates with a Western-style bed and blankets instead of the futon. Instead of participating in the twice-weekly communal bath, the Americans may take daily showers, twice a week for fifteen minutes and five times a week for five minutes. Instead of the usual close crop, long hair is allowed for the Americans when official permission is granted. Bedtime for the American inmates is extended an hour beyond the usual 9:00 P.M.

The American armed forces provide American inmates with additional food beyond the usual diet. When a medical crisis requires, the American will be transferred to the American Navy Hospital. Military chaplains come on weekdays for counseling and to provide Protestant and Roman Catholic services in a room simply furnished as a chapel; the chaplains serve their own congregations on Sundays. Japanese and foreign volunteers offer counseling, entertainment events, and special meals on birthdays. The director of the Yokosuka Branch of the American Red Cross and three American volunteers counsel the American inmates on any personal problems.

In Japanese prisons, visiting usually is limited to relatives and lawyers; a special room has tables with perforated plastic partitions between the inmates and the visitors; a correctional officer is present. At Yokosuka the embassy's representatives and American military officials may visit in an ordinary conference room. A prison officer is present as an observer. This arrangement is in accord with the formal agreement between Japan and the United States.

In the two blocks of one-man cells allocated the Americans, showers are substituted for the traditional congregate bathing pools. Western-style toilets are in each cell, each of which is an ordinary room with the exception of a metal door. Each cell is furnished with a bed, a table, a chair, and bookshelves. All prisoners may listen to a radio system in their cells; the Americans hear the Far East Network, the radio system of the American military.

Work assignments include processing clothing and rugs in a laundry, operating a small print shop, working in a metal shop (making springs for a private contractor when I visited Yokosuka), assembling paper boxes, doing yard work, and performing kitchen and janitorial tasks. Vocational training is offered in photography and lithographic printing.

In addition to being excused from work on the regular Japanese holidays, the American military inmates are excused on Washington's Birthday, Memorial Day, Independence Day, Labor Day, Thanksgiving, and Christmas. On the athletic field within the wall, the Americans are more inclined than the Japanese to play softball and basketball or to engage in weight lifting. The officials believe the Americans' military experiences lead to a preference for intensive physical exertion. A gymnasium provides opportunities for lectures by outsiders, entertainment, and films in English rented from the U.S. Air Force Base at Yokota.[8] Individuals at the base supplement the prison library by contributing works in English.

7

Elderly Inmates: Demographic Change Creeps into Prisons

"Perhaps the greatest challenge facing Japan," declares Martin (1989, 6), "is how to provide for the increasing numbers of elderly in the 21st century when close to one-quarter of the population will be over age 60." As a spin-off of that general development, the Correction Bureau and the Rehabilitation Bureau are already encountering a rising tide of elderly Japanese convicted for transgressions of the criminal law. The qualitative impact of more elderly on correctional practices in the twenty-first century will match the quantitative impact of that age-group's sheer numbers.

The Increasing Presence of the Elderly

The aging of the population has required a much shorter period in Japan than in Western Europe, points out Okazaki (1990, 8–9), and, unlike in Europe, the elderly's share of the Japanese population will continue to escalate until the year 2020. Both birthrates and death rates have declined; together they have altered the age distribution of adults (see table 7.1). The proportion of younger adults less than fifty years of age dropped from 73.7 percent in 1966 to 61.7 percent in 1992. Adults aged fifty to fifty-nine years have in-

ELDERLY INMATES

Table 7.1
Male Population Distribution and
Rate of Prison Admissions, 1966–92

Year	Total Adult Male Population[a]	% Distribution of Males by Age[b] 18–49	50–59	60+	Rate of Admissions per 100,000 Male Population 18–49	50–59	60+
1966	32,726	73.7	12.7	13.6	131.6	32.2	9.9
1967	33,624	73.9	12.4	13.7	112.9	29.5	8.9
1968	34,396	74.1	12.2	13.7	106.1	27.1	8.5
1969	35,102	74.3	11.9	13.8	95.5	23.6	6.1
1970	35,609	74.2	11.8	14.0	91.2	22.0	5.5
1971	36,121	74.2	11.7	14.1	94.8	22.6	6.2
1972	36,823	74.1	11.6	14.3	96.9	25.6	5.7
1973	37,366	73.8	11.7	14.5	88.3	23.5	5.8
1974	37,833	73.4	11.9	14.7	85.8	24.2	6.3
1975	38,665	73.0	12.1	14.9	85.2	27.2	6.1
1976	39,125	72.3	12.6	15.1	88.6	28.2	6.5
1977	39,591	71.6	13.1	15.3	89.2	26.6	6.7
1978	40,037	70.8	13.7	15.5	93.3	27.8	6.3
1979	40,478	70.1	14.4	15.5	92.3	30.0	6.8
1980	40,788	69.3	14.9	15.8	89.3	29.7	7.1
1981	41,324	68.6	15.5	15.9	93.8	35.1	7.8
1982	41,813	67.9	16.0	16.1	96.0	37.9	7.3
1983	42,349	67.1	16.5	16.4	92.4	39.1	8.1
1984	42,692	66.4	16.8	16.8	96.0	41.3	8.3
1985	43,220	65.7	17.0	17.3	93.0	43.9	8.9

Table 7.1 cont. on next page

ELDERLY INMATES

Table 7.1 continued

Year	Total Adult Male Population[a]	% Distribution of Males by Age[b] 18–49	50–59	60+	Rate of Admissions per 100,000 Male Population 18–49	50–59	60+
1986	43,792	65.0	17.1	17.9	88.2	46.6	9.5
1987	44,361	64.4	17.2	18.4	84.9	46.0	8.5
1988	44,942	63.9	17.1	19.0	79.3	45.5	8.9
1989	45,546	63.6	16.9	19.5	67.6	41.3	8.9
1990	45,873	62.9	17.0	20.1	61.8	39.3	9.1
1991	46,694	62.3	17.0	20.7	57.1	35.1	7.8
1992	47,307	61.7	17.1	21.2	55.1	36.9	8.8

Sources: Research and Statistics Section 1971a, 1976a, 1981a, 1986a, 1991a, 1993a; population reports from the Statistics Bureau of the Management and Coordination Agency.

[a] In thousands.

[b] Percentages equal 100 for each year.

creased their share from 12.7 to 17.1 percent. The adults sixty years old and older have moved from 13.6 percent in 1966 to 21.2 percent in 1992.

The declining birthrates are due to an interacting combination of changes underway in Japanese society and in the social psychology of contemporary young adults. The abortion rate is high, and the divorce rate is rising. The high cost of housing and children's education favors the small family. Young women especially prefer to delay marriage for the sake of the pleasures of single life.[1] The delay reduces chances for a multichild family. The greater employment of women outside family enterprises has encouraged the development of the nuclear family and the women's independence from the extended family.

Those babies who are born have improved chances of surviving into adulthood and even into the senior years, because of gains in medical care and living conditions. The higher birthrates of previous decades now deliver more adults to the total population than the current birthrates will deliver in the future. As table 7.1 shows, the total number of Japanese males, ages 18–49 years, was 32,726,000 in 1966 and 47,307,000 in 1992. Although the number has grown, the rate of increase is decreasing over the years. In 1967 the increase over 1966 was 2.7 percent, but in 1992 the increase was only 1.3 percent over 1991.

Decreasing death rates have added to the share of the adult population held by the aged. In Japan in the early twentieth century, the expectancy of the life span was forty-five years, and women gave birth to an average of 5.1 children during their childbearing years. By 1950 life expectancy was sixty years and the birthrate had dropped to 3.7 children. In 1987 the life expectancy was seventy-six years for males and eighty-two years for females; the births were 1.8 per woman, or less than the replacement level for the parents. "Most Japanese demographers expect fertility to remain below the replacement level for the foreseeable future," says Martin (1989, 7).

The escalating number of elderly raises serious public issues. Somehow a balance must be found between the growing numbers of the socially dependent elderly and the relatively few workers in the economically productive ages. Other issues must be addressed: the greater importance of pensions, the heavy costs of medical treatment of the elderly, the increased need to provide care for terminal patients without a chance for recovery and for the bedridden and mentally disabled, and the need to accommodate a dramatic increase in the number of aged persons living alone or with only a spouse.

Social change will have great impact in Japan, where the elderly traditionally have held a place of honor. "Young and old Japanese appear to be less certain about a child's obligation to support aging parents," says Martin (1989, 15). Urbanization and changes in laws weakened the customary supports for the multigenerational family and encouraged the contemporary popularity of the nuclear family.

As a consequence of the declining births, fewer adult children share with siblings the family responsibility for aged parents. By lengthening the years that both parents and their adult children are alive, reduction of the death rate has aggravated the pressure on the adult children. Inadequate housing and greater employment of women—traditional caregivers of the elderly—have added to the stress on families and have weakened the quality of the care the families can deliver. The social psychology of the nuclear family opposes acceptance of that responsibility.

There has been a dramatic increase in the number of elderly people living alone or with a spouse, says Okazaki (1990, 13), both in absolute terms and also in the percentage of households with aged members. Surveys attest to the inadequacies of Japanese housing for the elderly. One-third of the households moved between 1979 and 1983. One-third of the moves was due to marriage, job transfer, change of employer, and moving in with parents or children. Another 45 percent were due to inadequate home size, housing dilapidation, inconvenience in commuting, eviction, high rent, and bad environment. For persons sixty-five years old and older, eviction was the main cause (Hayakawa 1990, 35–36).

"Many elderly patients are chronic sufferers, usually of more than one disease or ailment, and require long periods of hospitalization," says Otomo (1990, 23). Those patients severely test the three components for managing health care: access of services for the ill, the quality of services, and the level of costs. Special nursing homes are recommended for aged patients whose acute symptoms have stabilized but whose families are unable to provide necessary care.

In keeping with the general policy of turning over to the private sector some of the functions usually assumed by government (see chapter 1), the family, community, and private employers have been expected to assume primary responsibility for services for the needy elderly. The elderly in Japan are apt to support themselves economically, but with the decline of agricultural employment and the improvement in public pensions, the likelihood is dropping. The costs of governmental services will mount. Social expenditures took up 14 percent of the gross national product in 1983 and are expected to take up 27 percent in 2025 (Martin 1989, 6).

Until the 1970s Japan's social security program was primitive, but Jones (1988, 962–64) reports considerable improvement, especially with the Pension Reform Act of 1985. The social security tax rate, borne equally by employer and employee, will escalate sharply early in the next century, because of the retirement of the postwar baby boomers. Full-time workers will be a smaller proportion of the population and will bear a heavier burden of taxes.

Aging: Implications for the Elderly Inmates

Sociological research has focused on the relationships between, first, how the life course of individuals experiencing aging is influenced by the social structure and, second, the effects of changes in society on the social positions held by aging individuals.[2] In the two general respects, the elderly are vulnerable to the socioeconomic world they inhabit as citizens of Japan; the same can be said about the small minority of elderly who become prisoners. The prison system also is vulnerable to the conditions in the society, including the developments that send more elderly Japanese to prison.

Technologically advanced society promotes greater freedom from the limits of poverty, illness, and dominance by an autocracy, but that kind of society also gives a great share of its people a sense of powerlessness, greater illness, and the experience of confinement. Addressing the relationship between health and gerontology, Kiefer (1987, 89) describes what the Japanese call the "ugly decline" (*ben na kako*): "No advanced culture has yet resisted the power of technology to postpone death; yet none has found a way to guarantee freedom and dignity to even a sizeable minority of the resulting masses of disabled, frail, and terminally ill."

Medical advances have delayed death for many persons, but by bringing about an unprecedented number of elderly, they have also multiplied the number of disabled, frail, and terminally ill. Only some of the medically dependent are well cared for by families and have access to professional help, but, Kiefer declares, the "ugly decline" lies in the "injustice" that others do not. "Ugliness" stems from a value judgment that all the disabled, frail, and terminally ill among the elderly should benefit from medical advantages and available professional help. When the concept of "ugly decline" is extended to aged prisoners, the value judgment would brand, as intolerable penalization beyond punishment for their crimes, the failure to grant them the benefits of quality medical care.

The management of elderly prisoners can benefit from the conclusions of research on the elderly. Popular wisdom underestimates the individual plasticity of the aged. Since biological decline is not inevitable, healthy individuals defy the unexamined assumption that all older prisoners are frail and senile. However, many prisoners are drawn from the low-income segment of the population; many elderly reach the prison with a history of inadequate medical care because of a lack of medical accessibility and because of their own neglect of their physical well-being. The diversity in backgrounds and personalities of older inmates tends to be overlooked in classification and assignment to housing and work. The keepers' attitudes and actions influence the inmates' self-images, but perhaps the increasing number of senior prisoners will revise attitudes and official policy.[3]

In discussing old age in a changing society, Blau (1973, 210) uses the term *role exit*, which she defines as the ending of "any stable pattern of interaction and shared activities between two or more persons." The emotional and social costs of role exit are similar to those experienced after the death of a loved one; "bereavement is caused not only by the death itself but also by the termination of any enduring pattern of activity between one person and a significant other." As examples, she refers to widowhood or orphanhood after death of a role partner; desertion as a voluntary action by a role partner; and expulsion by a group, as in banishment or excommunication.

The imprisonment of a latecomer to crime qualifies as expulsion by groups: the elderly offender is officially labeled as a criminal and is also rejected as socially unworthy by the reference groups of great emotional and social importance to the offender. The loss of the concern and esteem of others—common to all versions of role exit—is aggravated by social rejection. For some latecomers, that double effect of role exit is supplemented even further: elderly persons entering prison for the first time become sharply aware of their emotional and social vulnerability to rejection by the community in general and to rejection by their particular intimate groups especially.

Demographic Impact on Corrections

Correctional agencies are susceptible to demographic changes, as they are to other major social trends in society at large. The increasing representation of the elderly in Japanese society already has been extended to the prisons, with important consequences. The absolute number of elderly prisoners will grow even without increase in the elderly persons' proclivity for crime and without change in criminal justice policy.

The age-groups are defined as sixty years old and older,

fifty through fifty-nine years, and eighteen through forty-nine years. Offenders less than eighteen years of age may be sentenced to prison, but their representation among admissions have become so few that eighteen years has become the appropriate lower age limit. The number of males less than eighteen years old and entering prisons declined from ninety-five in 1966 to nine in 1976, five in 1986, and one in 1994 (Research and Statistics Section 1971a, 1981a, 1991a, and 1995a). Retirement is set at age sixty in Japan, but some American researchers have included the ages fifty through fifty-nine among the elderly years. Those years of age sometimes present the physical and social attributes of the elderly. This chapter will treat the fifty to fifty-nine age-group as intermediate in qualities between the oldest and younger inmates.

Only males are considered in the following analysis, because elderly women are too few among prison admissions to support multivariable tabulations. The two sexes differ in characteristics of arriving inmates; limiting analysis to the much more numerous males avoids the distorting effect. The very limited number of elderly womens' admissions varied greatly and irregularly over the years, from a minimum of thirteen in 1974 to sixty-two in 1989 (Research and Statistics Section 1976a, 1990).

The conjunction of two statistics is represented by imprisonment rates. The numerator measures the number of convicted adults entering Japanese prisons, and the percentage distributions by age of the admitted males varies over the years (see table 7.2). The total number of male admissions has dropped over the years, but the men aged fifty to fifty-nine years and sixty years and over have become more numerous in the long term.

The analysis in this chapter is concerned most directly with the relative importance of the senior ages among the admissions. The variance over the years might be due to changes in the tendencies of the elderly Japanese to break the criminal law; in the policies of the police, public prose-

ELDERLY INMATES

Table 7.2
Male Admissions to Prison by Age, 1966–92

Year	No. of Male Admissions 18–49	50–59	60+	% Distribution 18–49	50–59	60+	Mean Age
1966	31,719	1,344	442	94.7	4.0	1.3	31.6
1967	28,050	1,233	408	94.5	4.1	1.4	31.6
1968	27,041	1,134	401	94.6	4.0	1.4	31.8
1969	24,921	983	298	95.1	3.8	1.1	31.5
1970	24,108	922	274	95.3	3.6	1.1	31.7
1971	25,403	953	315	95.2	3.6	1.2	31.7
1972	26,443	1,098	303	95.0	3.9	1.1	32.3
1973	24,360	1,226	318	94.8	4.0	1.2	32.8
1974	23,816	1,087	349	94.3	4.3	1.4	33.5
1975	24,027	1,275	354	93.6	5.0	1.4	34.2
1976	25,050	1,392	387	93.4	5.2	1.4	34.6
1977	25,272	1,383	409	93.4	5.1	1.5	35.0
1978	26,473	1,526	387	93.2	5.4	1.4	35.5
1979	26,060	1,750	427	92.3	6.2	1.5	36.1
1980	25,271	1,799	460	91.8	6.5	1.7	36.3
1981	26,592	2,232	514	90.6	7.6	1.8	36.8
1982	27,221	2,539	513	89.9	8.4	1.7	37.1
1983	26,280	2,725	560	88.9	9.2	1.9	37.4
1984	27,200	2,967	592	88.4	9.7	1.9	37.7
1985	26,404	3,220	668	87.2	10.6	2.2	38.0
1986	25,109	3,498	740	85.6	11.9	2.5	38.3
1987	24,252	3,507	693	85.2	12.3	2.5	38.5
1988	22,786	3,501	761	84.3	12.9	2.8	38.8

Table 7.2 cont. on next page

ELDERLY INMATES

Table 7.2 continued

Year	No. of Male Admissions 18–49	50–59	60+	% Distribution 18–49	50–59	60+	Mean Age
1989	19,596	3,181	787	83.2	13.5	3.3	39.1
1990	17,839	3,061	844	82.0	14.1	3.9	39.2
1991	16,627	2,789	753	82.5	13.8	3.7	39.1
1992	16,073	2,992	884	80.6	15.0	4.4	39.6

Sources: Research and Statistics Section 1971a, 1976a, 1981a, 1986a, 1991a, 1993a.

cutors, or sentencing judges; and in the evaluation of the Japanese public toward the elderly in general and toward aged offenders particularly.

The denominator of the imprisonment rate tells us the number of males in Japan from whom the arriving prisoners were drawn. Table 7.1 lists the total number of males (eighteen years old and older) in the Japanese population for each of the years. The percentage distributions show that men eighteen to forty-nine years old continue to be in the majority, but that the men over 49 years old have taken over greater proportions of the population. Men sixty years old and older held a 13.6 percent share in 1966 but a 21.2 percent share in 1992.

As I already noted, the size of the population is determined by the birthrates and death rates, with in-migration and out-migration exerting minor influence. Each age-cohort has experienced differently the changes in birthrates and death rates as the members of the cohort moved through the continuum of chronological ages. For example, men aged sixty or more years in 1966 would have been born in 1906 or earlier; their biography would have been influenced by the political and economic developments in Japanese society and the quality of health care in the early stages of Japan's modernization. At the opposite end of the age continuum, the eighteen-year-old cohort in 1966 would have been born in 1948 (after World War II) and would have grown up in the era of Japan's "economic miracle" and advances in medical care.

The adults aged eighteen to fifty years compose the majority of all male prisoners, as well as of all Japanese males. That age category conforms to the general trend for all Japanese prisoners: its members are entering prison at a declining rate per one hundred thousand Japanese males, from a rate of 131.6 in 1966 to 55.1 in 1992 (see table 7.1). The agegroup eighteen to forty-nine years produced the general upward trend. The two younger groups broke from the general trend. For the 1970–86 period, both of the older agegroups confirm our hypothesis that the older prisoners have increased imprisonment rates in contrast to the declining rate of the younger males.

For the intermediate group—males aged fifty to fifty-nine years—the imprisonment rates dropped from 32.2 per one hundred thousand males, ages fifty to fifty-nine, in 1966 to 22 in 1970. Thereafter, a climb toward higher rates was begun. The upward trend was roughly consistent until it culminated in a rate of 46.1 in 1986. Thereafter, the rates dropped to reach 36.9 in 1992. Chapter 8 will consider that recent decline. The men aged sixty years and over followed the trend for men ages fifty to fifty-nine years. Their imprisonment rates tended downward from 9.9 in 1966 to 5.5 in 1970, began an irregular climb to 9.5 in 1986, and dropped thereafter.

The greater gain of the oldest inmates in that regard has been due, at least in large part, to the high increase of their numbers in Japan's total male population. The greater value of the denominator would reduce the imprisonment rate. In that respect, table 7.1 reports the percentage distributions of the three age-groups in the population between 1966 and 1992. The men aged sixty years and over held 13.6 percent of the population in 1966 and 21.2 percent in 1992; in absolute numbers the increase was from 4,445,882 to 10,013,149, a percentage increase of 125. The increase for men aged fifty to fifty-nine years was from 4,174,417 to 8,100,428, a percentage increase of 94. The men aged eighteen to fifty years expanded their numbers from 32,726,047 to 47,307,375, a percentage increase of only 44.6.

Table 7.2 presents the absolute numbers of prison admissions for the three age-groups. The men aged sixty years and over trail the other two age-groups in these numbers. Men aged sixty years and over matched the men fifty to fifty-nine years of age in percentage increase of absolute numbers. The men aged eighteen to forty-nine years dropped from 31,719 in 1966 to 15,973 in 1992, a decrease rate of 49.6 percent. The two older groups again confirmed our hypothesis, but they had about the same percentage increase. Men aged sixty years and over numbered 442 in 1966 and 884 in 1992, an increase at a rate of 100 percent. The number of men aged fifty to fifty-nine years grew from 1,344 to 3,092, for an upsurge rate of 130 percent. In that way, both of the older age-groups deviated from the decline in prison admissions of the most numerous age-group, eighteen to forty-nine years.

Responsive Incarceration: The Interrelationship Between Two Population Trends

The association between the demographic trends and the greater number of elderly inmates is an example of responsive incarceration. Greater numbers are subject to criminal sanctions because of developments in Japanese society, not because of the increased criminality of cohort members or because of revised criminal policy. Since the process of criminalization is not relevant here, the increase in the elderly cohort is due to responsive incarceration.

The concept of responsive incarceration rests on the

conjunction of two trends sufficient to explain the greater number of elderly prisoners: change of the proportion of the elderly in Japanese society and change over the years of the proportion of the elderly among Japanese prisoners, probationers, and parolees. The increase in the number of elderly prisoners mirrors the increase in the number of elderly in society as a whole, without any increased tendency of the elderly to commit crimes. To test the hypothesis, data for the first trend is drawn from the demographic statistics published by the Statistics Bureau of the Management and Co-ordination Agency. For the second trend, annual reports of statistics on correction, published by the Research and Statistics Section of the Secretariat of the Ministry of Justice, trace prison admissions.

To test the association, Pearson product moment correlation coefficients (r) were computed for three male age-groups for 1970, 1975, 1980, 1985, 1990, and 1992. For the youngest group, the r value of 0.6732 is statistically significant at the 0.001 level (21 degrees of freedom). The negative value is consistent with the decline of the general imprisonment rates. Both of the other age-groups (ages fifty to fifty-nine years and sixty and over years) have very high and positive r values (0.9738 and 0.9746, respectively) that are statistically significant at less than the 0.001 level (21 degrees of freedom). The positive values are consistent with the hypothesis that elderly prisoners—whether aged fifty to fifty-nine years or sixty years and over—deviate from the general decline.

Population projections extend the past trends of birthrates and death rates into the future when predicting demographic trends.[4] The number of Japanese adult males is expected to peak in the year 2010 at 63,681,000 and to decline to 58,261,000 by 2035. Males fifteen to sixty-five years of age will begin a decline in absolute numbers as early as the year 2000. Males aged sixty-five years and over are expected to gain shares from 12.2 percent in 1995 to 23.3 percent in the year 2035, but their absolute numbers will peak at 13,971,000

ELDERLY INMATES

Table 7.3
*Estimates of Future Number of Men Aged
65 Years and Over Admitted to Prison*

	No. of Elderly Men (in 1000s)	Prison Admissions by Alternative Rates[a] Low (4.10%)	Medium (4.99%)	High (5.25%)
2010	11,814	484	589	620
2020	13,971	573	697	733
2030	13,458	552	671	706
2040	14,012	574	699	736
2050	13,374	548	667	702
2060	11,374	466	568	597
2070	10,774	442	538	566
2080	10,747	441	536	564
2090	9,864	404	492	518

Source: *Japan Statistical Yearbook, 1991* (41st ed.).

[a] The rates (number of males aged 65 years and over entering prisons per 100,000 in Japan's total male population) were selected by their size from the years 1985-92. The estimated absolute numbers were computed by multiplying the estimated total elderly males by each of the alternative imprisonment rates.

in 2020. The estimated number will fluctuate until 2040 and then join the general erosion of absolute numbers.

By accepting the association between changes in the number of elderly male Japanese and the number of elderly male inmates, we have a way to estimate crudely the number of men more than sixty-four years of age who will enter the prisons in the future (see table 7.3). We must deal with the group sixty-five years old and older—not those sixty years old and older, as in our other analyses—because the Statistics Bureau of the Management and Coordination Agency published predictions for that age-group.

The limitations of population predictions—estimates based on the continuation of known trends of the past—must be considered in their application. Unanticipated events can affect the efficacy of past death rates and birthrates as forecasts of the future rates on which population trends are forecast. Prediction of future prison admissions is even more hazardous, because new policies may affect the police and courts. Public opinion about crimes of the senior citizens may become less tolerant. Perhaps new conditions will generate greater incarceration of the deviant conduct of elders. Imprisonment rates are erratic after 1986 for the two groups of older inmates (see table 7.1). The upward trend may have bottomed out.

Demographers usually hedge against the imponderables of population predictions by postulating low, medium, and high levels of change in future population rates. In adopting that strategy, I offer choice among three rates of imprisonment for men sixty-five years old and older in the future. The lowest rate is 4.1 per one hundred thousand elderly men; that rate is applied to the estimated number of elderly Japanese for a modest prediction of prison admissions of men sixty-five years old and over (see table 7.3). The number is expected to meander from 484 in 2010 to 574 in the year 2040. Thereafter, the erosion of the number of elderly men in Japan will decrease their admissions to prison to 404 by the year 2090.

The medium estimate was chosen from 1992, when the imprisonment rate was 4.99 per one hundred thousand Japanese males. The number of expected admissions to prison is greater under this estimate—589 in 2010, rising to a maximum of 699 in 2040, and ending at 492 in the year 2090. The high estimate follows a rate per one hundred thousand population of 5.25 in 1986. The peak number, 736, is predicted for 2040, and the number drops thereafter to 518 for the year 2090.

By linking the demographic trends for Japanese males with prison admissions, the age-specific rates in table 7.1

credit adult males less than fifty years of age for the downward trend for general imprisonment rates. The drop in their rates is not completely consistent, but the general direction is down. The two older age-groups show general upward movement until peaking in 1986. Thereafter, they tend to stabilize, which raises uncertainty about their future course.

Variety among Elderly Prisoners

The aged have been popularly stereotyped as frail, passive, and dependent on others, despite their great variety. Rather recently has come wider recognition that they too are capable of crime and can become prisoners. "In all probability, since the numbers of older prisoners are so few and the problems of the correctional system so many," comments Rubenstein (1984, 153), "awareness and efforts would naturally gravitate to the general population." Although continuing to be a minority, the aged are gaining absolute numbers sufficiently to test the readiness of the administration to meet their unique needs.

The aged prisoners and their offenses defy simple categorization derived from any belief that they are unique in their differences from younger inmates. Case histories assembled by the Research and Training Institute illustrate their heterogeneity in personal characteristics and criminal incidents.

At age sixty-two years, an inmate was released after serving his fifteenth sentence for a series of crimes against property. The first sentence, at age twenty-one years, was for burglary. After a total of twelve years in prison, he became a construction laborer. Rain sharply reduced his income. Unmarried and without family contacts, he had no other financial resources, such as a pension. Invading an unlocked building, he stole clothing, a wallet, and other items with a total worth of 6,127 yen. He was arrested on the scene, and the loot was returned to the victim. He was sentenced to two and a half years.

Another sixty-two-year-old man had been granted suspended prison sentences at age twenty-five for fraud and at age thirty-one for theft. Married at age thirty-four years, he worked as an office clerk and had two sons and a daughter. When fifty-nine he was divorced because of his relationship with another woman. After the divorce he lived alone and became decadent. In 1990 he stole a shoulder bag from a man sleeping on a train. His one-year prison sentence was suspended with probation for three years. While under probationary supervision at a hostel, he was a construction laborer. He stole a vest worth 7,900 yen from a wholesale textile shop. The suspension for the previous crime was revoked, and he was imprisoned.

Since age forty years, the operator of a small construction business had been fined four times for drunk driving, speeding, and causing a traffic accident with his truck. He lost his driver's license but continued to drive his truck and became involved in another accident. Sentenced to a year in prison, he was granted a suspension for five years but again was arrested for driving without an operator's license. He was given three years plus a year for the earlier suspension.

A construction laborer had been fined for assault and battery at age thirty years and for aggravated assault and battery at age forty years. At age sixty-one years, he was drinking with fellow workers in a temporary construction shed. In a quarrel, a thirty-five-year-old man struck him in the face, and he stabbed the younger man in the stomach, causing a wound that required three months to heal. The victim acknowledged that he had provoked the violence and asked that severe punishment be withheld. The sentence was for a year in prison.

A man hospitalized frequently for pulmonary tuberculosis since age thirty-five years had never married, had irregular employment, relied chiefly on social security benefits, and had no previous criminal record. At age sixty-seven years, he entered a home for the elderly, where he fell in love with a sixty-one-year-old resident who rejected him for another resident. As she washed at a basin, he stabbed her in the neck and, pursuing her, cut her face. She died from loss of blood. He was sentenced to ten years in prison.

Particular Challenges the Elderly Present for Japanese Corrections

The Correction Bureau of Japan will be especially tested because, as the Research and Training Institute (1991, 39–41) attests, the representation of the elderly is remarkably high among Japanese prisoners. For comparison with Japan's situation, four European prison systems were selected for their long average life spans, high standard of living, advanced social welfare system, and aging population. Korea was added because of its location near Japan. The adult prisoners of Japan included 5 percent who were at least sixty years in age and 16.2 percent aged fifty to fifty-nine years. The respective percentages were 1.5 and 5 in Sweden, 1.3 and 6.3 in the Federal Republic of Germany, 1.2 and 4.6 in France, 1.2 and 5 in Korea, and 1.1 and 4 in the United Kingdom.

As elsewhere, Japanese agencies are accustomed to managing young and healthy individuals physically capable of industrial labor; persons in the terminal stage of life are not necessarily physically eligible. Japan is especially dedicated to the industrial prison; two-thirds of the inmates are in the workshops for forty hours a week. Among those elderly capable of work, most perform tasks in the cells, usually assembling paper shopping bags, but also working with metal or textile fabric. One-fifth of them are engaged in cooking, laundry, and similar maintenance of prison operations (Research and Training Institute 1991, 39).

To consider all elderly prisoners to be geriatric patients

is an example of stereotyping. Senility constitutes the loss of mental faculties and physical capacities as consequences of disease. Seniors come in a great variety, and for many aging is a natural process (senescence) free of the pathologies of disease. Some seniors are in prison for the first time. Those who have aged in prison are more likely to have pessimistic attitudes and expectations about their future when restored to the community.

The prison has the unique combination of obligations. It must protect society against aggressive criminals and also provide for the basic needs of prisoners as physical organisms and human beings. Whether considering aged people in society or in prisons, gerontologists debate whether they should be placed in housing for the elderly only or should be distributed throughout the general population. By housing older prisoners in isolation from the general population, medical services can be more cost-effective and available; diet, exercise, and recreation can be specialized; staff can be oriented to the unique needs of the elderly; and physical facilities can be designed for them.[5]

The responsibilities of care, as distinct from custodial or supervisory responsibilities, raise new demands on correctional agencies. Among the elderly offenders, there is an unusual proportion of probationers, prisoners, and parolees with chronic and serious disabilities. Lower-income individuals, from whom a great share of offenders are drawn, have lacked the economic means or motivation for early medical care. When eligible to be returned to the community, elderly inmates often lack family ties or families ready and willing to assume responsibility for their medical care.

The Research and Training Institute (1991, 39) describes the Correction Bureau's policy requiring each prison to consider carefully the characteristics of prisoners aged sixty years and over: "For example, they are given (1) six hours of prison work (in general ordinary prisoners are given eight hours a day), (2) light kinds of work because of their physical condition, (3) additional clothes, (4) regular medical examination for adult diseases, (5) light exercise such as gate ball [croquet] for advanced age, specific opportunities to watch TV, movies, and to attend consolatory events."

Prison Admissions: Age by Three Variables

What kinds of crimes are most characteristic of elderly Japanese prisoners? The sample drawn by the Research and Training Institute offers preliminary information. The sample of 1,024 prisoners (including fifty-six women) were at least sixty years of age when arriving at the prisons as of 1 August 1987. Of those in the sample, 89 percent had been convicted of theft (564), fraud (135), murder (97), stimulant drugs (80), and arson (32). A variety of other less frequent crimes were specified: robbery (36), traffic (14), bodily injury (12), embezzlement and breach of trust (8), indecent assault (7), rape and extortion (6 each), and housebreaking (5) (Research and Training Institute 1992b).

Questionnaires completed by 971 inmates provided information on recidivism. Only 134 (13.8 percent) were in prison for the first time; almost half were in for murder or arson. Senior prisoners are expected to have aged in prison (often because of a long sentence for a violent crime) or to be a serial inmate in and out of the correctional institutions over the years. The sample indicates that multiple incarceration is most common among elderly inmates in Japan: 20 percent had been imprisoned two through five times, 20.6 percent six through nine times, and 45.6 percent ten or more times. Persons with the most frequent stays in prison were serving terms for larceny-theft.

Statistics published by the Ministry of Justice sustain my analysis of the relationship between age at prison admission and three variables: crimes, length of sentence, and number of times in prison. The three relationships will be traced from 1970 to 1994 at five-year intervals. Admissions of men aged sixty years and over were 274 in 1970, 354 in 1975, 460 in 1980, 668 in 1985, 844 in 1990, and 1,113 in 1994.

Table 7.4 arrays the crimes of aged men admitted to prison according to their frequency in 1970. Larceny continues to be most common in subsequent years, despite a trend toward less frequency. Larceny is in a prominent position because of the variety of offenses against property under the general term: sneak theft from homes, offices, and automobiles; picking pockets; automobile and bicycle theft; shoplifting; stealing from shrines; and so on. Although not rivaling larceny in number of prison admissions, fraud also is an offense against property covering many circumstances applicable to elderly persons: failing to pay a restaurant or hotel bill, jumping a turnstile for a free subway ride, confidence trickery, swindles by pretending to borrow an item, and so on.

Arson is particularly feared in light of the light construction of the traditional residences in Japan. The elderly had a low and declining degree of involvement—only 8 of 150 admissions of men in 1970 and 11 of 191 in 1994.[6] In the Penal Code, the crime of arson includes the burning of both inhabited and uninhabited structures. Setting fire to an inhabited structure, or in a structure with persons present, could draw a life sentence or at least five years. Firing of an uninhabited structure could result in imprisonment for six months to seven years; if the structure belongs to the offender and is burned without endangering the public, punishment is not required.

Other property offenses hold only a minor place among admissions of elderly men. Intrusion moved from zero in 1970 to twenty-eight in 1994; the increase probably includes disputes as well as the thievery of housebreaking. The Penal Code defines housebreaking as intrusion "without good reason upon a human habitation or upon the premises, structure or vessel guarded by another, or [the act of a person] who refuses to leave such a place upon demand." Embezzlement and, especially, forgery have very few num-

Table 7.4
Distribution of Prison Admissions of Men Aged 60 Years and Over, 1970–94

Offenses[a]	\% Distribution					
	1970	1975	1980	1985	1990	1994
Larceny	49.6	55.4	48.5	45.8	46.7	44.4
Fraud	27.7	16.7	21.7	21.9	14.7	15.7
Homicide	4.4	2.6	4.3	3.9	3.7	3.9
Gambling	2.6	2.6	1.7	0.5	1.1	0.1
Bodily Injury	2.2	4.5	1.5	2.6	3.1	3.3
Forgery	1.8	0.8	1.3	0.8	0.9	0.4
Traffic	1.1	3.7	6.5	4.6	8.1	8.3
Embezzlement	1.1	3.1	0.9	1.3	1.4	1.2
Arson	1.1	0.8	1.3	1.8	0.7	0.9
Prostitution	1.1	0.6	0.2	—	—	0.4
Robbery	0.7	1.4	1.3	2.2	1.4	2.2
Sex[b]	0.7	0.8	1.1	1.2	1.2	0.9
Extortion	0.4	—	0.7	1.2	1.5	1.0
Drugs	—	1.4	4.6	7.5	10.3	11.6
Intrusion	—	1.4	0.7	1.2	2.0	2.5
Other Violent[c]	0.7	0.8	1.1	1.6	1.3	1.7
Other Property[d]	1.1	0.8	0.4	—	—	—
Other[e]	3.3	2.6	2.2	1.9	1.9	1.5
Total Violent	8.4	9.3	8.9	11.5	11.0	12.1
Total Property	82.5	79.1	74.8	72.8	66.5	44.4

Sources: Research and Statistics Section 1971a, 1976a, 1981a, 1986a, 1990, 1995a.

[a] Arrayed according to frequency in 1970.

[b] Rape and indecent assault.

[c] Assault; violations of the violence law; kidnapping; illegal possession of firearms and swords; or explosives; intimidation; prison escape; and riot.

[d] Counterfeiting and possession of stolen property.

[e] Pornography and violations of public order, other penal laws, and other special laws.

bers, suggesting low involvement of the elderly in serious commercial crimes except for fraud. The category of total property crimes assumes dimensions demonstrating the dominance of these offenses in prison admissions, but the dominance has been challenged, primarily by drug and traffic offenses.

Drug offenses sent few elderly men to prison in the 1970s, but they assumed increasing importance in later decades. None of the 274 elderly inmates in 1970 were imprisoned for drugs, but 129 of 1,113 were in 1994. The campaign against stimulant drugs has swept up the elderly as well as offenders in general. To a lesser degree, traffic offenses followed suit; there were 3 cases out of 274 in 1970 and 92 out of 1,113 in 1994. The upsurge in drug and traffic offenses has contributed in part to the proportional loss of larceny and fraud among prison admissions, but the elderly inmates fell far short of the nonelderly inmates in that respect.

The crimes of rape and indecent assault are frequently linked with senility among the aged, but only 2 of the 274 admissions of elderly men in 1970 and 11 of the 1,113 admissions in 1994 were for those offenses. Another crime related to sex—prostitution—brought three seniors to prison in 1970 and five in 1994. Violations of the Antiprostitution Law are mostly for management of illicit sex operations; elderly men are unlikely to be imprisoned for this offense. Gambling and lottery crimes also are associated with organized crime, and admissions of the elderly for this offense have declined.

Total violence crimes moved from 8.4 percent of 1970 elderly admissions to 12.1 percent in 1994. More admissions for bodily injury and robbery account for the minimum gain. Homicide is the most expected of elderly crimes of violence; there were twelve cases in 1970 and forty-four in 1994, for a small decline in the proportions among all elderly offenses. The aggression of bodily injury recorded a modest percentage increase, from six admissions in 1970 to thirty-seven in 1994. Robbery increased from only two admissions in 1970 to twenty-four in 1994.

Compared with the admissions of younger adults, are the elderly becoming more prevalent among Japanese prisoners? How are any relative gains distributed among the major offenses? To answer these questions, I compare the prison admissions by crimes of senior inmates with the admissions of men aged eighteen to forty-nine years, the number of elderly per one hundred men aged eighteen to forty-nine years. The figures in table 7.5 are the percentages held by the oldest prisoners relative to the admissions of nonelderly prisoners. I have dropped from the comparison the "intermediate" age-groups—the men aged fifty to fifty-nine years.

Over the course of the five-year periods, the elderly have narrowed their numerical disadvantage to the younger men, from 1.14 percent in 1970 to 7.05 percent in 1994. Yet the senior inmates continue to be much less numerous than the younger age-group: despite their gain, in 1994 there were only seven elderly men entering the prisons for every one hundred men aged eighteen to forty-nine years.

The comparisons by crime should be regarded with caution when only a small absolute number of admissions is involved. For example, for senior admissions for embezzlement only 1.09 percent per one hundred men aged eighteen to forty-nine years in 1970 rose tenfold to 10.57 in 1994. The increase alerts us to an erosion of the younger group's dominance of the offense, but the small absolute numbers undermine the long-term reliability of the comparison. As table 7.4 implies, the absolute numbers of the seniors were only 3 of 274 admissions in 1970 and 13 of 1,113 admissions in 1994.

The representation of the elderly among all property offenses increased by six and a half times in the twenty-four years, but larceny and fraud (in the majority among property offenses) were sufficient to account for that trend. Both

Table 7.5
Number of Men Aged 60 Years and Over per 100
Men Aged 18–49 Admitted to Prison, 1970–94

Offenses[a]	Ratios					
	1970	1975	1980	1985	1990	1994
Larceny	1.51	2.39	3.20	4.49	8.61	11.38
Fraud	5.04	3.75	7.04	9.26	14.40	21.26
Homicide	1.84	1.51	3.58	4.50	8.73	15.44
Gambling	1.35	2.73	4.49	1.87	9.78	1.96
Bodily Injury	0.27	0.71	0.35	0.84	1.76	3.18
Forgery	2.08	1.27	3.35	2.92	9.09	5.40
Traffic	0.10	0.34	0.83	0.97	3.13	6.06
Embezzlement	1.09	4.82	1.80	4.09	10.91	10.57
Arson	2.11	1.99	3.08	5.74	4.11	6.58
Prostitution	5.00	5.13	1.82	—	—	9.09
Robbery	0.26	0.73	1.15	2.74	2.22	4.47
Sex[b]	0.15	0.28	0.80	1.54	2.18	2.16
Extortion	0.08	—	0.29	0.71	1.60	1.88
Drugs	—	0.31	0.37	0.70	1.92	3.18
Intrusion	—	3.31	1.41	5.37	15.04	27.45
Other Violent[c]	0.19	0.15	0.39	0.97	1.38	2.92
Other Property[d]	3.09	6.25	10.52	—	—	—
Other[e]	2.42	1.91	1.81	1.82	2.07	2.22
Total	1.14	1.47	1.82	2.53	4.73	7.05
Total Violent	0.38	0.54	0.76	1.42	2.46	4.19
Total Property	1.98	2.65	3.74	5.31	9.50	12.87

Sources: Research and Statistics Section 1971a, 1976a, 1981a, 1986a, 1990a, 1995a.

[a] Arrayed according to frequency in 1970.

[b] Rape and indecent assault.

[c] Assault, violations of the violence law; kidnapping; illegal possession of firearms and swords; or explosives; intimidation; prison escape; and riot.

[d] Counterfeiting and possession of stolen property.

[e] Pornography and violations of public order, other penal laws, and other special laws.

offenses cover a wide variety of prohibited acts. The aged have gained on the men aged eighteen to forty-nine years in admissions for intrusion and embezzlement, but the absolute numbers are insufficient for display of a convincing development.

Total violent crimes drew fewer admissions of aged offenders than did crimes against property, but the representation of the elderly definitely rose over the decades, mostly because of homicide, a violent crime expected of the aged offenders. To a lesser degree, robbery and bodily injury showed similar gains.

Officials report that elderly persons are becoming more and more responsible for the traffic crisis reported in chapter 4. "It is assumed that the elderly are having more and more opportunities to move about," reports the Traffic Safety Policy Office (1992, 17), "as a result of the increase in their employment, participation in social activities, and more time for outings.... With the progress in motorization, the traffic behavior of the elderly has also diversified." There were 830,000 driver's license holders over sixty-four years of age in 1979 and 3.16 million in 1991. The Traffic Safety Policy Office notes that although the elderly drivers continue to be a minority, their numbers have increased by two and a half times in a dozen years.

A greater number of senior drivers have been responsible for fatal accidents. The "first party" in accidents bears the greatest liability or has been found to have suffered the least damage where the degree of negligence is equal. The "second party" bears the lesser liability or has been found to suffer the greater damage where the degree of negligence is equal. Instances of first-party responsibility of elderly drivers were 342 in 1979 and rose consistently to 1,074 in 1991. Second-party events were more common; they increased from 1,256 in 1979 to 1,784 in 1991. The proportions of first parties in all instances of the elderly's responsibility moved from 21.4 percent in 1979 to 37.6 percent in 1991 (Traffic Safety Policy Office 1992, 27).

Traffic and drug offenses color especially the admissions of younger adults, but they also increasingly bring the elderly to Japanese prisons. The same pattern exists for rape and indecent assault, but to a lesser extent. The elderly have gained shares for gambling and lotteries and for prostitution, but the trends have been spotty and due primarily to the small number of admissions.

Medical Care and the Aged Inmates

Five medical facilities serve adult prisoners: Hachiojo Medical Prison, Jono Medical Prison in Kitakyushu City, Okazaki Medical Prison, Kikuchi Medical Branch Prison, and Osaka Medical Branch Prison. Hachiojo and Osaka receive both the physically and mentally ill. Jono and Okazaki deal exclusively with mental disorders. Kikuchi specializes in leprosy; at present no inmates suffer leprosy. To deliver medical services to adult prisoners, the Correction Bureau employs 226 physicians, 35 pharmacists, 36 technicians, 16 dietitians, and 216 nurses. In Japanese society and the prisons, the number of persons suffering from hypertension, diabetes, or malignant neoplasm has been increasing gradually. Because of the "habitual unhealthy life in society" of some inmates, tuberculosis (TB) remains a problem in prisons (Iwahori 1988, 1).

As in Japan, American prisons are vulnerable to outbreaks of TB, HIV/AIDS, hepatitis B and C, syphilis, and other sexually transmitted diseases. Tuberculosis was headed for eradication in the United States until the 1980s. The resurgence has been explained as interrelated with HIV infection, drug abuse, poverty, homelessness, poor access to health care, the dismantling of TB control programs, and drug-resistant TB. Hammett and Harrold (1994, 2–3) describe prisons and jails as high-risk settings, especially when crowded and poorly ventilated.[7] "Moreover, many inmates already have elevated risk for TB," they say, "be-

ELDERLY INMATES

Table 7.6
Hospitalizations of Male Prisoners, 1987–94

		Ages of Hospitalized Males			
Year	Total Males	18–49	50–59	60–69	70+
1987					
No.	10,772	8,486	1,727	424	135
Rate	24.46	23.20	28.65	35.13	63.68
1989					
No.	10,304	7,824	1,788	524	168
Rate	25.20	23.58	29.78	35.40	71.19
1991					
No.	9,159	6,732	1,655	622	150
Rate	25.31	23.65	28.32	37.79	61.98
1993					
No.	11,188	8,269	1,993	765	161
Rate	31.39	30.44	32.51	37.19	55.14
1994					
No.	8,725	6,041	1,766	734	184
Rate	24.35	22.53	27.32	33.18	55.09

Sources: Research and Statistics Section 1988, 1990, 1993a, 1994a, 1995a.

Note: The rates equal the number of hospital referrals per 100 inmates of given ages at year-end.

cause of their lifestyles, inadequate prior health care, and increased prevalence of HIV/AIDS." They note that TB rates are higher for prisoners with frequent incarceration and longer total time in prison.

The relative demand of aged prisoners for medical services generates referrals to prison hospitals. Table 7.6 includes referrals to hospitals in the free community when exceptional surgical problems exceed the resources of the prisons. The age-specific rates per one hundred male inmates rise consistently with age. The men aged sixty to sixty-nine years enter hospitals more frequently than men in younger age-groups. Men in the most advanced ages are much more apt to require elaborate medical services, even more frequently than men aged sixty to sixty-nine years. The incidence of illness and other medical crises is subject to such a variety of factors that reliable general trends over the years cannot be expected; the comparatively few inmates in elderly ages tend to aggravate the fluctuation of hospitalization rates.

Hospitalization for diseases of the circulatory organs and for tumors were more prevalent for the most advanced age. Men in their fifties were especially vulnerable to ailments of the digestive system and glandular disorders. The younger men were inclined toward diseases of the respiratory system. Cases of injury, poisoning, or mental disorder were few, but the men aged less than fifty years were most prone to those incidents.

Inspection of Osaka Medical Branch Prison revealed peculiar problems associated with care of the ailing elderly. Within the capacity for 191 patients, fifty-five beds are for the physically ill. The illness frequently requires protracted hospitalization; otherwise their physical condition will deteriorate, and surgery is not always appropriate. Patients serving longer sentences, especially those suffering cancer, take up more and more of the available bed space.

Patients are released on expiration of sentence, not when they have recovered from disease. As elsewhere, prison physicians have difficulties in referring them to community hospitals, which are reluctant to mingle former prisoners with regular patients. Prison hospitals receive ill inmates from all parts of Japan. Hospitals adjacent to the prison medical facilities are concerned that released patients will be concentrated in their wards. Elderly patients are especially unlikely to have relatives able or willing to care for them. In the event of a terminal illness, the public prosecutor is asked to arrange suspension of the prison sentence on basis of a medical certification that the patient is physically unable to complete the sentence, the family's financial capability and willingness to provide care, and acceptance of the inmate by a community hospital.

A Unit Specializing in the Elderly

In the Hiroshima Correction Region, Onomichi Branch Prison[8] received a few elderly from the Kure Branch Detention Center when it was renovated. Onomichi thereafter became the only contemporary prison in Japan serving the elderly as a major function. When elderly are admitted to prison, the detention centers in the region refer them to Onomichi. When other prisoners become elderly and difficult to manage, referrals to Onomichi must be authorized by the Hiroshima Region Headquarters. The seniors are assuming a greater share of the unit's population, 18 percent in 1985 and 28 percent in 1992. At the time of my November 1992 visit, 49 elderly were among the 113 inmates present. The elderly manufacture carpet slippers, tatami cushions, and paper shopping bags.

The present plant is overcrowded and obsolete; I was shown an architect's model for the proposed renovation of the branch prison. The plan calls for three sections: one for the elderly, one for other inmates, and one for pretrial detention. The section for the elderly will have a recreation area and living area on the second floor; the first floor will have the workshop, kitchen, and dining room. The elderly will be able to exercise on a porch without leaving the section. It was debated whether the elderly should be merged with younger inmates or should be separated in their own facility. It was decided to raise Onomichi's capacity for aged inmates from fifty to seventy and ultimately to one hundred.

A physician and two male paramedical nurses serve the

branch. A dentist comes twice a month. The branch has an X-ray machine, an electrocardiograph, and dental equipment. For serious medical problems, the inmates are sent to a community hospital. On admission to the branch, they are given a medical examination, and blood pressures are checked every four weeks. Some 90 percent of the elderly inmates require medication, creating a serious budgetary problem. Japanese prisons usually are unheated, except by kerosene heaters on especially frigid days. The frail elderly need additional clothing and are furnished a *yutampo*, a metal "hot water bottle" that is used to keep the feet warm in ordinary houses. The elderly inmates hold the device to their chest while asleep.

The elderly raise particular problems as inmates, the Onomichi staff said. The staff reported "stubbornness" in relationships with other persons. The elderly are apt to quarrel with one another and to "talk back" to staff but are not inclined toward physical violence. They move more slowly and need longer time for work tasks. Often there are no family ties that would meet their needs if paroled. Rehabilitation aid hostels are reluctant to accept them because of their unusual medical needs. Six of the forty-nine elderly at Onomichi were serving life sentences; one had been imprisoned for thirty-six years for murder. Two-thirds of them were recidivists, usually for a series of property offenses.

Relevancy of the Increase in the Aged for Community Corrections

Elderly probationers and parolees have been increasing in recent years despite the long-term decline in caseloads generally. The admissions to adult parole per one hundred thousand Japanese caseloads declined from 95.4 in 1950 to 13.2 in 1993. Parolees aged sixty years and older numbered 337 in 1984 (0.4 per one hundred thousand Japanese) and 564 in 1993 (0.6). The rates for adult probation admissions per one hundred thousand Japanese rose from 0.5 in 1950 to 115.2 in 1960 and thereafter dropped to 5.2 by 1993. Aged probationers numbered 85 (0.1 per one hundred thousand Japanese) in 1984 and 109 (0.11) in 1993 (Shikita and Tsuchiya 1990, 174; Research and Training Institute 1985, 114; 1994, 81).

The numbers and rates for the seniors are in low magnitude, especially for probation. As the number of elderly offenders are added to caseloads, the necessity to revise familiar practices for community corrections will be more apparent.

In Japan the prison warden, not the inmate, files an application with the regional parole board (RPB). Some 95 percent of the applications are approved; the remainder are either denied by the RPB or withdrawn by the warden because of the inmate's new rule violations. The elderly and the nonelderly had about the same approval rate in 1993, but the elderly had to survive a greater number of denials of applications (4.5 denials versus 2.5 average appearances before the board) before the final approval (Research and Statistics Section 1994b, 26–29).

The senior inmates collectively were slightly more likely than the younger prisoners to have avoided any contact with the criminal justice system before their current sentence, but those who had been involved in previous cases were more likely to have been served at least one previous prison sentence. Many of the nonelderly prisoners receiving a parole in 1993 had experienced previous imprisonment (47 percent of them versus 61.7 percent of the senior-aged parolees), but the nonelderly exceeded the elderly in having been granted a suspended prison sentence or a fine for a previous offense. The younger the parolees, the less the percentage who had served an earlier prison sentence (Research and Statistics Section 1994c, 90).

All offenders beginning adult probation in 1993 had fewer court appearances than parolees. The policy of judges makes that difference. Only 47.2 percent of the elderly probationers (versus 61.7 percent of the elderly parolees) had previously been in prison. Sixteen percent of the older probationers and 35 percent of the younger men and women had avoided previous contact with criminal justice agencies. Fines and suspended sentences were more characteristic of the nonelderly (Research and Statistics Section 1994c, 90).

Supervision of probationers and parolees is largely the responsibility of unsalaried volunteer probation officers (VPOs). The active participation of VPOs in supervision is consistent with the principles of community corrections, but the increased prevalence of aged probationers and parolees has raised questions about the effectiveness of VPOs. The increased prevalence is a derivative of the community undergoing change. As I already noted, the proportion of the elderly in society is matched with the proportion of elderly in prisons and in the community programs of probation and parole. In matching those two elements, responsive incarceration raises questions about the policy of relying heavily on VPOs.

The advanced age of probationers and parolees raises demands on the style and quality of case supervision. The characteristics of aged prisoners complicates the employment-residence plan, especially for long-term prisoners who face intensive changes in the community they hope to rejoin. The past lifestyle of habitual offenders and the effects of violent crimes have unraveled the ties with family that, in the past, were considered the fundamental basis for successful reentry into the community. When the elderly prisoner requires intensive medical care, community agencies are especially reluctant to invest personnel and financial resources in a convicted criminal.

The rehabilitation aid associations, private organizations partially subsidized by the Rehabilitation Bureau, operate hostels expected to fill the vacuum in services when the family is not available. The volunteers attempt to mobilize the needed resources. The elderly made up 3.2 percent of parolees in 1993 and 14 percent of the parolees entering hostels. Convicted offenders granted suspension of sentences included 2.2 percent aged sixty or more years and 11.7 percent of those admitted to hostels. The difficulties faced by the elderly is further indicated by the length of stay in the hostels before finding a more stable place in the community. Whereas the nonelderly parolees averaged a stay of fifty-two days, the elderly spent sixty days. Of those with suspended sentences, the elderly were there for 32.3 days and the nonelderly for 24 days.

8

Deviation from Deviation: A Personal Comment

Japan is reluctant to choose imprisonment as a major response to criminality, whereas major industrialized nations of the West confine a large share of their convicted criminals. That difference invites objective inquiry and, in large measure, gave me a strong interest in seizing the opportunity to study the operations of the Correction Bureau and the Rehabilitation Bureau.[1]

In the course of the research, I discovered that certain subpopulations of prisoners—I have called them "cohorts"—had become more numerous while the total number of prisoners were having lower annual rates per one hundred thousand Japanese. These unanticipated exceptions constituted a discovery worthy of examination in its own terms. This book has taken up, in turn, six cohorts: offenders among the yakuza, women offenders, adult traffic offenders, traffic and drug offenders among juveniles, foreign offenders, and elderly offenders.

Analysis of the six cohorts revealed another unanticipated trend; in recent years, four of the six cohorts have abandoned their deviation from the general decline in the resort to imprisonment. This final chapter has been assigned the task of explaining this deviation from the previous deviation. First, the background for a tentative explanation will be developed.

Criminalization and Marginal Deviance

The concept of criminalization appeared to be a promising means of explaining the unanticipated increase in prison admissions for certain cohorts. "Traditional crimes," such as homicide and larceny, have been defined by penal codes for a very long time. Through criminalization, "new crimes" are added—or the definition of "old crimes" broadened—to extend the authority of the police and courts and to increase the flow of convicted defendants to correctional agencies. Foreigners and the elderly are exceptional; referring to the creation of new crimes or new criminal justice policy is not necessary to explain the growth of their numbers as prisoners.

The cohorts are members of a larger group of "marginal deviants" enjoying public tolerance, although their typical behavior stands between that of complete conformists and flagrant rejectors of the dominant sociocultural norms. Selected members of the group have been exposed to the criminal law because they personify a public issue in the opinion of a political constituency.

Responsive Incarceration: Sensitivity to Society's Trends

Foreigners and elderly Japanese have become more numerous in prisons. Perhaps the two cohorts will engage in new crimes in the future or will become more active in their characteristic crimes. Perhaps the police, public prosecutors, and judges will adopt a more stern policy in disposing of the cases of elderly defendants. Either possibility could cause an increase in the number of prison admissions for these cohorts. But even without such changes, the expansion of the number of foreigners and elderly Japanese in the society has already added to the number of prisoners.

In 1983 foreign inmates constituted 3.35 percent of all

prisoners present at the end of the year; in 1994 they held a 4.19 percent share (see table 6.1). The elderly Japanese also are a minority compared with the number of younger prisoners, but their imprisonment rate per one hundred thousand males aged sixty years and over rose from 5.5 in 1970 to 9.5 in 1986 (see table 7.1). Meanwhile, the imprisonment rate for males aged eighteen to forty-nine years dropped from 91.2 in 1970 to 88.2 in 1986. The two opposing trends are increasing the representation of the elderly among prisoners to a remarkable extent.

Accelerated Criminalization: The Yakuza

Criminalization of organized crime is not a new development in Japan, but new legislation gave the police, public prosecutors, and courts greater possibility of at least curbing its excesses. The Diet took action with unprecedented enthusiasm in response to new aspects of the syndicates' operations. Gangs were being consolidated into nationwide "families," and intergang violence had surged. In the search for illicit income, the gangs were preying on legitimate businesses beyond the scope of delivering those illegal goods and services that have been in public demand. Yakuza traditions had placed limits on the gangsters conduct that earned them a modicum of public respect and even admiration, but the traditions have lost much moral influence.

Earlier legislation had been directed against the intimidation of witnesses and against unlawful assembly with dangerous weapons for the purpose of killing or injuring other persons. In 1991 the Diet authorized the definition of yakuza gangs as antisocial organizations. Public safety commissions were authorized to assist victims, to prevent intergang violence, to obstruct gang recruitment, to encourage the resignation of gang members, and generally to facilitate community opposition to the yakuza.

DEVIATION FROM DEVIATION

Table 8.1
Public Prosecutors' Dispositions of Yakuza Cases, 1983–93

Year	Total Cases	% Distribution of Dispositions by Public Prosecutors			
		Prosecution	Formal Trial	Non-prosecution	Prosecution Suspended
1983	16,706	84.7	(62.5)	15.3	(9.6)
1984	17,930	84.5	(61.3)	15.5	(9.6)
1986	16,569	84.0	(63.7)	16.0	(10.0)
1987	16,681	82.2	(63.9)	17.8	(11.6)
1988	16,430	81.2	(62.5)	18.8	(12.1)
1989	13,523	83.0	(62.6)	17.0	(10.4)
1990	12,506	81.0	(60.8)	19.0	(11.4)
1991	12,471	81.3	(61.8)	18.7	(11.3)
1992	12,140	77.2	(57.6)	22.8	(15.0)
1993	10,916	75.0	(52.8)	25.0	(15.5)

Sources: Research and Training Institute 1984, 48; 1985, 53; 1987, 69; 1988, 72; 1989, 79; 1990a, 66; 1991, 75; 1992a, 69; 1993, 57; 1994, 92.

Note: Statistics were not available for 1985.

Gangsters' share of total admissions to prison escalated from 16.4 percent in 1970 to 27.4 percent in 1988 (see table 2.1). Their shares of class-B prisoners (evaluated as the least promising inmates) have been even greater, rising from 28.2 percent in 1975 to 45 percent in 1989; over 90 percent of the gangster-inmates have been relegated to class-B status (see table 2.2). Gangster-inmates have recorded increasing imprisonment rates per one hundred thousand adult males from 12.32 in 1970 to 14.38 in 1989, while the nonyakuza rates dropped from 62.92 in 1970 to 39.74 in 1989 (see table 2.1). Since 1989 the gangsters have lost their percentage share of prison admissions; the share declined from 27.4

percent in 1989 to 18.8 percent in 1994. Their rates per one hundred thousand adult males dropped from 18.26 in 1987 to 8.19 in 1994, while the male nonyakuza inmates followed suit less drastically, their rates dropping from 48.78 in 1987 to 35.48 in 1994.

The authority of the public prosecutors is among the possible explanations for the changes in flow of gangsters into Japanese prisons. The defendant may be given outright release or may be sent to summary courts, where fines are the usual reaction. Referrals to district courts almost inevitably result in conviction; the judge may suspend a prison sentence and either release the convicted offenders or place them on probation.

As of 1989 the public prosecutors decided fewer cases (see table 8.1); the police referred fewer gangsters to the public prosecutors. In addition, the public prosecutors decided that a greater proportion of the cases should not be prosecuted; those suspects were released into the community. Furthermore, decisions to prosecute include referrals to summary courts that avoided the possibility of imprisonment. Thus, the referrals for formal trial in district courts dropped from 63.9 percent of the dispositions in 1987 to 52.8 percent in 1993. The recent net result has been fewer gangsters entering prison.

The trend also mirrors a redistribution of the offenses for which the yakuza are being imprisoned. Table 8.2 lists only those offenses reported in the *Summary of the White Paper on Crime*, published in English by the Research and Training Institute from the more voluminous *White Paper on Crime*, published in Japanese. Only the few convictions for illegal operation of horse-race gambling scored an increase in absolute number of imprisonments in 1992 over 1983. The Stimulant Drug Control Law continued to be the chief basis for imprisonment, but the absolute number of those gangsters dropped by a third. Crimes intimately related to the gangsters also lost shares: extortion by 57.2 percent, gambling and lottery by 50.7 percent, and violation of the Bicycle Race Law by 20.1 percent. Illicit trade in commercialized sex resulted in few cases, but they had a 21.5 percent increase in absolute numbers.

The laws intended to control the yakuza imprisoned fewer gangsters. In 1958 the crime of unlawful assembly with dangerous weapons was added to the Penal Code and heavier penalties were added to the Firearms and Swords Control Ordinance. In 1964 an amendment to the Law for Punishment of Acts of Violence added the aggravated crime of bodily injury committed with firearms and swords and stiffened penalties for habitual crimes of violence (Shikita and Tsuchiya 1990, 81). Imprisonment for unlawful assembly declined by 79.5 percent, for violent acts by 44.4 percent, and for possession of firearms and swords by 35.4 percent.

Extended Criminalization: Three Cohorts

In addition to the yakuza, three other cohorts have been selected for penalization as criminals from larger groups occupying the marginal position between full-fledged conformity and outright rejection of conventional Japanese norms. The three cohorts are adult traffic offenders, women drug offenders, and juveniles identified with either traffic or drug offenses. They have been exposed to extended criminalization, which involves increasing the responsibilities of the police, strengthening the courts' sentencing authority, and adding to the flow of convicted traffic offenders to the correctional agencies.

Adult traffic offenses. Usually, the violators of traffic laws are tolerated as minor rulebreakers and may be admired for risk taking in driving maneuvers. As realization of a serious traffic crisis widened, criminalization targeted the most flagrant of marginal deviants. Earlier laws were replaced by the Road Traffic Control Law in 1948; that law was replaced in turn by the contemporary Road Traffic Law in 1960. The latter has been further revised.

Table 8.2
Public Prosecutors' Referrals of Yakuza Defendants
for Formal Trial, 1983 and 1992 Compared

	1983 Decisions			1992 Decisions			% Change[b]
		Sent to Trial			Sent to Trial		
Offenses	No. of Cases (A)	No.	%[a]	No. Cases (B)	No.	%[a]	
Stimulant Drug	3,771	3,419	90.7	2,513	2,121	84.4	−33.4
Bodily Injury	3,058	1,594	52.1	2,240	1,168	52.1	−26.7
Extortion	1,825	1,285	70.4	1,336	781	58.5	−57.2
Violent	1,388	561	40.4	771	303	39.3	−44.4
Firearms, Swords	910	653	71.8	588	396	67.3	−35.4
Gambling, Lottery	891	435	48.8	439	201	45.8	−50.7
Assault	712	117	16.4	467	111	23.8	−34.4

Table 8.2 cont. on next page

Table 8.2 continued

| | 1983 Decisions | | | 1992 Decisions | | | |
| | | Sent to Trial | | | Sent to Trial | | |
Offenses	No. of Cases (A)	No.	%[a]	No. Cases (B)	No.	%[a]	% Change[b]
Larceny	487	373	76.6	412	304	73.8	−15.4
Homicide	232	206	88.8	66	51	77.3	−71.5
Horse Racing	226	187	82.7	236	184	78.0	4.4
Bicycle Racing	129	105	81.4	103	78	75.7	−20.1
Unlawful Assembly	117	74	63.2	24	10	41.7	−79.5
Prostitution	65	35	53.8	79	42	53.2	−21.5

Sources: Research and Training Institute 1984, 48; 1993, 57.
[a] Equals number of referrals for formal trial divided by number of cases.
[b] Equals A minus B and divided by A.

For traffic offenses in general, the increase in the number of male admissions to prison survived only until 1972 (see table 4.2). When prison admissions for professional negligence are distinguished from the Road Traffic Law, we find that the Road Traffic Law was sending more men to prison until 1982 (see table 4.3). The rates per one hundred thousand followed suit from 1969 to 1981; thereafter, admissions declined rather consistently. The deviation from the deviation occurred.

Women drug offenses. As in other countries, women prisoners in Japan are a small fraction of all prisoners, but that share has increased significantly (see tables 3.1 and 3.2). More to the immediate point here, that development has been largely due to a remarkable upsurge in the representation of stimulant drug convicts among admissions to women's prisons (see tables 3.3 and 3.4). The absolute numbers of the drug admissions to women's prisons began their strong upsurge in 1977 and reached their peak in 1985.

Several aspects of that trend should be noted. First, the impact of that upsurge first struck the women's prisons in 1977; the absolute numbers escalated until 1985, then receded while holding to high numbers (see table 3.3). Second, the men also experienced increased admissions of drug offenders, but the admissions to women's prisons drew proportionately more drug offenders. Table 3.5 matches high ratios for women with the great absolute number of drug admissions. Third, the image of public crisis had brought drug abuse to the fore of public concerns. Laws had been modified in the style of extended criminalization, but the rise of prison admissions of women drug offenders came later through a change in public policy. The policy change drew on linkages between (a) the public identification of stimulant drugs with individual and social pathology and (b) the general belief that female drug offenders are especially evil in their rejection of "proper" feminine roles.

As table 8.3 documents, the police have sent progres-

DEVIATION FROM DEVIATION

Table 8.3
Police Referrals to Public Prosecutors of Female Drug Defendants among Female Special-Law Defendants, 1979–91

Year	Total Special-Law Referrals	Drug Referrals No.	%[a]	% of Referrals Stimulants	Organic Solvents
1979	27,003	6,178	22.9	48.9	51.1
1980	27,610	7,364	26.7	42.1	57.9
1981	21,021	7,644	36.4	47.0	53.0
1982	20,520	8,533	41.6	44.2	55.8
1983	28,501	9,672	33.9	41.1	58.9
1984	24,591	10,141	41.2	42.1	57.9
1985	18,960	9,697	51.3	42.6	57.4
1986	20,404	8,890	43.6	40.0	60.0
1987	22,424	9,656	43.1	36.9	63.1
1988	17,821	11,017	61.8	30.4	69.6
1989	16,707	10,590	63.4	26.9	73.1
1990	18,284	11,272	61.6	23.6	76.4
1991	18,686	10,813	57.9	26.2	73.8

Sources: Research and Training Institute 1984, 55; 1985, 77; 1990a, 110; 1992a, 89.

[a] Equals total female drug referrals divided by total female special-law referrals.

sively fewer women to the public prosecutors for violations of the special laws.[2] The decline has been irregular and most marked after 1987. The total drug referrals by the police coincided with my proposition that cohorts increase their representation among prisoners despite the decline of the general imprisonment rate. The referrals of all drug suspects among women have increased rather consistently from 6,178 in 1979 to 10,813 in 1991. The pace exceeded that of referrals of all special-law referrals of women; the percentage share devoted to drug offenders rose from 22.9 percent in 1979 to 57.9 percent in 1991. That increase occurred despite the decreasing importance of stimulant drugs among total drug referrals. In 1979 the stimulant drug cases held 48.9 percent of all drug referrals by the police. By 1991 the share had dipped to 26.2 percent. The police referrals for organic solvent offenses were responsible for the general gain of total drug cases; in 1979 their share was 51.1 percent; by 1991 their share had reached 73.8 percent.

Juvenile traffic and drug offenses. Both a traffic crisis and an illicit-drug crisis have had major effect on admissions to juvenile training schools and juvenile probation. In absolute number of admissions, the traffic crisis first struck the juvenile training schools in 1971, peaked in 1985, and remained high thereafter (see table 5.1). The drug crisis first brought hundreds of juveniles to the training schools in 1978, reached a high in 1984, and continued a high level in subsequent years.

The dispositions of the family courts, of course, have significant effect on the flow of juveniles into the training schools. The juvenile training school referrals of traffic offenders rose quantitatively from 1980 to 1985, in opposition to the usual dip in incarceration. From 1985 the traffic referrals joined the usual decline. Referrals of all drug offenders were more ambivalent in pattern but did drop from 1982 through 1987 and then moved upward.

Admissions of traffic offenders to juvenile probation have been drastically increased—especially for the Road Traffic Law cases—by a special program. The surfacing of organic solvent abuse is noteworthy. The juvenile justice system expresses special concern for the ultimate welfare of youngsters. That concern particularly benefited the young abusers of organic solvents.

Family courts have continued the preference for probation over the training schools but also have increased referrals to training schools (see table 5.3). The family court took unusual care in traffic dispositions. Compared with drug offenses, traffic cases were more likely to be dismissed, experiencing the most lenient disposition, but dismissals after a hearing were more frequent than dismissals without a hearing. Stimulant drug cases, in comparison, received more stern dispositions in the form of referrals to training schools and probation (see table 5.2).

The dispositions of juvenile traffic cases by the family courts are traced in table 8.4 from 1980 through 1990. The special program for young traffic offenders has greatly enhanced probation's advantage, but traffic admissions to training schools rose from 69 in 1970 to 527 in 1990 (see table 5.5). Probation had a smaller advantage over training schools for drug offenders, but the quantitative gain in training school admissions were impressive for both versions of juvenile corrections.

Professional negligence cases were less numerous than the violations of the Road Traffic Law, but only the professional negligence cases recorded fairly continuous increases throughout the decade. The Road Traffic Law cases grew until 1984 and were fewer after that year. Thus, the Road Traffic Law brought about the recent quantitative decline in family court activities.

Referrals to training schools were very exceptional in contrast to probation. Referrals to probation offices were especially frequent for the professional negligence cases, increasing from 24.98 percent in 1980 to 28.93 percent in 1990. A very small portion of Road Traffic Law cases go to training schools, but that portion has increased slightly over the years. The decline in the Road Traffic Law referrals further reduced the impact of that slight increase.

The serious traffic cases (professional negligence) were more likely than Road Traffic Law cases to receive the most stern dispositions (referrals to training schools) or the second most stern action (probation), instead of the tolerance of dismissals without a hearing. In contrast to the handling

Table 8.4
Juvenile Traffic Defendants Adjudicated by Family Courts, 1980–90

Year	No. of Cases	% Distribution of Dispositions by Family Courts				
		Prosecutors	JTS	Probation	Hearing	No Hearing

Professional Negligence Offenses

Year	No. of Cases	Prosecutors	JTS	Probation	Hearing	No Hearing
1980	48,190	11.23	0.39	24.98	54.69	8.71
1981	50,420	11.12	0.31	25.51	54.43	8.63
1982	52,625	11.14	0.28	25.78	53.80	9.00
1983	55,151	11.61	0.30	26.47	52.86	8.76
1984	53,681	12.16	0.26	25.92	51.82	9.84
1985	53,243	11.34	0.29	26.82	51.59	9.96
1986	54,188	10.67	0.26	28.62	52.23	8.22
1987	60,792	9.16	0.19	28.52	52.92	9.21
1988	59,749	6.74	0.20	28.46	54.45	10.15
1989	61,565	5.60	0.16	29.31	53.67	11.26
1990	60,005	4.88	0.16	28.93	54.10	11.93

Road Traffic Law Violations

Year	No. of Cases	Prosecutors	JTS	Probation	Hearing	No Hearing
1980	256,255	13.78	0.08	11.70	55.84	18.60
1981	276,038	14.47	0.09	11.63	55.02	18.79
1982	287,418	14.96	0.09	12.01	54.50	18.44
1983	315,758	16.11	0.10	12.74	52.54	18.51
1984	332,349	17.13	0.10	12.24	50.99	19.54
1985	330,810	17.15	0.09	12.65	51.08	19.03
1986	321,943	15.65	0.10	12.92	51.63	19.70
1987	257,728	14.15	0.12	15.18	51.78	18.77
1988	208,910	11.90	0.12	17.67	50.03	20.28
1989	191,733	11.84	0.17	20.29	48.24	19.46
1990	192,748	12.26	0.19	22.81	46.50	18.24

Sources: Research and Training Institute 1984, 145; 1987, 143; 1990, 167; 1992a, 149.

of professional negligence, as the years passed the Road Traffic Law cases were more likely to be granted probation or dismissal without a hearing. Dismissals after a hearing are the dominant referrals for both professional negligence and Road Traffic Law cases; dismissals without a hearing are the most lenient disposition. The family courts preferred the slightly less degree of leniency granted by dismissals after a hearing, particularly for professional negligence incidents.

Referral of juvenile traffic offenders to public prosecutors became less frequent over the years, although they made up a large share of all juvenile referrals. The family courts had two general reasons for returning their cases to the public prosecutors: first, if the characteristics of the offender or the nature of the offense was considered justification for handling the case as for adult offenders; second, if the offender was older than twenty years of age and, therefore, not a juvenile. The first reason was applied most often, but as time passed, the transfers to the public prosecutor were more frequently based on advanced age.

As table 8.5 shows, juvenile drug offenders were less likely than traffic offenders to be returned to the public prosecutors, and organic solvent users were least likely to be referred. The stimulant drug group drew fewer of the referrals as the years passed. The family courts adjudicated fewer drug than traffic offenders, partly because of the special probation program for juvenile traffic offenders, but also because of the greater popularity of motor vehicles over illicit drugs among adolescents.

The caseload for organic solvent abuse greatly exceeded in absolute number the stimulant drug cases. Both kinds of drug abuse recorded declining numbers; the decline was especially marked for stimulant drugs. That reduction suggests the family courts' evaluation of stimulant drugs as the more grave variety of juvenile drug abuse.

The organic solvents drew by far the greater number of dismissals, especially dismissals without a formal hearing.

Table 8.5
Juvenile Drug Defendants Adjudicated by Family Courts, 1982-92

		% Distribution of Dispositions by Family Courts				
Year	No. of Cases[a]	Prosecutors	JTS	Probation	Hearing	No Hearing
		Stimulant Drug Offenses				
1982	2,087	8.9	26.3	40.6	17.7	6.5
1983	1,966	8.7	28.6	40.4	17.1	5.2
1985	1,521	7.2	34.2	40.8	12.5	5.3
1986	1,247	6.7	36.2	42.8	11.0	3.3
1987	1,090	7.6	35.9	40.2	12.6	3.7
1988	882	8.7	32.5	43.1	11.7	4.0
1989	741	7.6	33.3	44.4	12.1	2.6
1990	583	5.1	34.0	44.4	13.9	2.6
1991	784	7.4	40.3	39.3	10.5	2.5
1992	768	5.2	38.5	43.1	10.2	3.0
		Organic Solvent Offenses				
1982	18,396	0.7	1.5	11.1	34.9	51.8
1983	17,417	1.9	1.6	12.1	35.2	49.2
1985	15,185	1.8	2.3	13.0	36.6	46.3
1986	14,177	1.6	2.2	12.5	35.2	48.5
1987	13,804	1.7	2.3	12.9	36.2	46.9
1988	14,834	1.4	2.2	13.1	35.8	47.5
1989	15,365	1.3	2.1	12.5	34.7	49.4
1990	17,032	1.2	1.9	12.0	34.6	50.3
1991	16,891	1.0	2.1	12.7	34.5	49.7
1992	13,769	1.5	2.4	13.3	35.5	47.3

Sources: Research and Training Institute 1984, 144; 1985, 135; 1987, 142; 1988, 145; 1989, 149; 1990a, 166; 1991, 150; 1992a, 148; 1993, 98; 1994, 106.

Note: Statistics were not available for 1984.

[a] Excludes the few referrals to other agencies.

Organic solvents produced a few training school and probation referrals, whereas the two kinds of referrals dominated stimulant drug dispositions. Probation was used more frequently than the training schools for stimulant drugs and organic solvents, but as I already noted, the courts consider probation less stern than incarceration.

Two Fundamental Ideas and Their Implications

This chapter's title—"Deviation from Deviation: A Personal Comment"—is intended to convey two ideas. First, as I already explained, the six cohorts have been entering prisons in increasing numbers; they have deviated from the general decline of the imprisonment rate. In exploring that deviation, I discovered that, in recent years, four cohorts have joined the general trend toward lessening imprisonment. They have deviated from their previous deviation.

Second, in seeking an explanation for the deviation, I must go beyond reliable evidence available to me and offer my opinion, derived, in part, from an exploration of the history, culture, and structure of Japan. In this chapter, I have drawn on publications issued by the Ministry of Justice for evidence that fewer members of cohorts are entering the prisons. I have attributed that trend to the processing by public prosecutors and judges.

A very important question remains, however: what has happened within Japanese society that has blunted the impact of criminalization on the four cohorts? Finding a reliable answer to that question would require an informational base beyond the resources provided by the Ministry of Justice. Another major research enterprise would have to focus primarily on the history, culture, and structure of Japanese society. I have followed the approach of *applied research* in concentrating on the correctional agencies and considering the broader context of Japanese society only to make sense of the policies and practices of the Correctional Bureau and the Rehabilitation Bureau.

The reports of my findings have been in a mold of applied research that has benefited from the opportunity to observe directly the operations of the bureaus through unusual access to the annual statistics and other reports published by the Ministry of Justice. Their availability brought the research within my individual capacities and skirted the necessity for costly and time-consuming collection of original statistics.

The fundamental issue was empirical: what is the significance of the low and declining imprisonment rate for Japanese corrections? From that issue, other general questions were raised: What are the characteristics of the major programmatic elements? How do various personnel carry out their programmatic responsibilities? Why are the various duties and activities carried out in a particular way? During the exploration of the implications of those questions, the unanticipated patterning of the six cohorts emerged to become the subject of this book.

A new research effort would have to be an example of *theoretical research*. My applied research has focused on the operations of the two correctional agencies; theoretical research takes in the larger context of Japanese society. Study of correctional agencies calls for the knowledge base of criminology; understanding the broader tapestry of the society draws on the many social and behavioral disciplines for their bodies of knowledge and verified truths. When of genuine quality, applied research and theoretical research (frequently called "pure" research) share the benefits of sound theory and methodology.

Theory moves beyond the mere collection of separate experiences and sets out to capture the essence of a subject matter. It provides premises to guide the probing of the nature of and the causes behind a fact or event. Theory reaches into a scattering of facts and relates selected facts to one another because, according to a particular premise, their relationship has special meaning that will fill a gap in knowledge. The premise presupposes the meaning and ultimate significance of the relationship. Research is required to either confirm or reject the premise.

Methodology is the body of systematic procedures and principles whereby research attains its purposes in a logical, orderly, and cogent way. Academic research usually is described as "pure" in that the factors being related are not mixed with other, extraneous factors. The word *pure* also conveys a second meaning, "abstract," which emphasizes the interrelationships among selected facts or events. The methodology is tailored to probe the essence of a phenomena, rather than only accumulating many discrete facts or events.

Theoretical research begins with a hypothesis that, if confirmed by reliable and valid evidence, would advance scientific knowledge by pushing back the boundary of the unknown. To test the hypothesis, the investigator must plan the collection of data to focus precisely on the predetermined hypothesis.

In taking advantage of administrative statistics of unusual completeness and quality, I had to accept certain restrictions. My research was limited to the parameters of published data. Hypotheses had to be framed within the scope of variables already determined. Concepts were chosen to bear on that data, in contrast to the approach of theoretical research, which selects appropriate concepts and afterward collects original data. The administrative statistics have another limitation: the tabulations relate only two variables (in addition to gender) at a time, such as age and crimes, marital status and crimes, or admissions to probation and years of schooling. For example, analysis of the elderly cohort could not relate age, marital status, and crime; analysis of any cohort could not relate age, crime, and number of admissions to prison; and analysis of the juvenile cohort could not measure the outcome of juvenile probation by both year of termination and offense.

Applied research has the advantage for corrections of focusing on problems of the here and now that stem from the responsibilities of executives and staff members to do something. By cultivating sound research design and methodology, an agency gains reliable testing of traditional practices and of alternatives to current policy. Theoretical researchers can benefit from direct contacts with action agencies; theories can be tested when relevant to corrections, especially when sampling and methodology squares with the environmental realities of the prison or probation office.

When not conforming to enunciated principles of responsible inquiry, theoretical researchers can raise difficulties for correctional agencies. They may engage in methodological narcissism that converts the abstractions of theoretical science into unnecessarily abstruse verbiage. Some of these theoreticians assume that anyone of ordinary knowledge cannot comprehend the research procedures. In that vein, external researchers take advantage of the correctional environment to test abstract ideas, then return to their institutes to issue reports that disappear into academic archives.

Propositions for Future Research

A basic principle of research is that it never ends; today's conclusions reveal further questions that may be even more profound. The principle evokes the frustration of endless effort, but as an appetizer adds zest to the main dish, the latest discovery injects enthusiasm to the continued search for an elusive truth.

The deviation of four prison cohorts from their previous deviation in terms of admissions promises to be another example of the principle. Persons expert in a body of relevant knowledge, competent in research, and well acquainted with Japan's history, culture, and social structure are invited to undertake investigation of the unanticipated discovery. The following propositions are advanced as speculative hypotheses to be tested, rather than as already established truths.

Proposition 1: Emphasis on self-discipline opposes criminalization. In Japan the prevention of deviance and the control of criminality is linked to the grip of custom, the integration of values within personalities through socialization, and the importance most Japanese place on being accepted by reference groups. The popular and official faith is that most criminals are capable of—and prepared to undertake— self-correction without intervention by outside parties.

Two possibilities explain the decline in prison admissions of the cohorts. First, the Japanese faith in self-discipline persuades the criminal justice agents to rely decreasingly on the expansion of criminalization. Second, as evidence of the deterrent effect of expanded criminalization, fewer members of the cohorts are breaking the law. The effect may exceed that in Western societies, because the marginal deviants are especially responsive to the threat of punishment when subject to Japanese conditions.

"Any Japanese who has once suffered the psychic torment of social disapproval or rejection," says Christopher (1987, 164), "is unlikely to risk facing the experience again." Referring to this form of social control as "shaming," Braithwaite (1989, 100–101) writes: "Most shaming is by individuals within interdependent communities of concern." He defines two varieties of shaming. *Reintegrative shaming* is dedicated to decertifying ultimately the offenders as criminals while "signifying" (to show conventional signals) the evil of deeds not of persons. *Stigmatizing shaming* is disintegrative in that degradation ceremonies obstruct the offenders' reconciliation with the community.

Disagreeing with the aforementioned interpretations of "the way deviants are treated in Japan," Miyazawa (1994, 91) calls for ethnographic studies comparing "Japanese reality" to that of other countries. "Japanese people conform because they know that conformity will be highly rewarded while non-conformity costs enormously," he says (89). He reports that companies and schools, as major informal-control agencies, treat harshly the "members who defy the existing power structure and social arrangements."

Proposition 2: Less reliance on the law, preference for institutional cohesion. The resort to criminalization implies faith that the threat to punishment will persuade deviants to abandon the prohibited conduct. As criminalization efforts, the amendment of old laws and the passage of new laws represent deliberate, calculated attempts to eliminate quickly the targeted deviant conduct. Societies differ in their reliance on written law as a primary means of welding their citizens into integrated and effective social organizations. I hypothesize that because Japan does not place a premium on written law, criminalization lost salience over time and the prison admissions dropped off.

America was settled by millions of migrants from many nations who introduced an advanced economy into a relatively virgin continent previously inhabited by Indians engaged in hunting, food gathering, or primitive agriculture. Politically, a nation emerged from thirteen separate colonies of European nations and through the gradual settlement of frontier territories. In the West local governments were established before migration from the Atlantic Coast built the populations and economies that justified the creation of state governments. Migration, the haphazard mode of settlement, and the lack of common traditions among the settlors gave the United States fundamental difficulties in building a nation almost from scratch and in welding diverse populations into a society. In the absence of common traditions, the written law was summoned to be part of a deliberate effort to create a social order. As part of that effort, criminalization would be likely to have persistent effect.

A full-fledged body of written law was not framed in

Japan until 1868, when modernization of the society was begun with greater abruptness and at a more rapid pace than in Europe. Many Western ideas, some elements of Western institutions (including law and corrections institutions), and much of the technology of the West were imported but modified to suit Japanese traditions. Japan began the creation of a modern society, but with a heritage of traditions and customs (the "living law") as the foundation of the social order. "There may be a marked difference between modern and the old level of state law," says Noda (1976, 39), "but at the level of living law there was no break in the continuity." With tradition and custom continuing to challenge the eminence of the formal law, the public and legal establishment would be prepared to accept, with relative ease, the return to the lenient management of marginal deviants that existed before their criminalization was undertaken.

Proposition 3: Limited external pressure on criminal justice agencies decreases prison admissions. Correctional agencies in Japan do not control the flow of convicted criminals into prisons and community-based programs. They are dependent on other governmental decision makers for resources and must accommodate their policies and practices to the expectations of the public and the influential power groups in the society.

The recent reversal of prison admission trends for the four cohorts reflects, in part, changes by the police, public prosecutors, and judges in the criteria applied to the offenders they are processing. This chapter has exploited limited access to official data to test that proposition. The possibility could be explored further by fuller access to the data and by amassing illustrative cases.

The proposition assumes that the criminal justice agencies are relatively free to return to previous practices that sent back a major share of the cohorts to the free community or, at least, restricted the cohorts' admissions to prison. If the proposition is valid, the agencies in Japan are able to soften the ultimate impact of the criminalization stimulated by the perception of a social crisis.

To obtain resources and ideological support, correctional agencies are among the special-interest groups that present themselves as indispensable instruments for attaining high social ideals. Otherwise, the Correction Bureau and Rehabilitation Bureau are less involved than American counterparts in the competition among interest groups. The crime rate is relatively low; the Tokugawa heritage insulates the bureaus from intensive political pressure. "The ruler was, by definition, virtuous," explains Yanaga (1956, 17–18), "and knew better than anyone else what was good for the people. Since the ruler's job was to rule, there was no need for the citizen to be concerned about the affairs of government which are the concern of the ruler and his officials."

Pharr (1990, 4–5, 168–70) asserts that the level of discontent in Japan is higher than "elsewhere in the industrial capitalist world," but she finds the nation governable because of the strategy of "privatizing social conflict" despite considerable protest at the grass roots. She believes that instead of seeking open discourse, negotiations, and engaging in confrontations, Japanese authorities deal with conflicts on a case-by-case basis. The protesters have difficulty in gaining broader support, and the concessions they may win are not extended to a broader constituency. Further protests are warded off.

Proposition 4: The legal establishment prefers limited criminalization. As a corollary of the previous proposition, it may be argued that the Japanese public prosecutors and judges retained their preference for diverting the major portion of offenders from imprisonment. The new theme is that the professional philosophy of these officials was operative in opposing criminalization. The most frequent procedures for public prosecutors were suspension of prosecution or referral to summary courts, with referral of only a minority for formal trial. The judges would suspend prison sentences either for unconditional release or for probationary supervision.

The corollary is also justified by the conservative nature of the governmental regime and the power structure of Japan. American conservatives call for a heavy investment in more prison sentences, in keeping with the political preference for a "tough" policy in managing criminals. Japanese conservatives prefer to avoid that overwhelming investment. The Japanese procedures and philosophy are possible because the procuracy and judiciary are populated by professionals free of the necessity to be elected to office. Appealing to voters, district attorneys and judges in the United States promise to put more criminals behind bars.

Another corollary draws on the difference between law as it is enacted and law as it is practiced. When legislators broaden the scope of criminalization, they define general principles, whereas those persons confronting face-to-face the newly defined criminals must make realistic interpretations. In enforcing the broadened scope of the laws, the police, public prosecutors, and judges may find that law as it is practiced is identifying fewer offenders.

Notes

References

Index

Notes

1.
Introduction: Exceptions to an Exceptional Reluctance to Imprison Offenders

1. On 3 December 1995, the Department of Justice reported that as of 30 June 1995 the state and federal prisons of the United States held 1,104,074 men and women. From 30 June 1994 to 30 June 1995, the increase had been 89,707—the largest twelve-month increase on record, requiring 1,725 new prison beds each week.

2. Table 1.1 is based on the year-end population of the respective prison system. In this book, other statistical tables are based on admissions to prisons, juvenile training schools, or probation offices. Annual statistical reports of Japan's Correction Bureau and its Rehabilitation Bureau rely mostly on admissions. Lynch (1988, 184) prefers admissions for measuring changes in the quantity and quality of caseload: "Flow of studies using annual admissions are not affected by the accumulation of more serious offenders." Such offenders would have longer sentences.

3. The organization and functions of the two correctional agencies are only briefly considered here; for detailed treatment, see Johnson 1996. The summary here is intended only to be background for the analysis of the six cohorts.

4. In the 1930s the direction of cross-national influence was reversed when Jijiruo Ogawa, a Japanese scholar who taught in the

Peking Law School, was especially instrumental in introducing Western principles during a period of penal reform (Dutton 1992).

5. For a more detailed discussion of VPOs and hostels, see Johnson 1996, chapters 8 and 9. The rise and operations of the Correctional Association Prison Industrial Cooperation are considered in Johnson 1996, chapter 5.

6. I do not intend to imply that Americans (and Westerners in general) agree on the prostitution issue. Jolin 1994 summarizes the controversies in the Western history of prostitution and in the feminist movement.

7. Lieutenant Ethel B. Weed, American Women's Army Corps, as the women's affairs information officer in the Civil Information and Education Section of the Supreme Commander for Allied Powers, had the duty to get out the vote of women. As a civilian, she had been a reporter on the *Cleveland Plain Dealer* (Robins-Mowry 1983, 90–92).

8. Fumiya Ibe, interview by author, tape recording, Tokyo, May 1990. Ibe, superintendent of the Women's Guidance Home in Hachioji (Tokyo), provided invaluable orientation to the history and operations of women's guidance homes in Japan. Professor Akira Ishii of Aoyamagakuin University, Tokyo, translated my questions during the interview and later the cassette recording of the Japanese conversation.

9. Despite the Antiprostitution Law, Japanese traditions do not taboo erotic pleasure, and, untouched by the law, commercial sex draws relatively mild censure. Katoh (1991, 73) describes prostitution and pornography as part of everyday life that is available "with payment of enough money" to crime syndicates.

2.
The Yakuza and Accelerated Criminalization

1. The origin of the term *yakuza* suggests a negative public judgment. *Ya-Ku-Sa* (eight-nine-three) referred to a losing (no-good) hand in gambling and denotes "good-for-nothing" persons (DeVos with Mizushima 1973, 293).

2. Similarly, from 1750 to 1950, before the creation of formal police departments, England relied on "criminal policemen." A robber, thief, embezzler, or murderer could earn a pardon by be-

traying accomplices or spying on companions (Pringle 1958; Radzinowicz 1956, 40).

3. Similarly, American crime syndicates have threatened reprisals against witnesses; their success in the past stimulated a witness protection program (Levin 1985).

4. The public presence of the gangs is described in "Japanese Gangsters" 1990 and "Tycoons of Crime" 1992.

5. In distinguishing gang-related juveniles and non-gang-related juveniles at juvenile classification homes in two months of 1989, the Research and Training Institute (1990b, 12–13) found the gang-related juveniles usually were not living with natural parents, had a low standard of living, and felt negatively about their families and themselves.

6. The review of postwar trends of the criminal groups was drawn mostly from Research and Training Institute 1990, 338–56.

7. Although intergang violence has become less common, incidents like the following do occur. En route from Kawagoe Juvenile Prison to the rail station, Koichi Watanabe, my guide and translator, and I encountered a policeman who told us a gangster had murdered a police officer responding to a call about a shooting. On the next day (1 October 1988), the *Japan Times* reported that Masaru Mokoyama, a member of the Takashi-gumi gang (an affiliate of the Sumiyoshi Rengo Syndicate), had earlier wounded a man and woman.

8. The Stimulant Drug Control Law regulates the import, possession, manufacture, transfer, receipt, and use of stimulant drugs. Since both traffic and abuse are subject to criminal sanctions, the number of police clearances involves a remarkably high proportion of yakuza members, although their proportion has declined from 59.7 percent of 8,218 clearances in 1975 to 50.2 percent of 19,921 clearances in 1980, 48.7 percent of 22,980 clearances in 1985, and 43.8 percent of 15,038 clearances in 1990 (Research and Training Institute 1985, 62; 1992a, 74).

9. Dr. Kanehiro Hoshino, director of Criminology, National Research Institute of Police Science in Tokyo, provided the translation. I am solely responsible for the abridgement.

10. The reports precede the summaries and were written in Japanese. Hiroyuki Katayama translated the two reports for me.

11. Kobayashi (1990, 139) summarizes conclusions of research on why any gangsters abandon affiliation: "difficulty of accumu-

lating wealth is a crucial factor in their seceding from their gangs, and they secede when they find organized crime is not a rewarding business."

3.
Women Drug Offenders
and Extended Criminalization

1. Woronoff (1980, 287) speaks of the "ominous trends" since 1974 (growth of juvenile delinquency, runaway children, and illicit use of stimulant drugs) that "foreshadow more crime to come."

2. Several laws have been directed against various drugs: the Opium Law (1897) and Chapter 14 of the Penal Code deal with crimes relating to smoking opium. The Narcotic Drugs and Psychological Substances Control Act is directed against morphine, heroin, cocaine, and lysergic acid diethylamide (LSD). Other drug laws are the Hemp Control Law (1948); the Poisonous and Hazardous Substance Control Law (1947), which was replaced in 1950 with the Poisonous and Injurious Substance Control Law, to cope with abuse of paint thinner (primarily by juveniles); and the Stimulant Drug Control Law (1951, amended in 1954, 1955, and 1973).

3. The "factory girls," teenagers or younger, sang songs such as "Working in the factory is nothing less than being cast into a prison, without being bound with a chain" (Robins-Mowry 1983, 38).

4. The Japanese continue to boast strong values and love of children, but as the *Economist* (12 November 1994, 46) reports, the current fertility rate fails to replace the parents' generation; young women are delaying marriage because those in their twenties want to preserve both their jobs and their comforts. The number of single women aged twenty-five to twenty-nine years who were still single was 18 percent in 1970 and 40 percent in 1990. By age forty to forty-four, only 5.8 percent are single.

5. Kocher (1961) described Tochigi Women's Prison before it was relocated outside the city in 1979.

6. A more recent survey (Wooldredge and Masters 1993) obtained the following information on sixty-one of the one hundred women's prisons receiving mailed questionnaires: 21 percent pro-

vide prenatal counseling, 15 percent help mothers find suitable placement for the infant after birth, 15 percent lighten or abolish the mother's work obligation, 13 percent allocate separate living quarters, and 11 percent offer postnatal counseling.

7. Probation offices are responsible for supervision of both probationers and parolees.

8. Masaru Matumoto, director of the Supervision Department, Rehabilitation Bureau, Tokyo, and his staff provided the information on which this summary is based.

4.
Traffic Offenders:
The Impulse
for Penal Innovation

1. This statement reflects the fines at the time the Penal Code was enacted originally. Periodically, the laws related to fines are revised, subject to approval by the Diet, to recognize the effects of inflation. On 7 May 1991, for example, maximum fines were raised to range from one hundred thousand yen to one million yen.

2. Bixby (1971) describes Ohi's program as it originally operated.

5.
Juvenile Offenders:
Reactions to Drug
and Traffic Offenses

1. The comparisons in this paragraph and in the immediately following paragraphs are based on statistics reported in Research and Statistics Section 1994b.

2. The third pattern has been that admissions to correctional agencies are largely male. My statistical analysis does not distinguish the sexes, because the published data on probation and parole deal with only the total caseload.

3. Yokoyama (1992, 17) points out that, despite the greater penalization, some juveniles persisted in drug abuse. Because they had begun abusing cough medicine, the Ministry of Health and Welfare instructed drug stores to sell only one bottle to juveniles.

6.
Foreigners in Japanese Prisons: Adaptation and Accommodation

1. The Tochigi, Fuchu, and Yokosuka Prisons supplied data on the class-F inmates.

2. On remand after appearing in court, two Iranians said they expected to be released to their apartments in Tokyo. When continued on pretrial detention, they inflicted injuries on themselves.

3. Japanese officials acknowledge that their officers also may misunderstand the precise meaning of the foreigners' acts as intended by the foreigners.

4. The staff of Fuchu Prison assembled these statistics for me. Nakano has been abolished; now on its grounds are a neighborhood park and the headquarters of the Tokyo Correction Region and of the Japanese Correction Association. Only Nakano's gate remains as a monument.

5. The statistics in this paragraph and in the immediately following paragraphs are from Research and Statistics Section 1988, 1993a.

6. The original site was split by a railroad. Two unsentenced Japanese prisoners escaped in 1978 by taking advantage of the noise of a passing train. This was the first and last escape at Yokosuka.

7. In 1995 Deputy Warden Tetsuya Ozaki provided recent information on procedures and the qualities of inmates at Yokosuka.

8. The Japanese inmates may watch the films in English if they desire; similarly, the Americans may observe the films in Japanese if they desire.

7.
Elderly Inmates: Demographic Change Creeps into Prisons

1. Schwartz (1991, 20) cites other reasons for Japan's low birthrate: a hyperactive work ethic, women tending to see Japanese marriage as "a raw deal," and single men trying to save on

NOTES TO PAGES 222–261

rents by living in company dormitories, where female visitors are banned.

2. For a detailed analysis of the research, see Riley, Foner, and Waring 1988.

3. An example of change is that the upward trend of the lower limit for the ages of elderly inmates has been raised in research from fifty or fifty-five years to sixty or sixty-five years.

4. This discussion is based on estimates in the *Japan Statistical Yearbook, 1991*, 41st ed., 25.

5. For geriatric patients, Kelsey (1986, 56) calls for twenty-four-hour nursing care, lockable bedrails, walkers, bedside commodes, and lift-type bathing facilities.

6. The statistics in this paragraph and in the immediately following paragraphs are from Research and Statistics Section 1971a, 1995a.

7. Japanese prisons provide a smoke-free environment because tobacco smoking is forbidden to prisoners, subject to punishment. Earlier prisons were of wooden construction, and fire was a major hazard.

8. Onomichi, is a branch prison for Okayama Prison. Okayama was established about 112 years ago, during the Meiji Restoration. It was relocated with modern design on its present site in 1960.

8.
Deviation from Deviation:
A Personal Comment

1. What I discovered is reported in Johnson 1996.

2. In addition to amendments to the Penal Code of 1907, special laws outside the Penal Code have been enacted by the Diet. These extensions of the criminal law's reach, comments Suzuki (1973, 292), are "more likely to produce political controversy."

References

Public Documents Published by the
Ministry of Justice, Tokyo

Correction Bureau. 1967. *Correctional Administration in Japan.*
———. 1982. *Correctional Institutions in Japan.*
———. 1990. *Correctional Institutions in Japan.*
Rehabilitation Bureau. 1990. *Community-Based Treatment of Offenders in Japan.*
Research and Statistics Section. 1971a. *Annual Report of Statistics on Correction for 1970.* Vol. 1.
———. 1971b. *Annual Report of Statistics on Correction for 1970.* Vol. 2.
———. 1971c. *Annual Report of Statistics on Rehabilitation for 1970.*
———. 1976a. *Annual Report of Statistics on Correction for 1975.* Vol. 1.
———. 1976b. *Annual Report of Statistics on Correction for 1975.* Vol. 2.
———. 1976c. *Annual Report of Statistics on Rehabilitation for 1975.*
———. 1981a. *Annual Report of Statistics on Correction for 1980.* Vol. 1.
———. 1981b. *Annual Report of Statistics on Correction for 1980.* Vol. 2.
———. 1981c. *Annual Report of Statistics on Rehabilitation for 1980.*
———. 1986a. *Annual Report of Statistics on Correction for 1985.* Vol. 1.
———. 1986b. *Annual Report of Statistics on Correction for 1985.* Vol. 2.
———. 1986c. *Annual Report of Statistics on Rehabilitation for 1985.*
———. 1987a. *Annual Report of Statistics on Correction for 1986.* Vol. 1.
———. 1987b. *Annual Report of Statistics on Correction for 1986.* Vol. 2.
———. 1988. *Annual Report of Statistics on Correction for 1987.* Vol. 1.
———. 1990. *Annual Report of Statistics on Correction for 1989.* Vol. 1.

REFERENCES

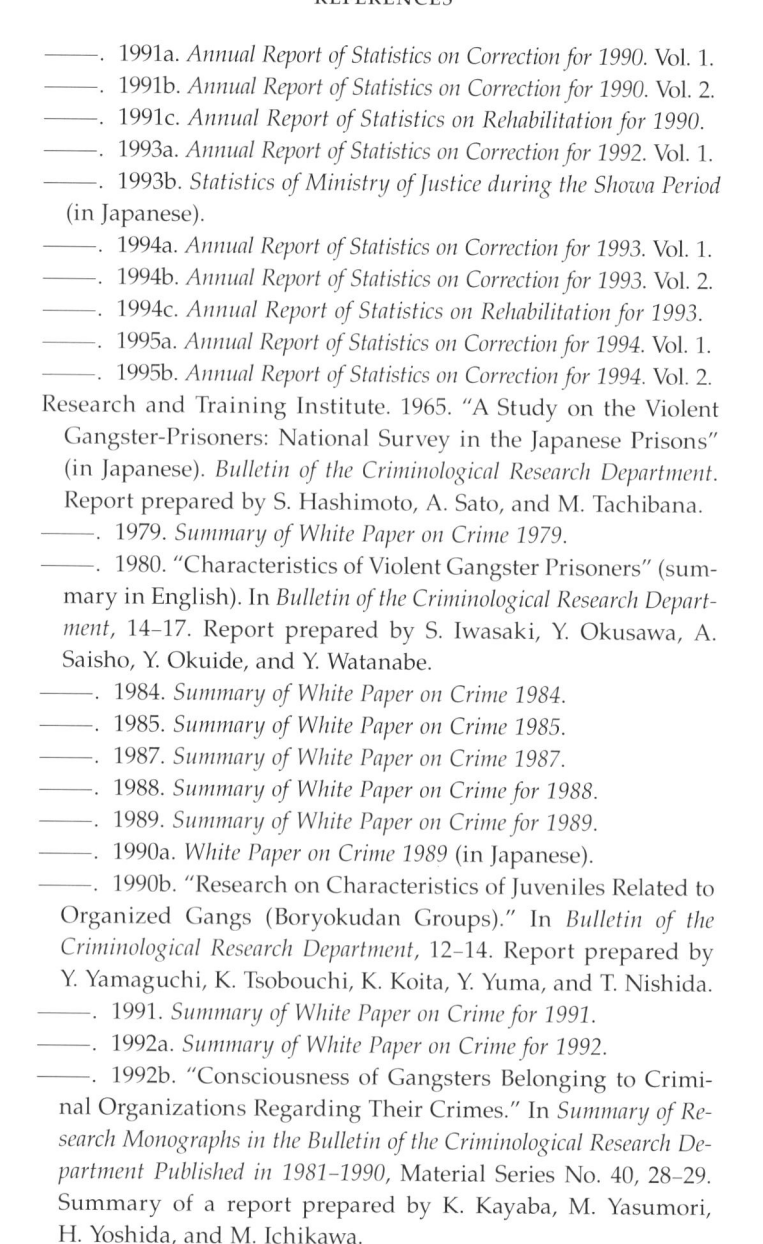

———. 1991a. *Annual Report of Statistics on Correction for 1990*. Vol. 1.
———. 1991b. *Annual Report of Statistics on Correction for 1990*. Vol. 2.
———. 1991c. *Annual Report of Statistics on Rehabilitation for 1990*.
———. 1993a. *Annual Report of Statistics on Correction for 1992*. Vol. 1.
———. 1993b. *Statistics of Ministry of Justice during the Showa Period* (in Japanese).
———. 1994a. *Annual Report of Statistics on Correction for 1993*. Vol. 1.
———. 1994b. *Annual Report of Statistics on Correction for 1993*. Vol. 2.
———. 1994c. *Annual Report of Statistics on Rehabilitation for 1993*.
———. 1995a. *Annual Report of Statistics on Correction for 1994*. Vol. 1.
———. 1995b. *Annual Report of Statistics on Correction for 1994*. Vol. 2.
Research and Training Institute. 1965. "A Study on the Violent Gangster-Prisoners: National Survey in the Japanese Prisons" (in Japanese). *Bulletin of the Criminological Research Department*. Report prepared by S. Hashimoto, A. Sato, and M. Tachibana.
———. 1979. *Summary of White Paper on Crime 1979*.
———. 1980. "Characteristics of Violent Gangster Prisoners" (summary in English). In *Bulletin of the Criminological Research Department*, 14–17. Report prepared by S. Iwasaki, Y. Okusawa, A. Saisho, Y. Okuide, and Y. Watanabe.
———. 1984. *Summary of White Paper on Crime 1984*.
———. 1985. *Summary of White Paper on Crime 1985*.
———. 1987. *Summary of White Paper on Crime 1987*.
———. 1988. *Summary of White Paper on Crime for 1988*.
———. 1989. *Summary of White Paper on Crime for 1989*.
———. 1990a. *White Paper on Crime 1989* (in Japanese).
———. 1990b. "Research on Characteristics of Juveniles Related to Organized Gangs (Boryokudan Groups)." In *Bulletin of the Criminological Research Department*, 12–14. Report prepared by Y. Yamaguchi, K. Tsobouchi, K. Koita, Y. Yuma, and T. Nishida.
———. 1991. *Summary of White Paper on Crime for 1991*.
———. 1992a. *Summary of White Paper on Crime for 1992*.
———. 1992b. "Consciousness of Gangsters Belonging to Criminal Organizations Regarding Their Crimes." In *Summary of Research Monographs in the Bulletin of the Criminological Research Department Published in 1981–1990*, Material Series No. 40, 28–29. Summary of a report prepared by K. Kayaba, M. Yasumori, H. Yoshida, and M. Ichikawa.
———. 1992c. "Annual Conditions Regarding Elderly Prisoners." In *Summary of Research Monographs in the Bulletin of the Crimino-

logical Research Department Published in 1981–1990, Material Series No. 40, 49–51. Summary of a report prepared by Y. Nozaka, T. Otsuki, F. Kashiwagi, S. Hashisako, and M. Ichikawa.
———. 1993. *Summary of White Paper on Crime for 1993.*
———. 1994. *Summary of White Paper on Crime for 1994.*

Other Works Cited

Abadinsky, Howard. 1981. *The Mafia in America: An Oral History.* New York: Praeger.

Adler, Freda. 1975. *Sisters in Crime: Rise of the New Female Criminal.* New York: McGraw-Hill.

Albanese, Jay. 1985. *Organized Crime in America.* Cincinnati: Anderson Publishing Company.

Albini, Joseph L. 1975. "Mafia as Method: A Comparison Between Great Britain and U.S.A. Regarding the Existence and Structure of Types of Organized Crime." *International Journal of Criminology and Penology* 3:295–305.

Albrecht, Hans-Jorg. 1987. "Foreign Minorities and the Criminal Justice System in the Federal Republic of Germany." *Howard Journal of Criminal Justice* 26:272–86.

Araki, Nobuyoshi. 1985. "The Flow of Criminal Cases in the Japanese Criminal Justice System." *Crime and Delinquency* 31:601–27.

Bayley, David H. 1976. *Forces of Order: Police Behavior in Japan and the United States.* Berkeley: University of California Press.

Beasley, William G. 1972. *The Meiji Restoration.* Stanford, Calif.: Stanford University Press.

Becker, Howard S. 1963. *Outsiders: Studies in the Sociology of Deviance.* New York: Free Press.

Befu, Harumi. 1971. *Japan: An Anthropological Introduction.* San Francisco: Chandler Publishing Company.

Bellah, Robert N. 1971. "Continuity and Change in Japanese Society." In *Stability and Social Change*, edited by Bernard Barber and Alex Inkeles, 377–404. Boston: Little, Brown.

Benedict, Ruth. 1967. *Chrysanthemum and the Sword: Patterns of Japanese Culture.* New York: World Publishing.

Bixby, F. Lowell. 1971. "Two Modern Correctional Facilities in Japan." *Federal Probation* 35:13–15.

Blau, Zona Smith. 1973. *Old Age in a Changing Society.* New York: New Viewpoints.

REFERENCES

Boudouris, James. 1985. *Prisons and Kids: Programs for Inmate Parents*. College Park, Md.: American Correctional Association.
Braithwaite, John. 1989. *Crime, Shame, and Reintegration*. New York: Cambridge University Press.
Brinton, Mary C. 1993. *Women and the Economic Miracle: Gender and Work in Postwar Japan*. Berkeley: University of California Press.
Buruma, Ian. 1984. *A Japanese Mirror: Heroes and Villains in Japanese Culture*. London: Jonathan Cape.
———. 1984–85. "Tattoos in Pinstripes." *Far Eastern Economic Review* 126, no. 52:37, 47.
Bynum, Timothy S. 1987. "Controversies in the Field of Organized Crime." In *Organized Crime in America: Concepts and Controversies*, edited by Timothy S. Bynum, 3–11. Monsey, N.Y.: Criminal Justice Press.
Carney, Larry S., and Charlotte G. O'Kelly. 1987. "Barriers and Constraints to the Recruitment and Mobility of Female Managers in the Japanese Labor Force." *Human Resource Management* 26:193–216.
Christie, Nils. 1993. *Crime Control as Industry*. London: Routledge.
Christopher, Robert C. 1987. *The Japanese Mind: The Goliath Explained*. Tokyo: Charles E. Tuttle.
Clark, Ronald. 1979. *The Japanese Company*. New Haven, Conn.: Yale University Press.
Clemmer, Donald. 1958. *The Prison Community*. New York: Rinehart and Company.
Council of Europe. 1992. "Statistics Concerning Prison Populations in the Member States of the Council of Europe." *Prison Information Bulletin* 16: 4–16.
Cressey, Donald R. 1974. "Law, Order, and the Motorist." In *Crime, Criminology, and Public Policy*, edited by Roger Hood, 213–34. London: Heinemann.
Dalby, Liza Crihfield. 1983. *Geisha*. Berkeley: University of California Press.
DeVos, George A., with Keiichi Mizushima. 1973. "Organization and Social Function of Japanese Gangs: Historical Development and Modern Parallels." In *Socialization for Achievement: Essays on the Social Psychology of the Japanese*, edited by George A. DeVos, 280–310. Berkeley: University of California Press.
Dutton, Michael R. 1992. *Policing and Punishment in China: From Patriarchy to "The People."* New York: Cambridge University Press.

REFERENCES

Duus, Peter. 1969. *Feudalism in Japan*. New York: Alfred A. Knopf.
Feinman, Clarice. 1986. *Women in the Criminal Justice System*. 2d ed. New York: Praeger.
Fletcher, Beverly R., and Dreama G. Moon. 1993. Introduction to *Women Prisoners: A Forgotten Population*, edited by Beverly R. Fletcher, Lynn Dixon Shaver, and Dreama G. Moon. Westport, Conn.: Praeger.
Fujita, Taki. 1968. "Women and Politics in Japan." *Annals of American Academy of Political and Social Science* 375:91–95.
Fukutake, Tadashi. 1967. *Japanese Rural Society*. Translated by Ronald P. Dore. London: Oxford University Press.
———. 1989. *The Japanese Social Structure: Its Evolution in the Modern Culture*. 2d ed. Translated by Ronald P. Dore. Tokyo: University of Tokyo Press.
General Secretariat. 1989. *Guide to the Family Court of Japan*. Tokyo: Supreme Court of Japan.
George, B. J. 1988. "Discretionary Authority of Public Prosecutor in Japan." In *Law and Society in Contemporary Japan: American Perspectives*, edited by John O. Haley, 263–88. Dubuque, Iowa: Kendal-Hunt.
Hagan, Frank E. 1983. "The Organized Crime Continuum: A Further Specification of a New Conceptual Model." *Criminal Justice Review* 8:52–57.
Haley, John Owen. 1991. *Authority Without Power: Law and the Japanese Paradox*. New York: Oxford University Press.
Hammett, Theodore M., and Lynne Harrold. 1994. *Tuberculosis in Correctional Facilities*. Washington, D.C.: National Institute of Justice, U.S. Department of Justice.
Hartz-Karp, Janette. 1981. "Women in Constraints." In *Women and Crime*, edited by Satyanshu K. Mukherjee and Jocelynne A. Scutt, 167–95. Sydney: George Allen and Unwin.
Hayakawa, Kazuo. 1990. "Housing for the Elderly." In *Responding to the Needs of an Aging Society*, edited by Yoichi Okazaki et al., 30–36. Tokyo: Foreign Press Center.
Hayashi, Shuji. 1988. *Culture and Management in Japan*. Translated by Frank Baldwin. Tokyo: University of Tokyo Press.
Hazama, Hiroshi. 1976. "Historical Changes on the Life Style of Industrial Workers." In *Japanese Industrialization and Its Social Consequences*, edited by Hugh Patrick, 21–51. Berkeley: University of California Press.

REFERENCES

Herbert, David L., and Howard Tritt. 1984. *Corporation of Corruption: A Systematic Study of Organized Crime*. Springfield, Ill.: Charles C. Thomas.

Hobson, Barbara Meil. 1987. *Uneasy Virtue: The Politics of Prostitution and the American Reform Tradition*. New York: Basic Books.

Holden, Karen C. 1983. "Changing Employment Patterns of Women." In *Work and Lifecourse in Japan*, edited by David W. Plath, 34–46. Albany: State University of New York Press.

Huang, Frank F. Y., and Michael S. Vaughn. 1992. "A Descriptive Analysis of Japanese Organized Crime: The Boryokudan from 1945 to 1988." *International Criminal Justice Review* 2:19–57.

Ino, Kenji. 1974. *Yakuza and Japanese* (in Japanese). Tokyo: Mikasa Syobo.

Ishida, Takeshi. 1983. *Japanese Political Culture*. New Brunswick, N.J.: Transaction Books.

Ishii, Akira, and Dieter Bindzus. 1987. "Prisons in Japan: Resocialization by the Means of Treatment." *Aoyama Law Review* 29:328–62.

Iwahori, Takeshi, M.D. 1988. "Introduction to Medical and Health Care Services of Correctional Institutions in Japan." United Nations Asia and Far East Institute for Prevention of Crime and Treatment of Offenders, Tokyo. Photocopy.

Iwai, Hiroaki. 1966. "Delinquent Groups and Organized Crime." In *Japanese Sociological Studies*, edited by Paul Halmos, Sociological Review Monograph Series, no. 10, 199–212. Keele, England: University of Keele.

———. 1986. "Organized Crime in Japan." In *Organized Crime: A Global Perspective*, edited by Robert J. Kelly, 208–33. Totowa, N.J.: Rowman and Littlefield.

"Japanese Gangsters: Honorable Mob." 1990. *Economist*, 27 January, 19–20.

Johnson, Elmer H. 1996. *Japanese Corrections: Managing Convicted Offenders in an Orderly Society*. Carbondale: Southern Illinois University Press.

Johnson, Elmer H., and Hisashi Hasegawa. 1992. "Prison Administration in Contemporary Japan: Six Issues." In *Prisons Around the World: Studies in International Penology*, edited by Michael K. Carlie and Kevin I. Minor, 208–18. Dubuque, Iowa: William C. Brown.

REFERENCES

Jolin, Annette. 1994. "On the Backs of Working Prostitutes: Feminist Theory and Prostitution Policy." *Crime and Delinquency* 40:69–83.

Jones, Howard, Paul Corres, and Richard Stockford. 1977. *Open Prison*. London: Routledge and Kegan Paul.

Jones, Randall S. 1988. "The Economic Implications of Japan's Aging Population." *Asian Survey* 28:958–69.

Kaplan, David E., and Alex Dubro. 1986. *Yakuza: The Explosive Account of Japan's Criminal Underworld*. Reading, Mass.: Addison Wesley.

Katoh, Hisao. 1991. "The Development of Delinquency and Criminal Justice in Japan." In *Crime and Control in Comparative Perspectives*, edited by Hans-Gunther Heiland, Louise I. Shelley, and Hisao Katoh, 69–81. Berlin: Walter de Gruyterr.

Kelsey, O. W. 1986. "Elderly Inmates: Profiling Safe and Humane Care." *Corrections Today* 48:56, 58.

Kersten, Joachim. 1993. "Street Youths, Bosozoku, and Yakuza: Subculture Formation and Societal Reactions in Japan." *Crime and Delinquency* 39:277–95.

Kiefer, Christie W. 1987. "Care of the Aged in Japan." In *Health, Illness, and Medical Care in Japan*, edited by Edward Norbeck and Margaret Lock, 89–109. Honolulu: University of Hawaii Press.

Kobayashi, Juichi. 1990. "Characteristics of Organized Crime in Japan and Their Policy Implications." *Asian Journal of Crime Prevention and Criminal Justice* 8:135–47.

Kocher, Marjorie B. 1961. "Tochigi Women's Prison, Japan." *American Journal of Corrections* 23:20–22, 24–25.

Kondo, Dorinne K. 1990. *Crafting Selves: Power, Gender, and Discourses of Identity in a Japanese Workplace*. Chicago: University of Chicago Press.

Koshi, George M. 1970. *The Japanese Legal Advisor: Crimes and Punishments*. Tokyo: Charles E. Tuttle.

Kouhashi, Hiroshi. 1985. "Court's Selection of Offenders to be Placed Under Probationary Supervision." United Nations Asia and Far East Institute for Prevention of Crime and Treatment of Offenders, Tokyo. Photocopy.

Lauderdale, Pat. 1976. "Deviance and Moral Boundaries." *American Sociological Review* 41:660–76.

Lemert, Edwin M. 1951. *Social Pathology*. New York: McGraw-Hill.

Levin, Joshua M. 1985. "Organized Crime and Insulated Violence: Federal Liability for Illegal Conduct in the Witness Protection Program." *Journal of Criminal Law and Criminology* 76:208–50.

Levy, Marion J. 1970. "Contrasting Factors in the Modernization of China and Japan." In *Comparative Perspectives: Theories and Methods*, edited by Amitai Etzioni and Frederic L. Dubow, 224–67. Boston: Little, Brown.

Longstreet, Stephen, and Ethel Longstreet. 1970. *Yoshiwara: City of the Senses.* New York: David McKay.

Lynch, James P. 1988. "A Comparison of Prison Use in England, Canada, West Germany, and the United States: A Limited Test of the Punitive Hypothesis." *Journal of Criminal Law and Criminology* 79:180–217.

Maguire, Kathleen, and Ann L. Pastore. 1995. *Sourcebook of Criminal Justice Statistics—1994.* Washington, D.C.: Bureau of Justice Statistics, U.S. Department of Justice.

Martin, Linda G. 1989. "The Graying of Japan." *Population Bulletin* 94:3–42.

Masaki, Akira. 1964. *Reminiscences of a Japanese Penologist.* Tokyo: Criminal Policy Association.

Masland, John W. 1946. "Neighborhood Associations in Japan." *Far Eastern Survey* 15, no. 23:355–58.

McKelvey, Blake. 1977. *American Prisons: A History of Good Intentions (1936).* Montclair, N.J.: Patterson-Smith.

Menard, Scott. 1992. "Demographic and Theoretical Variables in the Age-Period-Cohort Analysis of Illegal Behavior." *Journal of Research in Crime and Delinquency* 29:178–99.

Ministry of Health and Welfare. 1979. *A Brief Account of Drug Abuse and Countermeasures.* Tokyo.

Miyawaki, Raisuke. 1979. "Crackdown Operations Against Organized Racketeer Groups (Yakuza) in Japan." *International Criminal Police Review* 329:167–69.

Miyazawa, Koichi, and Schura Euller Cook. 1990. "Juvenile Delinquency and Juvenile Justice in Japan." *International Annals of Criminology* 28:55–65.

Miyazawa, Setsuo. 1991. "The Private Sector and Law Enforcement in Japan." In *Privatization and Its Alternatives*, edited by William T. Gormley, Jr., 241–57. Madison: University of Wisconsin Press.

———. 1994. "Enigma of Japan as a Testing Ground for Cross-

REFERENCES

Cultural Criminological Studies." *International Annals of Criminology* 32:81–102.

Nagashima, Atsushi. 1990. "Criminal Justice in Japan." In *Crime Prevention and Control in the United States and Japan*, edited by Valarie Kusuda-Smick, 3–11. Dobbs Ferry, N.Y.: Transnational Juris Publications.

Nagel, Ilene, and John Hagan. 1983. "Gender and Crime: Offense Patterns and Criminal Court Sanctions." In *Crime and Justice: An Annual Review of Research*, edited by Michael Tonry and Norval Morris, 4:91–144. Chicago: University of Chicago Press.

Nakane, Chie. 1984. *Japanese Society*. Tokyo: Charles E. Tuttle.

National Police Agency. 1991. *White Paper on Police 1990 (Excerpt)*. Tokyo: Japan Times.

———. 1992. *White Paper on Police 1991 (Excerpt)*. Tokyo: Japan Times.

———. 1994. *White Paper on Police 1993 (Excerpt)*. Tokyo: Japan Times.

Nishikawa, Masakazu. 1990. "Adult Probation in Japan: A Case Study of Alternatives to Imprisonment." United Nations Asia and Far East Institute for Prevention of Crime and Treatment of Offenders, Tokyo. Photocopy.

Noda, Tosiyuki. 1976. *Introduction to Japanese Law*. Translated by Anthony H. Angelo. Tokyo: University of Tokyo Press.

O'Brien, Robert M. 1989. "Relative Cohort Size and Age-Specific Crime Rates: An Age-Period-Relative-Cohort-Size Model." *Criminology* 27:57–78.

O'Callaghan, Sean. 1968. *The Yellow Slave Trade: A Survey of the Traffic in Women and Children in the East*. London: Anthony Blond.

Okazaki, Yoichi. 1990. "Social Factors Behind the Aging of Society." In *Responding to the Needs of An Aging Society*, edited by Yoichi Okazaki et al., 7–14. Tokyo: Foreign Press Center.

Otomo, Eiichi. 1990. "Caring for the Aged." In *Responding to the Needs of an Aging Society*, edited by Yoichi Okazaki et al., 23–29. Tokyo: Foreign Press Center.

Ozaki, Robert S. 1978. *The Japanese: A Cultural Portrait*. Tokyo: Charles E. Tuttle.

Parisi, Nicolette. 1982. "Are Females Treated Differently? A Review of the Theories and Evidence on Sentencing and Parole Decisions." In *Judge, Lawyer, Victim, Thief: Women, Gender Roles, and Criminal Justice*, edited by Nicole Hahn Rafter and Elizabeth Anne Stanko, 205–20. Boston: Northeastern University Press.

Park, Robert E. 1967. "Human Migration and the Marginal Man."

In *Robert E. Park on Social Control and Collective Behavior: Selected Papers*, edited by Ralph H. Turner, 194–206. Chicago: University of Chicago Press.

Pempel, T. J. 1982. *Policy and Politics in Japan: Creative Conservation.* Philadelphia: Temple University Press.

Perry, John Curtis. 1980. *Beneath the Eagle's Wings: Americans in Occupied Japan.* New York: Dodd Mead.

Pharr, Susan J. 1981. *Political Women in Japan.* Berkeley: University of California Press.

———. 1990. *Losing Face: Status Politics in Japan.* Berkeley: University of California Press.

Pringle, Patrick. 1958. *The Thief Takers.* London: Museum Press.

Radzinowicz, Leon. 1956. *A History of English Criminal Law and Its Administration from 1970.* Vol. 2. London: Stevens and Sons.

Raz, Jacob. 1992. "Self-Presentation and Performance in the Yakuza Way of Life: Fieldwork with a Japanese Underworld Group." In *Ideology and Practice in Modern Japan*, edited by Roger Goodman and Refsing Kirsten, 210–34. London: Routledge.

Riley, Matilda White, Anne Foner, and Joan Waring. 1988. "Sociology of Age." In *Handbook of Sociology*, edited by Neil Smelser, 243–90. New York: Macmillan.

Robins-Mowry, Dorothy. 1983. *The Hidden Sun: Women of Modern Japan.* Boulder, Colo.: Westview Press.

Rome, Florence. 1975. *The Tattooed Men.* New York: Delacorte Press.

Rose, Gordon. 1970. "Penal Reform as History." *British Journal of Criminology* 10:348–71.

Rubenstein, Dan. 1984. "The Elderly in Prison: A Review of the Literature." In *Elderly Criminals*, edited by Evelyn S. Newman, Donald J. Newman, Mindy L. Gewirtz, and associates, 153–68. Cambridge, Mass.: Oelgeschlager, Gunn, and Hain.

Sansom, George. 1963a. *A History of Japan to 1334.* Tokyo: Charles E. Tuttle.

———. 1963b. *A History of Japan, 1334–1615.* Tokyo: Charles E. Tuttle.

———. 1963c. *A History of Japan, 1615–1867.* Tokyo: Charles E. Tuttle.

Saso, Mary. 1990. *Women in the Japanese Workplace.* London: Hilary Shipman.

Sassen, Saskia. 1994. "Economic Internationalization: The New Migration in Japan and the United States." *Social Justice* 21:62–82.

Sato, Ikuya. 1991. *Kamikaze Biker: Parody and Anomy in Affluent Japan.* Chicago: University of Chicago Press.

REFERENCES

Sato, Kinko Saito. 1981. "Emancipation of Women and Crime in Japan." In *The Incidence of Female Criminality in the Contemporary World*, edited by Freda Adler, 258–72. New York: New York University Press.

Sato, Tsuneo. 1990. "Tokugawa Villager and Agriculture." In *Tokugawa Japan: The Social and Economic Antecedents of Modern Japan*, edited by Chie Nakane and Shizaburo Oishi, 37–80. Tokyo: University of Tokyo Press.

Schneider, Hans Joachim. 1993. "Organized Crime in International Criminological Perspective." Resource Material Series, no. 43, 133–48. Tokyo: United Nations Asia and Far East Institute for Prevention of Crime and Treatment of Offenders.

Schwartz, Joe. 1991. "Why Japan's Birthrate Is So Low." *American Demographics* 13:20.

Seward, Jack. 1972. *The Japanese*. New York: William Morrow.

Shikita, Minoru, and Shinichi Tsuchiya. 1990. *Crime and Criminal Policy in Japan from 1926 to 1988*. Tokyo: Japan Criminal Policy Society.

Sievers, Sharon L. 1983. *Flowers in Salt: The Beginnings of Feminist Consciousness in Modern Japan*. Stanford, Calif.: Stanford University Press.

Simmel, George. 1908. *Sociologie*. Leipzig: Duncker and Humbolt.

Simon, Rita James, and Navin Sharma. 1976. "Women and Crime: Does the American Experience Generalize?" In *Criminology of Deviant Women*, edited by Freda Adler and Rita James Simon, 391–400. Boston: Houghton Mifflin.

Singer, Kurt. 1981. *Mirror, Sword, and Jewel: The Geometry of Japanese Life*. Tokyo: Kodansha International.

Smart, Carol. 1982. "The New Female Offender: Reality or Myth?" In *The Criminal Justice System and Women*, edited by Barbara Raffel Price and Natalie J. Sokoloff, 105–16. New York: Clark Boardman Company.

Smith, Robert J. 1961. "The Japanese Rural Community: Norms, Sanctions, and Ostracism." *American Anthropologist* 63:522–33.

———. 1987. "Gender Inequality in Contemporary Japan." *Journal of Japanese Studies* 13:1–25.

Steffensmeier, Darrell J. 1978. "Crime and the Contemporary Woman: An Analysis of Female Property Crime, 1960–1975." *Social Force* 57:556–64.

Steffensmeier, Darrell J., Cathy Streifel, and Edward Shihadeh.

1992. "Cohort Size and Arrest Rates over the Life Course: The Easterlin Hypothesis Reconsidered." *American Sociological Review* 57:306-14.

Steiner, Kurt. 1965. *Local Government in Japan*. Stanford, Calif.: Stanford University Press.

Suttles, Gerald D. 1991. Preface to *Kamikaze Biker: Parody and Anomy in Affluent Japan*, by Ikuya Sato. Chicago: University of Chicago Press.

Suzuki, Yoshio. 1973. "Politics of Criminal Law and Reform—Japan." *American Journal of Comparative Law* 212:287-303.

———. 1979. "Corrections in Japan." In *International Corrections*, edited by Robert J. Wicks and H. H. A. Cooper, 141-61. Lexington, Mass.: Lexington Books.

Takeuchi, Hiroshi. 1986-87. "The Balance Sheet of the Yakuza Business." *Japanese Economic Studies* 15:49-65.

Tamura, Masayuki. 1992. "The Yakuza and Amphetamine Abuse in Japan." In *Drugs, Law, and the State*, edited by Harold H. Traver and Mark S. Gaylord, 99-117. New Brunswick, N.J.: Transaction Publishers.

Tamura, Masayuki, Kanehiro Hoshino, Ayako Uchiyama, and Seiji Yonezato. 1993. "The Impact of the Anti-Organized Crime Law on Boryokudan and Their Members' Intentions to Resign from the Organization." *Reports of the National Research Institute of Police Science* 34 (December): 1-12.

Tomasevski, Katarina. 1994. *Foreigners in Prison*. Helsinki: European Institute for Crime Prevention Control.

Tonomura, Hitomi. 1992. *Community and Commerce in Late Medieval Japan: The Corporate Villages of Tokuchini-Ho*. Stanford, Calif.: Stanford University Press.

Tournier, Pierre, and Marie Danielle Barre. 1990. "Survey of Prison Systems in the Member States of the Council of Europe: Comparative Prison Demography." *Prison Information Bulletin* 15:4-16.

Traffic Bureau, National Police Agency. 1986. *Statistics '85: Road Accidents: Japan*. Tokyo: International Association of Traffic and Safety Sciences.

———. 1994. *Statistics '93: Road Accidents: Japan*. Tokyo: International Association of Traffic and Safety Sciences.

Traffic Safety Policy Office. 1985. *White Paper on Transportation Safety in Japan '84*. Tokyo: International Association of Traffic and Safety Sciences.

REFERENCES

———. 1991. *White Paper on Transportation Safety in Japan '90*. Tokyo: International Association of Traffic and Safety Sciences.

———. 1992. *White Paper on Traffic Safety in Japan '91*. Abridged ed. Tokyo: International Association of Traffic and Safety Sciences.

———. 1994. *White Paper on Traffic Safety in Japan '93*. Tokyo: International Association of Traffic and Safety Sciences.

Tsurumi, E. Patricia. 1990. *Factory Girls: Women in the Thread Mills of Meiji Japan*. Princeton, N.J.: Princeton University Press.

"Tycoons of Crime." 1992. *Economist*, 28 February, 36–37.

Uchiyama, Ayako, Kenehiro Hosino, Masayuki Tamura, and Seiji Yonezato. 1993. "The Changes in Way of Life of Boryokudan Members after Enforcement of the Anti–Organized Crime Law." *Reports of the National Research Institute of Police Science* 34 (December): 13–26.

UNAFEI. N.d. *Criminal Justice Legislation of Japan*. Tokyo: United Nations Asia and Far East Institute for Prevention of Crime and Treatment of Offenders.

Usui, Chikado. 1994. "On the Current American Discussion of Women's Roles in Japanese Economy." Paper presented at the annual meeting of the Southern Sociological Society, Raleigh, N.C.

Van Wolferen, Karel. 1989. *The Enigma of Japanese Power: People and Politics in a Stateless Nation*. London: Macmillan.

Wagatsuma, Hiroshi, and Arthur Rosett. 1986. "The Implications of Apology: Law and Culture in Japan and the United States." *Law and Society* 20:461–98.

Watanuki, Joji. 1986. "Is There a 'Japanese-Type Welfare Society'?" *International Sociology* 1:259–69.

Watson, Billie J. 1971. "Japan's New Prison for Selected Traffic Offenders." *Traffic Digest and Review* 19:6–10.

Wilson, Nanci Koser. 1983. "An International Perspective on Women and Criminology." In *International Handbook of Contemporary Developments in Criminology*, edited by Elmer H. Johnson, 1:99–100. Westport, Conn.: Greenwood Press.

Wooldredge, John D., and Kimberly Masters. 1993. "Confronting Problems Faced by Pregnant Inmates in State Prisons." *Crime and Delinquency* 39:195–203.

Woronoff, Jon. 1980. *Japan: The Coming Social Crisis*. Tokyo: Yohan Publications.

Yanaga, Chitoshi. 1956. *Japanese People and Politics*. New York: John Wiley and Sons.

REFERENCES

Yokoo, Toshio. 1986. "The Japanese Police Campaign Against the Boryokudan." *International Criminal Police Review*, 41:38–45.

Yokoyama, Minoru. 1980. "Juvenile Justice System in Japan." Paper presented at the annual meeting of the Academy of Criminal Justice Sciences, Oklahoma City, Okla.

———. 1983. "Social Control of Juvenile Traffic Offenders in Japan." Paper presented at the International Symposium on the Impact of Criminal Justice Reform, San Francisco, Calif., 3–5 November 1983.

———. 1990. "Criminalization Against Traffic Offenders in Japanese Criminal Justice System." *Kokugakuin Journal of Law and Politics* 27:1–27.

———. 1991. "Emergence of Anti-Prostitution Law in Japan: Analysis from Sociology of Criminal Law." Paper presented at the Thirtieth International Congress, International Institute of Sociology, Kobe, Japan.

———. 1992. "Japan: Changing Drug Laws: Keeping Pace with Problems." *C J International* 8:11–18.

Yoshimura, Saneyuki. 1991. "The Institutional Treatment of Drug Offenders in Japan." United Nations Asia and Far East Institute for Prevention of Crime and Treatment of Offenders, Tokyo. Photocopy.

Index

Abadinsky, Howard, 34
Academic education, 73, 205–6, 208, 213
Accelerated criminalization, 11, 12, 32–33, 254–57
Adler, Freda, 76
Advanced criminal tendencies, 49–51, 97, 200, 210
Aftercare, 165, 236, 246–47, 250–51
Age as a variable, 1, 67, 97, 174, 204, 208, 213, 222–24, 224–25, 227–29, 237–44
Aging process, 222–24
Albanese, Jay, 34
Albinin, Joseph L., 34
Albrecht, Hans-Jora, 191
American military, 185, 201, 210–16
Antiboryokudan Law, 13, 42–47
Antiprostitution Law, 26, 28–29, 82, 89, 204, 240
Apology, 21, 22
Arai, Kiyoshi, 144
Araki, Nobuyoshi, 130
Arii Dockyard Camp, 143, 144

Arson, 77, 78, 81, 87, 110, 117, 119, 204, 237
Assault with Unlawful Assembly Law, 33, 42, 54, 257
Authority, 3, 10, 253, 256

Bailey, David H., 28
Barre, Marie Danielle, 188
Bayley, David H., 26, 126–27
Beasley, William G., 15
Becker, Howard S., 9
Bedford Hills Correctional Facility, 98
Befu, Harumi, 76
Bellah, Robert N., 16
Benedict, Ruth, 27
Ben na kako (ugly decline of elderly), 223
Bicycle Race Law, 257
Bindzus, Dieter, 147
Birth rates, 98, 217–19, 220, 221, 227, 232
Bixby, F. Lovell, 283
Blau, Zona Smith, 224
Bodily injury, 58, 82, 83, 86, 87, 207, 214, 237, 240, 243

301

INDEX

Boryokudan (violent gangs), 34
Bosozoku (wild tribe), 14, 169–71, 172, 173, 174
Boudouris, James, 98
Braithwaite, John, 271
Brinton, Mary C., 73
Bureaucracy, 17–18, 25
Buruma, Ian, 26, 31, 33, 38
Bynum, Timothy S., 34

Carney, Larry S., 74
Changes in Japanese society, 77, 124, 125, 169, 220–21, 222–23, 227–28, 229, 230, 267
Chiba Prison, 142
Christie, Nils, 5
Christopher, Robert C., 27, 271
Clark, Ronald, 72
Class-F prisoners, 185–87, 194, 201–4, 206, 207, 208–10, 213
Classification, 49–51, 146, 200–201, 204–5, 223
Clemmer, Donald, 108
Code of Criminal Procedure, 23, 33
Cohorts, 1–2, 8, 9–10, 42–43, 65–67, 157, 252, 267, 270, 271, 273
Community corrections, 164–66, 194–97, 248–51
Cook, Schura Euller, 19
Correction Bureau, 7–8, 29, 30, 98, 217, 244, 252
Corrections, dependency of, 3, 4–5, 273
Corres, Paul, 142
Council of Europe, 188–89
Cressey, Donald, 126
Criminalization, 3–4, 8–14, 123, 125, 126–27, 128, 162–63, 190, 253, 254, 267, 271, 272, 273, 274; exceptions to criminalization, 11–12
Criminal status, 9, 190, 224
Cultural strangers, 184, 191–92, 198–200
Culture, 4, 16–17, 19–23, 191–92, 270

Daimyo (feudal lords), 15, 17
Dalby, Liza Crihfield, 27
Death rates, 220, 221, 227, 232
Demography, 12, 224–29, 229–33
Deportation, 189, 203, 204, 207
Detention, 165, 210, 247
Deviance, 8–10, 20, 104, 111, 115
DeVos, George A., 36, 38, 39, 280
Diet, 26, 254, 285
Discretionary prosecution, 23–24
Discrimination, 191, 192–93
Driving education, 125, 146, 147–48
Drug offenses, 1, 2, 3, 13, 14, 34–35, 39–40, 41–42, 51–52, 67–72, 81, 82–83, 85–86, 87, 92, 93, 110, 117, 119, 120, 157, 159–60, 161–62, 163, 182–83, 188, 190, 196, 240, 244, 252, 257, 260–62, 265–67
Dubro, Alex, 37
Dutton, Michael R., 280
Duus, Peter, 35

Earthquake at Kobe, 38
Elderly population, 217–19, 220–22, 224–29, 233–35, 236–37, 238–44
Elderly prisoners, 1, 2, 10, 11–12, 217, 223, 224–33, 233–36, 237–44, 244–48, 252, 253
Embezzlement, 58, 78, 81, 83, 86,

INDEX

87, 110, 117, 119, 214, 237, 241, 243
Engineering, traffic, 124, 125
Equal Employment Law, 74
"Evil woman" thesis, 75, 109
Extended criminalization, 13–14, 26, 27–29, 67–68, 123, 126, 148, 157, 161, 257–67, 271
Extortion, 57, 78, 237, 256

Family, 25, 72–73, 120, 219, 221, 222, 236, 247, 250
Family courts, 7, 14, 96, 157, 161, 164–69, 171, 174, 177–79, 183, 262–67; dismissals, 166–67, 263, 265, 265–67; referrals to juvenile training schools, 166, 167, 169, 263, 267; referrals to probation, 262, 263–65, 267; referrals to public prosecutors, 165–66, 167, 265
Feinman, Clarice, 76
Feminists, 27–28, 77–78
Firearms, 42, 53–54, 214, 257
Firearms and Swords Control Law, 53–54, 59, 257
First admissions to prison, 89–93, 237
Fletcher, Beverly R., 76
Foner, Anne, 285
Foreigners, 184, 188, 188–89, 191–93, 194
Foreign prisoners, 1, 2, 11–12, 185, 186–87, 198–200, 201–3, 203–6, 207–9, 252, 253
Forgery, 58, 81, 83, 86, 87, 110, 117, 119
Fraud, 78, 81, 83, 86, 117, 119, 120, 207, 214, 237, 241
Fuchu Prison, 143, 185, 200–201, 206–10, 284

Fujita, Taki, 28
Fukutake, Tadashi, 27, 72, 73
Fumoto Women's Prison, 93, 95, 97, 98
Futons (comforters), 214

Gambling, 82, 83, 110, 240, 244, 256
Gang, juvenile, 169–71, 173, 174
Genders, 65, 73–74, 75, 99–100, 109
George, B. J., 24, 25
Gifu Prison, 144
Giri (duty), 20, 22, 76, 127
Gotoh, Nobuo, 143, 144
Group and self, 19–20

Hachioji Medical Prison, 204, 210, 244
Hagan, Frank E., 34
Hagan, John, 75
Hakodate Juvenile Prison, 142
Haley, John Owen, 3, 17
Halfway houses, 25–26, 120, 144, 250–51
Hammett, Theodore M., 244–45
Harima Training School, 173
Harmony, 19, 20
Harrold, Lynne, 244–45
Hartz-Karp, Janette, 76
Hasegawa, Hisashi, 37, 62, 97
Hashimoto, S., 288, 289
Hayakawa, Kazuo, 221
Hayashi, Shuji, 18
Hazama, Hiroshi, 72
Herbert, David L., 34
Hobson, Barbara Meil, 26
Holden, Karen C., 73
Homicide, 57, 77, 79, 81, 82, 83, 86, 87, 92, 93, 110, 117, 120,

121–22, 188, 194, 204, 213, 237, 240, 243, 253
Hoshino, Kanehiro, 45, 281
Housebreaking, 237, 238
Household registration, 18
Housing, 219, 221
Huang, Frank F. Y., 33

Ibe, Fumiya, 280
Ichihara Prison, 123–24, 139–43, 144–48
Ichihara Training School, 173
Ichikawa, Mamoru, 236, 288, 289
Ie (family orientation), 72–73
Illicit commerce, 26–29, 34, 35, 82, 83, 86, 87, 92, 110, 196, 204, 240, 244, 256
Immigration Control and Refugee Recognition Law, 188, 189
Imprisonment, 1, 3, 4, 5, 7, 65–67, 69–72, 109–10, 123, 130–35, 225–27, 228–29, 252, 253, 254, 255–56, 261–62, 267, 275
Indecent assault, 237, 240, 244
Infanticide, 77, 110
Informal control, 17–19, 145–47
Ino, Kenji, 35, 36
Interest groups, 274
Intrusion, 237, 238
Ishida, Takeshi, 18, 19
Ishii, Akira, 147, 280
Ishikawajima Workhouse, 206
Iwahori, Takeshi, 244
Iwai, Hiroaki, 37, 39
Iwakuni Women's Prison, 93, 95, 96
Iwaski, Shiro, 288

Japan Times, 20–23
Japan, U.S. compared to, 5, 20–23, 26–27, 272–73
Japanese social psychology, 20–23, 271
Johnson, Elmer H., 37, 280, 285
Jolin, Annette, 280
Jones, Howard, 142, 222
Jono Medical Prison, 244
Judges, 5, 10, 23, 24–25, 75, 81, 89, 109, 117, 128, 134, 135, 137, 191, 253, 254, 267, 273, 274
Juvenile classification homes, 7–8, 164–65, 174
Juvenile Law, 164, 165
Juvenile prisons, 95, 96
Juvenile Training School Law, 164
Juvenile training schools, 7, 14, 78, 123, 157, 160–61, 164, 166–67, 177, 179–82, 182–83, 262, 262–63, 267

Kagamihara Metal Industrial Camp, 143, 144
Kakogawa Prison, 142
Kakusei Society, 27
Kaplan, David E., 37
Kasamatsu Women's Prison, 93, 95, 98
Kashiwagi, Fumio, 236, 289
Katayama, Hiroyuki, 281
Katoh, Hisao, 13, 280
Katsuo, Ryozo, 139
Kayaba, K., 288
Kelsey, O. W., 285
Kersten, Joachim, 38, 39
Kiefer, Christie W., 223
Kikuchi Medical Branch Prison, 244
Kitsuregawa School, 143, 144
Kobayashi, Juichi, 281
Kocher, Marjorie B., 203, 282
Koita, Kiyofumi, 288
Kondo, Dorinne K., 72, 73

INDEX

Koshi, George M., 28
Kotatsu (well under table), 214
Kouhashi, Hiroshi, 24, 137, 165, 179
Kurubane Prison, 144
Kyofu Society, 27

Labeling theory, 8–9
Language as barrier, 185, 192, 201
Larceny, 77, 78, 81, 83, 86, 92, 110, 119, 188, 193, 194, 207, 214, 237, 241, 253
Lauderdale, Pat, 8, 9
Law, 8, 13, 14–17; traditional or formal, 10–11, 14–17, 272–73, 275; *see also* specific laws
Law for Punishment of Acts of Violence, 38, 54, 257
Lemert, Edwin M., 9
Levy, Marion J., 19
Life expectancy, 220, 221
Longsweet Stephen and Ethel, 31
Lynch, James P., 279

Management and Coordination Agency, 230, 231
Management of prisoners, 61–64, 223
Mandatory prosecution, 24
Marginal deviance, 8, 9–10, 253, 257, 271, 273
Marginal man, 191
Marijuana, 204, 207
Martin, Linda G., 217, 220, 221, 222
Masaki, Akira, 143
Masland, John W., 18
Masters, Kimberly, 282
Matsuyama Prison, 143, 144
Matsuyama Training School, 173
Matumoto, Masaru, 283

McKelvey, Blake, 95
Medical care, 29, 220, 221, 223, 227, 236, 244–48
Meiji Restoration, 15, 16, 27
Menard, Scott, 1
Mental Health Law, 69, 163
Migrant control, 188–90, 192
Miho Training School, 173
Minamoto, Yoritomo, 26
Ministry of Health and Welfare, 163
Miyawaki, Raisuke, 40
Miyazawa, Koichi, 19
Miyazawa, Setsuo, 20, 25, 271–72
Mizushima, Keiichi, 36, 38, 39, 280
Mokoyama, Masaru, 281
Monument of Atonement, 146
Moon, Dreama G., 76
Moral boundaries, 8, 9–10
Moral training, 29, 146–47

Nagashima, Atsushi, 19
Nagel, Ilene, 75
Naikan therapy, 147
Nakane, Chie, 20, 72
Nakano Prison, 201, 284
Narcotics, 163, 182, 194, 204, 207
Narcotics Control Law, 163
National Personnel Authorization Law, 25, 97, 146
National Police Agency, 40, 41, 69
National Research Institute of Police Science, 45–47
Neighborhood, 18–19
New York Times, 38
Nishi, Yukio, 144
Nishida, Taro, 288
Nishikawa, Masakazu, 23, 24, 137
Noda, Tosiyuki, 16, 20, 273

INDEX

"Nonhuman" offenders, 76, 109
Nozaka, Yoichi, 236, 289
Nuclear family, 219, 221
Nursing homes, 221

O'Brien, Robert M., 1
O'Callaghan, Sean, 26
Ogawa, Jijiruo, 279
Ohi Dockyard Camp, 143–44
Ohita Prison, 142
Ohtsuka, Toichi, 213
Oitama Training School, 173
Okayama Prison, 285
Okazaki Medical Prison, 244
Okazaki, Yoichi, 217, 221
O'Kelly, Charlotte G., 74
Okinawa Prison, 201
Okinawa Training School, 173
Okuide, Yasuo, 288
Okusawa, Yoshio, 288
Onomichi Branch Prison, 142, 247–48, 285
Open institution, 123, 139–42, 142–44, 145–46, 148, 173
Organic solvents, 163, 167, 174, 176, 182–83, 214, 265–67
Osaka Medical Branch Prison, 244, 246–47
Osaka Prison, 185, 200
Otomo, Eiichi, 221
Otsuki, Takashi, 236, 289
Oyabun-kobun (superior-follower statuses) ties, 36, 64
Ozaki, Robert S., 16
Ozaki, Tetsuya, 284

Parisi, Nicolette, 75
Park, Robert E., 191, 199
Parole, 7, 25, 55, 116, 119–22, 135, 165, 174, 248, 249–51
Paternalism, 20, 36, 77, 99

Pempel, T. J., 25
Penal Code, 23, 24, 29, 77, 82, 127, 128, 130, 188, 238, 257, 285
Pension Reform Act, 222
Perry, John Curtis, 28
Perry, Matthew C., 15, 210
Pharr, Susan J., 27, 274
Poisonous and Hazardous Substances Control Law, 14, 163, 166
Police, 5, 40, 42–47, 125–27, 128, 163, 170–71, 253, 254, 260–61, 273
Political institutions, 10–14, 190, 253, 274, 275
Population, 157, 159–61, 189, 220
Power, 3, 10–11, 20, 75
Preferential treatment, 68, 75
Prevention, 162, 165
Pringle, Patrick, 281
Prisoners as outcasts, 198–99, 224
Prisonization, 108
Prisons, 51–54, 79–83, 95, 97, 103, 111, 115, 123, 146; prison construction, 96, 206–7; prison industry, 25, 205, 206–7, 209, 215, 235
Privatization, 25, 221–22, 275
Probation, 7, 24, 25, 55, 116–19, 123, 135–39, 157, 163, 164, 165, 167, 169, 174, 176–77, 177–79, 181–82, 183, 194–97, 248–49, 249–50, 262, 263, 265, 267
Professional negligence, 128, 134, 135, 138–39, 167, 177, 179, 260, 263, 265
Prostitutes' union, 28
Prostitution, 26–29, 35, 83, 86, 87, 89, 92, 110, 196, 204, 240, 244

INDEX

Public crisis, 8, 12, 14, 42–43, 68–69, 109, 123–25, 125–27, 128, 157, 162, 243–44, 253, 257–60, 260, 262, 274
Public opinion, 126–27, 162, 163, 171, 232
Public policy, 4, 5, 8, 10, 13, 163, 260
Public prosecutors, 5, 10, 23–24, 54–55, 75, 81, 89, 96, 109, 128, 134, 135, 166, 167, 191–92, 246–47, 253, 254, 256, 261, 267, 273, 274
Public safety commissions, 43–45, 254
Purification, 19, 22

Radzinonicz, Leon, 281
Rape, 213, 237, 240, 244
Raz, Jacob, 36
Rebellious inmates, 100, 108
Recidivism, 89–93, 110–16, 237
Regional parole boards, 7
Rehabilitation aid hostels, 25–26, 120, 144, 250–51
Rehabilitation Bureau, 7, 25–26, 55, 116, 196, 217, 252
Research, 267–75
Responsive incarceration, 11–12, 185, 190, 229–33, 250, 253–54
Retirement, 222, 225
Riley, Matilda White, 285
Road Traffic Law, 127, 128, 134–35, 138, 162–63, 167, 170, 173, 174, 181, 257, 263–65
Robbery, 57, 78, 82, 83, 86, 87, 110, 188, 194, 204, 207, 208, 214, 237, 240, 243
Robins-Mowry, Dorothy, 27, 28, 282

Role exit, 224
Rome, Florence, 37, 38
Rose, Gordon, 4–5
Rosett, Arthur, 22, 109
Rubenstein, Dan, 233
Rule violations, 63, 97–108, 110–16

Saga Branch Prison, 97
Saijo Branch Prison, 142
Saisho, Atsuro, 288
Samurai (warriors), 17–18, 35–36, 38
Sansom, George, 16, 35
Sapporo Women's Branch Prison, 93, 98
Sasebo Prison, 201
Sasebo Training School, 173
Saso, Mary, 72, 73
Sassen, Saskia, 189
Sato, A., 288
Sato, Haruo, 139
Sato, Ikuya, 35, 169–70
Sato, Kinko Saito, 77
SCAP (Supreme Commander for Allied Powers), 27
Schneider, Hans Joachim, 34
Schwartz, Joe, 284
Self-correction, 19, 22, 126, 214, 271
Self-discipline, 8, 145
Senescence, 236
Senility, 223, 235–36, 240
Sentences, length of, 87–89, 104–8, 204, 207, 213, 237
Serial pisoners, 89–93, 110–16, 237
Seward, Jack, 201
Sex offenses, 58, 59, 82, 83, 207
Sharma, Navin, 77
Shihadeh, Edward, 1

INDEX

Shikita, Minoru, 28–29, 30, 33–34, 128, 130, 163, 249
Shoplifting, 79, 110
Sievers, Sharon L., 72, 73, 74
Simmel, George, 190
Simon, Rita James, 77
Singer, Kurt, 16
Smart, Carol, 77
Smith, Robert J., 18, 73, 74, 76
Social control, 125–26, 271
Social discipline, 18–19
Social psychology of Japanese, 219, 220–21
Special investigators, 164
Status of Forces Agreement, 211–13
Steffensmeier, Darrell J., 176–77
Steiner, Kurt, 18
Stimulant Drug Control Law, 13, 67–69, 163, 207, 256
Stimulant drugs, 2, 78, 163, 166, 167, 174, 176, 182–83, 194, 204, 214, 237, 240, 265–67
Stockford, Richard, 142
Strangers, 184, 190–91
Streifel, Cathy, 1
Sub-rosa economy, 103–4, 105, 111, 115
Suspended sentences, 24, 117, 137, 192, 193, 250, 256, 274–75
Suttles, Gerald D., 169
Suzuki, Yoshio, 17, 109, 199, 285

Tachibawa, M., 288
Takahashi, Yoshio, 144
Takeuchi, Hiroshi, 34
Tamura, Masayuchi, 41–42, 45
Tochigi Women's Prison, 93, 95, 98, 185, 200, 203–6, 284
Tokugawa, Ieyasu, 35
Tokugawa Era, 15–16, 35, 72–73
Tolerance, 9, 167, 253, 257

Tomaseuski, Katarina, 189, 190
Tonomura, Hitomi, 18, 35
Tournier, Pierre, 188
Toyogaoka Training School, 173
Toyohashi Prison, 142
Traffic Bureau, 162
Traffic infraction notifications, 130, 134, 135
Traffic offenders, 1, 2, 3, 13, 14, 54, 58, 82, 86, 87–89, 92, 93, 110, 123, 125–27, 128, 134, 135, 157, 161–63, 167, 171–72, 173, 177–82, 196, 207, 214, 237, 240, 243–44, 252, 257–60, 262–65
Traffic Safety Policies Law, 124–25
Traffic Safety Policy Office, 162, 163, 243
Training Institute for Correctional Personnel, 146
Tritt, Howard, 34
Tsubouchi, Hisao, 144
Tsubouchi, Kosuke, 288
Tsuchiya, Shinichi, 28–29, 30, 33, 34, 128, 130, 163, 249
Tsukigata School, 173
Tsurumi, E. Patricia, 72

Uchiyama, Ayako, 45
Ukyo Rengo (motorcycle gang group), 170
Usui, Chikado, 74
Utsunomiya Prison, 144

Van Wolferen, Karl, 16–17, 32–33
Vaughn, Michael S., 33
Visitation, 205, 210, 215
Vocational guidance, 29
Volunteer Probation Officer Law, 25, 116–17, 197
Volunteer probation officers

INDEX

(VPOs), 7, 25, 165, 250; volunteers in prison, 209, 215

Wagatsuma, Hiroshi, 22, 109
Wakayama Women's Prison, 93, 95, 97, 98
Waring, Joan, 285
Watanabe, Koichi, 281
Watanabe, Yoshiaki, 288
Watanuki, Joji, 25
Watson, Billie J., 145
Weed, Ethel B., 280
Welfare society, 25
Wilson, Nanci Koser, 77
Window of opportunity, 26, 148
Witness intimidation, 33, 254
Women, 72-74, 77, 219, 221; women's vote, 26, 27, 28
Women prisoners, 66-67, 83-86, 89-93, 96-100, 101-3, 105-8, 110-16, 119, 120
Women's guidance homes, 29-31

Wooldredge, John D., 282
Woronoff, Jon, 282

Yagishita, Takeji, 144
Yakuza, 1, 2, 3, 10, 12-13, 32-64, 78, 108, 163, 170, 252, 254-57
Yamagata Prison, 142
Yamaguchi, Yoshiteru, 288
Yanaga, Chitoshi, 274
Yasumori, M., 288
Yokohama Prison, 210
Yokoo, Toshio, 40
Yokosuka Prison, 185, 200, 201, 210-16
Yokota Air Force Base, 216
Yokoyama, Minoru, 27, 96, 130, 163, 170, 283
Yonezato, Seiji, 45
Yoshida, H., 288
Yoshimura, Saneyuki, 163
Yuma, Yoshikaza, 288

Elmer H. Johnson was born in Racine, Wisconsin, and received his Ph.D. in sociology from the University of Wisconsin at Madison in 1950. He taught at North Carolina State University at Raleigh from 1949 to 1966. To gain practical experience, he worked in the summer of 1956 as a parole supervisor for the North Carolina Board of Paroles and later took academic leave to serve as assistant director of the North Carolina Prison Department, 1958–60. He taught at Southern Illinois University at Carbondale, where he attained the rank of Distinguished Professor in the Center for the Study of Crime, Delinquency, and Corrections and in the Department of Sociology, from 1966 until his retirement in 1987. He has authored numerous articles and several books, including *Crime, Correction, and Society*, 4th ed. (1978), and *Japanese Corrections: Managing Convicted Offenders in an Orderly Society* (1996), and he edited the two-volume *International Handbook of Contemporary Developments in Criminology* (1983) and the *Handbook on Crime and Delinquency Prevention* (1987). He has published extensively on comparative criminal justice of Europe, Australia, China, and Japan.